STRANGER
AND
FRIEND

The Way of an Anthropologist

STRANGER
AND
FRIEND

The Way of an Anthropologist

HORTENSE POWDERMAKER

W · W · NORTON & COMPANY

New York · London

W. W. Norton & Company, Inc., 500 Fifth Avenue, New York, N.Y. 10110
W. W. Norton & Company Ltd., 37 Great Russell Street, London WC1B 3NU

Library of Congress Catalog Card No. 65-13030

Published simultaneously in Canada by Stoddart,
a subsidiary of General Publishing Co. Ltd,
Don Mills, Ontario.

PRINTED IN THE UNITED STATES OF AMERICA

234567890

ISBN 0-393-00410-4

CONTENTS

PART III

MISSISSIPPI

PART IV

HOLLYWOOD

PART V

NORTHERN RHODESIA, NOW ZAMBIA

ACKNOWLEDGMENTS

My greatest indebtedness is to the people with whom I lived and worked in the four field experiences discussed in this book. Their patience, help, and friendship made the field work possible. The writing of the book was much aided by the comments, criticisms, and encouragement of friends and colleagues, each of whom read certain sections of the book in early drafts. Among these people are: Sidney Axelrad, Sydel Silverman, and Robert Glasse of Queens College; Eric Wolf of the University of Michigan; Gerald Berreman, Herbert Phillips, and Seymour Lipset of the University of California, Berkeley; Benjamin Colby of the Laboratory of Anthropology in Santa Fe and Rudolph Kieve, also of Santa Fe; Colin Turnbull of the American Museum of Natural History; Jay Richard Kennedy of New York; and Theodora Kroeber of Berkeley. I am grateful to all of them.

Residence at various institutions during a sabbatical year and a summer provided excellent facilities for work and I am much indebted to them. In chronological order they are: The MacDowell Colony, The Institute of International Studies and Department of Anthropology at the University of California, Berkeley, the Huntington-Hartford Foundation in California, and the Rockefeller Foundation Villa Serbelloni in Italy. I appreciate, too, the kindness of Helena Burke (née Malinowski) in providing working space in the Malinowski villa during the couple of months I spent in the Dolomites. I am indebted to the Wenner-Gren Foundation for Anthropological Research for a research grant which aided in the writing of the book. My thanks go likewise to Sara Klein Geneshier who worked with diligence and faithfulness in the typing and many retypings of the manuscript.

PREFACE

*To understand a strange society, the anthropologist has tradi-
tionally immersed himself in it, learning, as far as possible,
to think, see, feel, and sometimes act as a member of its culture and at the same time as a trained anthropologist from
another culture.* This is the heart of the participant observation method—involvement and detachment. Its practice is
both an art and a science. Involvement is necessary to understand the psychological realities of a culture, that is, its
meanings for the indigenous members. Detachment is necessary to construct the abstract reality: a network of social relations including the rules and how they function—not necessarily real to the people studied.

Field work is a deeply human as well as a scientific experience and a detailed knowledge of both aspects is an important source of data in itself, and necessary for any comparative study of methodology. Yet we know less about participant
observation than about almost any other method in the social
sciences. Anthropologists have written only occasionally and
usually briefly about what actually happens in the field. Most
of the discussion of the actualities of field work has been
limited to private discussions between anthropologists, and
these usually touch only high spots or amusing anecdotes. A
scientific discussion of field work method should include considerable detail about the observer: the roles he plays, his
personality, and other relevant facts concerning his position
and functioning in the society studied. Now more aware
methodologically, anthropologists have written a number of
papers on the subject. But the number is not large and the
data are limited. (A selected bibliography is in the appendix
to this book.)

Sociologists and, increasingly, other social scientists—political scientists, social psychologists, and others—do field re-

search, sometimes quite different and other times quite similar
to the participant observation of the anthropologist. Always
more interested in methodology, sociologists have an enormous
literature on the subject, but as Robert K. Merton has noted,
it is concerned with how social scientists ought to think, feel,
and act and fails to give the necessary detail on what they
actually do, think, and feel.[1] Few practicing social scientists
today believe their research resembles the orderly intellectual
presentations in textbooks on method: choice of problem, formulation of hypotheses and testing of them, analysis and interpretation of data. All these do occur, and, obviously, research must be planned in advance. But, as Edward Shils
has pointed out, the research process is often quite dis-
orderly.[2]

The logical final report of the research has only a partial
resemblance to the original plans, and even less to the actual
process of getting the data. A sociologist working among
peasants in a Balkan village expressed confusion and some
resentment when she first learned a few of these facts. She
wrote: "The sociology methods I have been teaching in the
classroom do not work out as easily in practice and are
rather difficult to carry out. I am trying to set forth the
component of each family in the village I am studying and
find it impossible to do this quickly, accurately, or without
getting lots of extraneous information, which, with my methods, I would rather have at a later date."[3] Even in the survey
(not participant observation) on which she was engaged, it
was not possible to work on people as if they were chemical
or physical elements, to be arranged according to a predeter-
mined plan.

Little record exists of mistakes and of learning from them,
and of the role of chance and accident in stumbling upon
significant problems, in reformulating old ones, and in devising

---

[1] Robert K. Merton, "Foreword," Bernard Barber, *Science and the
Social Order* (rev. ed.; New York: Collier Books, 1962), p. 19.
[2] Edward Shils, "Primordial, Sacred and Civil Ties," *British Journal
of Sociology*, 1957, pp. 130–45.
[3] Quoted in Irwin T. Sanders "Research with Peasants in Under-
developed Areas," *Social Forces*, Vol. 35, Oct. 1956, p. 1.

new techniques, a process known as "serendipity." A lack of theory, or of imagination, an over commitment to a particular hypothesis, or a rigidity in personality may prevent a field worker from learning as he stumbles.

We know little also of the feelings of the anthropologist as he continuously participates, observes, and interviews, of his discouragements and pleasures, and of the possible relationship of these to the type of work he does. Only a few relatively complete accounts of the realities of a field project from its beginning to completion exist. One is by the sociologist W. F. Whyte and is contained in an appendix of seventy-nine pages in the second edition of *Street Corner Society*.[4] Whyte's account of how he lived and worked in a slum district not far from Harvard University, of the relation of his research to his personal background and his awareness of how "ideas grow up in part out of our immersion in the data and out of the whole process of living" (p. 281) is unique and a classic.

The long "Introduction" by Malinowski in his famous *Argonauts of the Western Pacific* is the most detailed report by any anthropologist of how he worked in the field.[5] A fictionalized account of a woman anthropologist's field experiences in West Africa, written under a pseudonym, describes her personal relations with the Africans and her feelings.[6] It rings true to most field workers, even though presented as a novel.

Recently, Phillip Hammond has edited a volume of informal essays by a group of distinguished sociologists, each of whom attempts to give the "feel" of and the "context of discovery" in a specific research experience.[7] Among all field workers— sociologists, anthropologists, and others—there is an increasing awareness of the need for personal chronicles of their research. The sociologist Buford Junker writes: "the behavior of field workers could be studied to delineate the 'bundles' of skills, sensitivity, sensibilities, and so on, that characterize

---

[4] Chicago: University of Chicago Press, 1956.

[5] Bronislaw Malinowski, *Argonauts of the Western Pacific* (London: G. Routledge and Sons, Ltd., 1922).

[6] Elenore Smith Bowen (pseudonym), *Return to Laughter* (New York: Harper & Bros., 1954).

[7] Phillip E. Hammond, ed., *Sociologists at Work: The Craft of Social Research* (New York: Basic Books, Inc., 1964).

them, as well as their apparent need and capacity for much sustained social interaction." [8]

In this book four major field research experiences are covered in detail: a late Stone-Age Melanesian society in the southwest Pacific (1929–30); a rural Mississippi community—half Negro and half white—(1933–34); Hollywood (1946–47); and an African mining township in Northern Rhodesia (1953–54). The time span of a quarter of a century began when I was a young woman who had just completed graduate studies, and I did the last field work, discussed here, as a middle-aged professor. During this period significant developments in anthropology and related disciplines naturally contributed to my intellectual growth, and the accelerated rate of social change throughout the world presents new problems for research. In addition, as is often true, the very process of living and growing older is a source of learning and increasing self-awareness.

The first field experience in the village of Lesu, on the island of New Ireland (Bismarck Archipelago, Mandated Territory of New Guinea) immediately followed the award of a Ph.D. at the University of London, where I studied under Malinowski. I was fortunate; Lesu was something of an idyl. The people were friendly and outgoing; no biracial situation existed: I was the first anthropologist and the first white person to live there, and could set my own role. The community was small, and I participated and observed easily; I was able to learn the language, by no means perfectly, but sufficiently well after a time to understand and be understood. I was trained to study a Melanesian people since Malinowski's work and his lectures were largely based on a Melanesian society (the Trobriand Islanders), and I was also familiar with the literature on the general area. At that time, anthropologists tended to pick an area or people for study, rather than a problem. A field worker could not have had a better initial experience than immersion in this late Stone-Age culture, in

---

[8] Buford H. Junker, *Field Work: An Introduction to the Social Sciences, With an Introduction by Everett C. Hughes* (Chicago: University of Chicago Press, 1960), p. 143. Junker further characterizes a field for future research as "the psychodynamics of social science field work roles."

being involved and detached, in learning to think, see, feel, and sometimes act as a Melanesian and yet retaining a capacity to stand outside and think, see, and act as a member of his own society and as a trained anthropologist.

The second field work in rural Mississippi was far more difficult and complex. True, I did not have to learn a new language and the community was a subsection of my culture with a known history. But I had to find my way and fit into a southern community which, even in the mid-thirties, was characterized by the deep fears and anxieties of both Negroes and whites. I had to live and work within the dominant white power structure and at the same time be an accepted part of the Negro community. I had to alternate between seeing and feeling as a Negro and as a white person in Mississippi, and then standing outside, both as myself with a personal value system, and myself as a social scientist. The alternate ways of seeing, thinking, feeling, and acting in Lesu were simple in contrast.

The attempt to study Hollywood anthropologically was even more difficult than field work in Mississippi. The research grew out of my interest in movies as culture patterns, first perceived as a problem in Mississippi when I listened to whites and Negroes talk about the movies that they and I had seen. The details of how this interest grew into the study of Hollywood are given in Part IV, as is the discussion of that field work. The problem of studying the social-psychological process out of which a movie emerges was legitimate. But, today, I regard this study as the least successful and satisfying (to me) of my field projects. The difficulties were very great; partly they were sociological and lay in the situation, and partly they were psychological and within me. An analysis of both may be as revealing, if not more so, than that of more successful field work.

An African copper-mining township in Northern Rhodesia (now Zambia) presented a quite different field experience from the preceding ones. The specific problem was the influence of the mass media in social change, set in the broader frame of leisure activities as an index of change. The study was frankly exploratory. The mining township numbered thirty thousand Africans and quantitative work was necessary to establish

patterns. A survey was followed by more qualitative work.
New problems arose in the field and the study of leisure was
expanded to become part of a broader study of change.

Although each field experience was unique, similarities
existed, too. Among the topics treated in this book are:

The selection of area and/or problem.

Problems of getting started, of establishing a routine of living
and a pattern of systematic work, and of functioning within the
indigenous power structure.

Development and changes in problems.

Techniques of interviewing in the larger context of the
anthropologist's role and his relations with informants.

Mistakes (such as, over-projection and hidden involvements)
and successes.

Discouragements and becoming fed-up, due to continuous
concentration on unending notetaking, to awareness of one's
limitations and those of anthropology, to tensions and anxieties,
and other problems which varied from one field experience to
another; ways of meeting these problems and of "escape."

Pleasures in getting the "feel" of the society, in close friendships with a few native peoples, of collecting some particularly
good data, and of seeing it in perspective.

The use of insight in determining the field worker's behavior
and in understanding his informants, when knowledge is in-
sufficient and theories and techniques inadequate.

The ever-present role of involvement and detachment, a
major theme throughout the book.

The continuing relation between personal feelings (sensory,
aesthetic, emotional) and intellectual perception is stressed—
how the anthropologist feels as well as what he does, since
he is part of the situation studied. In recounting my field experiences, I look inward as well as outward, with the benefit
of hindsight. An anthropological voyage may tack and turn in
several directions, and the effective field worker learns about
himself as well as about the people he studies.

Although there must, inevitably, be some selectivity in the
details presented, of prime importance in any account of research is its honesty. But no matter how good the memory,
how complete the journals, how deep the insight, how strong
the desire to be honest, we know man's fallibility in all
these respects. It is as impossible to be totally objective towards one's self as towards the people one studies. Within

these limitations, I have tried to be as accurate as possible.

Among the reasons for choosing to be an anthropologist—to step in and out of society and to study it—are those connected with family background and personality. Class, religion, and other social (as well as personal) factors define certain experiences, and reactions to them create new ones. In retrospect some of these appear to have been relevant to my becoming an anthropologist and to the type of work I have done within the discipline. Later, university training was, obviously, of major importance. Both are therefore briefly described in Part I. Finally, in a more technically written Epilogue, an attempt is made to analyze some of the general characteristics of the participant observation method, to view it in the perspective of other and newer methods, and to raise a few controversial questions.

A major contribution of anthropologists, sociologists, and other social scientists has been their ability to stand at a considerable distance from the society they study. This book is an attempt to stand outside and observe one anthropologist—myself, the only one I can really know—stepping *in* to societies and *out* of them. It puts under a sort of microscope the participation–observation method as used by an anthropologist in widely different societies. When I discussed the book with several anthropologists in my age group, some of them said, "This is the book I planned to write." I hope they carry through their plans. The more such studies, the better prepared we will be to generalize. A number of young anthropologists have mentioned their need and desire for such a book. It is primarily written for them and other young social scientists, and attempts to present a case history of how an anthropologist lives, works, and learns; how he thinks and feels, in the field. Other readers may also find it useful and interesting to go backstage with an anthropologist, and see what lies behind the finished performance.

PART I

INTRODUCTION

I

BACKGROUND

The anthropologist is a human instrument studying other human beings and their societies. Although he has developed techniques that give him considerable objectivity, it is an illusion for him to think he can remove his personality from his work and become a faceless robot or a machinelike recorder of human events. It is important to accept that this human instrument is as much a product of biological, psychological, and social conditioning as are the people he studies. Often we catch glimpses of an anthropologist or sociologist and have hunches about what he is like and of his biases as we read his books. In one focused on the participant observation method, a description of the field worker is in order since his personality is part of the research situation being studied.

Obviously, this personality is not formed in the field but has many years of conditioning behind it. These influence the anthropologist's choice of problems and of methods, even the choice of discipline itself. I include here a brief description of the factors in my background which (through hindsight) appear relevant to my becoming an anthropologist and to the type of work I have done within that discipline. As Everett Hughes writes, "It is doubtful whether one can become a good social reporter unless he has been able to look, in a reporting mood, at the social world in which he was reared." [1] The relevancy of the personal factors becomes clearer throughout the book.

Long before I ever heard of anthropology, I was being conditioned for the role of stepping in and out of society. It was part of my growing-up process to question the traditional

[1] Buford H. Junker *Field Work: An Introduction to the Social Sciences, With an Introduction by Everett C. Hughes* (Chicago: University of Chicago: University of Chicago Press, 1960), p. xi.

values and norms of the family and to experiment with behavior patterns and ideologies. This is a not uncommon process of finding one's self. A feeling of personal or social discomfort (or both) have been a prelude quite often to anthropological and sociological curiosity and interests in my generation, and, I think, in that of my teachers. Why should a contented and satisfied person think of standing outside his or any other society and studying it?

In her study of life histories of eminent scientists, Roe found that anthropologists and psychologists early showed considerable concern about social relations; open rebelliousness in the family was usual among the former, and occurred only slightly less often among the latter.[2] As she remarks, "An unresolved conflict over parental relations could be displaced to a concern with personal relations generally."[3] Biologists and physicists, on the other hand, had neither rebelliousness nor family difficulties and developed ways of life with less personal interaction. All the scientists stood somewhat apart from life, in contrast to successful businessmen. Among the latter, Roe found a trend to identification with the father and a comparative absence of rebellion against authority figures. Compensatory mechanisms are not necessarily undesirable, and the absorption of all the scientists in their work meant that it filled deep needs.[4] It is my hypothesis that some of the new trends in anthropology can be correlated with changing types of personalities in the discipline who have different needs to meet. This concept will be briefly discussed in the Epilogue.

The feeling of apartness from others described by Roe may have different causes and has nothing in common with the

---

[2] Anne Roe, "A Psychological Study of Eminent Psychologists and Anthropologists, and a Comparison with Biological and Physical Scientists," *Psychological Monographs* (American Psychological Association), No. 352, 1953, pp. 1–55.

[3] *Ibid.*, p. 48.

[4] The late Clyde Kluckhohn wrote, "The lure of the strange and far has a peculiar appeal for those who are dissatisfied with themselves or who do not feel at home in their own society." *Mirror for Men* (New York: Fawcett World Library, 1957), p. 11.

Ruth Benedict's answer to a student who asked her how she happened to study anthropology is of interest. He reports that Benedict said she was uncomfortable living in Westchester and wanted to find out how the other half lived.

trend to alienation and nihilism that exists among some young people in this mid-century. Often, apartness is part of an intellectual's personality and may take diverse forms, among which are the arts as well as the sciences. The form for me, eventually, was anthropology, and among the conditioning factors (some known and others unknown) was a rebellion against the family.

As a child, I did not accept the norms of my upper-middle- and middle-class German Jewish background. (A paternal grandmother was English Jewish.) I was second generation born in the United States. Grandparents on both sides seem to have been prosperous before migrating to Philadelphia, where the grandfathers were successful businessmen. I was early aware of the subtleties of class distinctions within the extended family. The business background was much the same for all, but levels of success varied. Actually these differences were not very large, but they were symbolically significant. My family was in the middle-middle group, though its fortunes went up and down. We moved away from Philadelphia when I was about five, and after seven or eight years of living in Reading, Pennsylvania, we settled in Baltimore.

I never had a sense of much real religious feeling in the family, although there was a definite sense of being Jewish, particularly for my mother. Her father had been president of a reform synagogue in Philadelphia and active in Jewish civic affairs. In Baltimore we belonged to a reform synagogue with a congregation of German descent, and I was confirmed in it. My family, other relatives, and their friends completely accepted the then current belief in the alleged social superiority of German Jews over more recent Jewish immigrants from eastern Europe. Knowledge of the social distinctions between these two groups preceded my awareness of the general social position of Jews in American culture. During childhood and adolescence, my friends were not restricted to any religious group.

My identity was polarized against this background, rebelling against the business values and the social snobbery. At the age of fourteen, after visiting an uncle and aunt, I wrote a poem called "Things," expressing scorn for the stress on acquiring and taking care of material things. School was a major interest in adolescence, and favorite subjects were literature, history, and Latin. I read omniverously, and the fictional worlds created by Romain Rolland, Hawthorne, Dostoevski, Thackeray, and many others provided a way of stepping outside of my immediate environment. Later, I went out of my way to meet recent Jewish working-class immigrants from eastern Europe, whom my family scorned. I liked them. They seemed to have a feeling of what I now call cultural roots, which I envied. They sang Russian songs, spoke Yiddish, and ate Jewish foods. Most of those I knew had a socialist ideology, and a few had intellectual interests. Their style of life seemed more definitive than the Americanized business culture of my family which bored me.

Goucher College strengthened the tendency to step in and out of my social group. My participation in college life through extra-curricular activities was rather perfunctory. The detachment from college social life occurred partly because as a day-student, living at home, I did not have the in-group feeling of dormitory life. But there was another reason. In my freshman year I was surprised at not being invited to join a sorority and belatedly discovered that sororities were not open to Jews. I was not sure that I wished to join one, but I wanted to be invited. (Sororities ceased to exist at Goucher College in 1950.) A relatively unimportant snub by college sororities was thus my first awareness of social restrictions on Jews, or at least, the first I remember.

Interested in learning more about society, and, probably, wanting to understand my position in it, I thought of majoring in sociology. But it was not well developed at the Goucher of that time, and the two courses I took contributed little to my understanding and left me dissatisfied. (Anthropology was non-existent in most undergraduate colleges then.) I changed to history, one of the top departments with a number of scholarly and stimulating teachers. From their courses I gained some sense of the comparative nature of civilizations and of historical depth. The Middle Ages and the Renaissance were my favorite periods. I read widely for other courses and on my own: literature, poetry, and philosophy. The humanistic bent was apparent. Fun and frivolity were part of life, too: parties, picnics, candy-pulls, canoeing on the Potomac river, walking trips through western Maryland, tennis, and other such doings.

At college I developed socialistic interests, shared by only a few fellow students. For several weeks, three of us debated with great seriousness whether it was right to accept inherited wealth. I took the negative position. I "discovered" the Baltimore slums and the trade-union movement. My belief in the latter was naïve, simple, and ardent: poverty could be eradicated and the world would be better, if all workers joined unions. I had little concern with Marxian theory, or the political party. My interest in the labor movement was in part an expression of rebellion from the family, which made it no less socially legitimate.

In dilettantish fashion I began to explore the world of the workers, and spent a spring vacation working in a small unorganized men's shirt factory. Never having used even a hand-operated sewing machine, and being totally ungifted in sewing, I was scared by the power machine, as well as by the forelady. My body rebelled against sitting at a machine all day. In urgent need of exercise, I often went dancing in the evenings and played tennis over weekends. The physical sensation of sitting continuously at a machine and the memory of the unending boredom of sewing one seam on the back yoke of shirts have never left me.

A pleasant memory of my stint at the shirt factory is of the friendly girls. A particular friend was an Italian, working next to me. She helped me when I got into trouble with the machine, and we often ate lunch together. Before long she decided that her brother, who owned a tobacco and newspaper shop in a small town between Baltimore and Washington, and I should marry. Accordingly, I was invited to a family dinner to meet him. Unable to go through with the deception that I had any intention of marrying her brother and helping him run his shop, I disappeared from the factory a couple of days before the dinner. But I was pleased that it had been easy to make friendly contacts in the first excursion outside of my own environment.

I helped to revive the local Women's Trade Union League and became its representative to the Baltimore Federation of Labor, where I observed delegates playing politics in their bid for power. My first public speech was made in a campaign of the Federation to organize women. Terrified, I stood in a truck, parked in a working-class neighborhood; a large Irish man from the Machinists' Union, whose deep voice made my girlish one seem silly, did his best to quiet my fears. Somehow I spoke, and survived. During this period I knew the local officers and some members of the International Ladies' Garment Workers' Union and the Amalgamated Clothing Workers of America, or more colloquially, the I.L.G.W.U. and A.C.W. of A.

After college, eager to leave home and Baltimore, I went to New York and applied for a position (any position) at the headquarters of the Amalgamated Clothing Workers. I became an assistant to the director of education, J. B. Salutsky (later known as J. B. S. Hardman), who ran what he called the "intellectual backyard" of the organization, including its publications. He was an interesting Russian intellectual with a quick imaginative brilliance. But it was not my idea of changing the world to sit in an office and write, edit, and pound a typewriter; I wanted a more direct experience.

So, after five or six months, I went to see the president, Sidney Hillman, and told him that I was dissatisfied with my job and wanted to organize workers. Hillman looked at me, inquired about my experience, thought a while, and asked if I could be ready to go to Cleveland by the end of the week and conduct an organizing campaign there. Eager, but scared, I mentioned my lack of experience. Hillman seemed unconcerned and said he was sure I could do the job.

In retrospect, the few years spent as a labor organizer seem not to have been without value for an anthropologist-to-be. They provided a knowledge of social realities not gained through text books. I saw and experienced the operation of power within the union and in the struggle between workers and employers. Active participation in the lives of factory workers helped me understand a segment of the American class system to which I did not belong—what it was not, as well as what it was. A social movement became a complex living force rather than an abstraction. I stepped into a part of society I had not known, and, after a time, I stepped out of it.

The labor movement which I entered in the early twenties was quite different from the powerful organizations which have now become an accepted and respected part of American society. During the years of World War I the unions had developed considerable strength and secured improvements in wages and work conditions. But when the war was over and labor no longer in short supply, business and management engaged in a strong and ruthless open-shop campaign. Conflicts between labor and management were frequently intense and violent.

At the same time, the Russian Revolution and the rise of the Labor party to power in England contributed to an intellectual ferment in certain sections of American labor. Pockets of militant unionism developed in the industrial centers of New York and Chicago and in the unions of the needle trades, machinists, and some of the railway workers. One of these unions was the Amalgamated Clothing Workers of America, which had broken away from the conservative United Garment Workers and was not accepted by the American Federation of Labor. (The C.I.O. had not yet been born.) The Amalgamated was led by Sidney Hillman, who developed new concepts of labor-management relations and expanded the functions of the union to include unemployment insurance, banks to serve the financial needs of members, adult education, cooperative housing, medical and other services. These benefits were centered primarily in New York, Chicago, and Rochester. In the hinterlands the union was weak or non-existent, employers were hostile, agencies of government unfriendly, liberals and intellectuals indifferent.

In the thirties it was fashionable for the latter to be involved in all kinds of social causes. But in the early and mid-twenties it was unusual for a middle class college girl to be a labor organizer. There was some similarity to the contemporary participation of Northern white college students in the civil rights movement in the deep South, except that the latter is respectable and approved by the President of the country, as well as by religious and many other leaders.

While my role as an organizer for the Amalgamated Clothing Workers of America was decidedly different from that of the anthropologist's participant observation, similarities were not altogether lacking. Aside from the couple of weeks in the shirt factory, this was my first experience in a sub-culture different

from my own and, in a limited sense, a kind of field work. I
tried to understand people whose backgrounds were unlike
mine and I participated—to some degree—in their lives. But
the goals and methods were completely dissimilar. As an organizer, I endeavored to induce change: to give workers, some
of them indifferent or apathetic, a sense of their own interests
which I thought could best be served by belonging to a col-
lectivity—the union—and to spot potential leaders and develop
them. Later, as an anthropologist, I tried, as far as possible, to
make no change in the society I studied. But even in the labor
movement days, I seem to have been a "natural" observer and
recorder. I kept a diary. It has long been lost, but excerpts
from it, published in *The Amalgamated Illustrated Almanac,*
have helped me to recall my work in the labor movement.[5]

In Cleveland a number of small shops in the men's clothing
industry were in the union, but the largest one was still unorganized. It paid higher wages than the union shops, had a big
welfare department, and was owned and run by two men who
considered themselves liberals. When Hillman described the
situation to me, he said he wanted the campaign conducted on
a "high" level and, if possible, without antagonizing the liberal
employers.

Feeling uncertain and yet confident, I arrived in Cleveland.
First, I met the manager of the local Amalgamated organization and the members of their joint board. Hillman came a day
or so later. Unconventionally, we called on the two men who
were owners and managers of the large factory we hoped to
organize. It was large, modern, with big windows, and in sharp
contrast to small, dingy union shops in the city. The two gentlemen proudly escorted us through their factory. The workers
thus saw two people, later to be identified as the president of
the union and an organizer, within the shop escorted by the
owner-managers. Hillman had hoped this would be an outcome
of the visit. After the tour of the factory, we chatted pleasantly
with the owners in their office. They said that, of course, they
would not organize their employees for us, but they would
recognize the union if we succeeded in forming an organization

---

[5] Hortense Powdermaker, "From the Diary of a Girl Organizer," *The
Amalgamated Illustrated Almanac,* Amalgamated Clothing Workers of
America, prepared by the Education Department under the direction of
J. B. Salutsky (New York: 1924).

in their shop. It was obvious that they considered this impossible and, as they looked at me, they appeared amused at the idea of my trying to do it. I remember how I looked: a young "flapper," dressed in a brown and white checked wool suit, and a brown upturned felt hat, perched a bit coquettishly on one side, over my bobbed hair.

The majority of the employees in the shop were young girls, many of Bohemian and Italian immigrant background, and the remainder American-born. The skilled cutters were usually of eastern European background and, of course, men. I do not remember just how I began, and the published excerpts from the diary do not describe this. But quite early in the campaign, I began writing short one-page circulars, printed in different colors. Each circular contained a message about unionism, simply written, and generally based on a quotation from Abraham Lincoln, George Washington, Thomas Jefferson, or another "father" of the country. I was trying to break the image of the union as a radical European organization and to stress its advantages to American workers. Standing in front of the factory exit at closing time, I passed out the circulars, and chatted with some of the workers. Almost no one refused the circular, and quite a few stopped to talk and said they would be glad to see me at home when I suggested a visit in the evening.

One cutter gave us a lead to his group. He had been an active socialist in Bohemia and believed in unions as a matter of principle. He was our first member, and through him we had access to other cutters. The girls were more difficult. They had never heard of Karl Marx, and were unaware of the concept of working-class solidarity. Like most girls, they were interested in beaus, clothes, having a good time, getting married; the younger ones hoped marriage would end their factory days. But they had their complaints—speeding up of work being a major one. The factory's elaborate welfare department seemed to have little meaning for them. As we became better acquainted, I was invited to some of their parties, or to go with them to the movies on a Sunday afternoon. We rented a hall and gave dances for them some Saturday evenings.

Excerpts from the published diary give the tone and manner of my participation in the life of these factory girls.[6]

---

[6] *Ibid.*, pp. 46–7.

Monday. Have been after one girl a long time. She has a lot of fire and is something of a leader. This was my third visit to her house. I did not discuss the union right away. We had discussed it rather fully at previous meetings. Tonight she was wearing silk stockings with some unusual clocks on them. We naturally fell into a discussion of hose and their clocks; at the end of an hour, she said, apropos of nothing, that she'd join up.

Sunday. Went to an Italian wedding tonight. Anne, who has joined the union, said that one of the girls in her section was getting married, and that a large number of girls from the shop were invited to the reception. Anne invited me to go with her as a "girl-friend." The bride, whom I had not met, kissed me and led me off in an Italian waltz. The wedding festivities last for a week —a party every night. After that, I'm told, the bride and groom go into retirement for a week. I went to a party on the third night, and the bride looked as if she needed to retire for a month!

Wednesday. Went after S. tonight and found that it was a case of getting mother and father. With mother I discussed the waywardness of the younger generation and with father the terrible effects of Prohibition and here and there edged in a word about the A.C.W. of A. Daughter joined. She is a leader in a little group of about twenty girls and she promises to get the others.

Monday. In front of shop this afternoon. Talking Union to one of the girls and we drifted into a discussion of clothes. She tells me that she is buying a $1,000 squirrel coat!

Sunday. Went to the movies this afternoon with four of the girls. They are a very independent sort and I like them. They take me in as one of them and would resent my treating or anything of that sort; so we go "Dutch."

Friday. Spoke to a girl today who told me that she could not join the union because the boss was her "friend." I questioned her on what she meant and, after some discussion, she told me he was her "friend" because he smiled at her whenever he saw her. Sometimes, there was even a pleasant "good-morning." That's all —but he was her "friend," and she would not be disloyal to him.

Tuesday. Gave out circulars today. Had a good bit of favorable comment and they created quite a stir. A large group gathered around to ask questions.

Afterwards Ruth lingered to tell me her hard-luck story. She had married simply to stop work; ten days after the wedding her husband lost his job. So Ruth is back in the factory with pessimistic ideas on the subject of marriage. She says that now she is for the union, married or single. (When I talked to her before she had not been interested, because she expected marriage would end her working days.)

Sunday. The shop is on vacation for a week and a bunch of the girls are at a Y.W.C.A. camp. So am I. Five of us are in one shack. The first day was a little strained. What was I, the union organizer, doing here? However, that night after lights were out, we lay talking in low tones—love affairs, of course—and the second day everything was okay. We are all friends now. I'm in demand as a tennis instructor and we are swimming, walking, doing the dishes together, and having a good bit of fun. Can't say that I object to this form of organization work!

I am going slow on the union stuff. So far have just talked indirectly about the I.L.G.W.U. "Unity House," pointing out the differences between this Y.W. camp and a union-owned summer home.[7] There is considerable dissatisfaction over some of the regulations here.

Wednesday. Had a show tonight—all the shacks competing in stunts. Our shack got first prize.

During the campaign, the company welfare workers in the factory "discovered" that I was not a "working girl," and tried to use this information against me. They told the factory workers that I had gone to college and was not a member of the working class. When the girls came to me with the welfare workers' "report," without any hesitancy I said it was true. But the girls had very little sense of class, particularly when compared to the welfare workers. I had mingled socially with them in evenings and over weekends; the welfare workers' rather formal contact ended when the factory whistle blew at five o'clock. The factory workers continued to more or less accept me as one of them. By this time some of us really were friends and liked each other. I had a vague impression that they were even pleased to know I was a college girl.

The employers' attitude is indicated by the following entry in my diary:

Saturday. Hillman was in town and we had a rather interesting and long conversation with the two owners of the shop. One took the initiative in talking. He came forward with this noble suggestion: He would call a meeting of workers in his shop and let them decide the issue of union or not. Of course, the meeting

---

[7] I had spent a weekend at the I.L.G.W.U. summer house and had been impressed with its many attractions. It apparently did not bother me that Unity House was owned by a different union than the one for which I was working.

would be in the shop and under his direction. Then, if the workers voted for a union, they could have it. But if they voted against the union, I was to be taken away from gracing the front lawn of the factory and all organization work stopped. Smart man, he is! Of course, there was nothing doing on his proposition.

I participated in some of the activities and meetings of the Cleveland union and its committees, and noted the minutiae of human relations underlying union business, as in the following diary excerpt:

Friday. Grievance committee meeting today very funny. S. L. brought charges against E. R. because he had called her a "horse." E. says that S. can't take a joke. Much discussion on just what calling a person a "horse" means.

But these activities were peripheral to the main job. An Italian male organizer was sent to assist. Gradually we were building an organization within the big shop. Naturally, we were most interested in those who were in key positions on the assembly line, and who seemed to be leaders. I suspected that one or two of our members were spies, but there was nothing tangible on which to base the suspicions. Also, I already knew that the presence of a spy was inevitable.

I was in touch with Hillman by letter and phone. My respect and liking for him grew with acquaintance. Not the charismatic type of leader, he was brilliant, dedicated, highly practical, and skilled whether in negotiations with employers or settling intra-union difficulties. Eventually we decided it was time for a showdown and we called a meeting which Hillman was to address. It was well advertised in advance and I expected all those who had joined the union to be present, and confidently hoped for many others.

Part of the publicity plan included a parade of workers from union shops around the big shop in the late afternoon of the meeting day. I had secured the necessary permit from the police for the parade. That morning, a policeman sought me out at the union office, demanded the permit, and then tore it up. He gave no explanation, and I assumed that the employers were behind the cancellation. As a substitute, I hired a half-dozen taxis to drive around the building a half-hour before quitting time, honking their horns continuously. The windows of the factory were promptly closed.

The meeting was a dismal failure. The day it was to take place, many of those who had joined the union, and all those who had shown leadership, were fired. In the almost empty hall, I wept. Hillman, however, did not seem surprised and tried to comfort me. He said the campaign had been a great success. Through my tears I asked how he could say that. He went on: it would take at least three or four campaigns before the shop would be organized; every other organizer whom he had asked to undertake the first campaign had refused, because they said the job was impossible.[8] Hillman had been quick to see that in my naïveté I did not know the job was impossible; so, in a sense, I had done it.

But I was depressed. I had worked for almost a year and had built an organization. Following Hillman's instructions I had carefully avoided any attack on the two men who headed the firm. I really had believed they would recognize the union, if we succeeded in getting a sufficient number of their workers to join. In spite of Hillman's comforting words about the "success" of this initial campaign, I felt low. My earlier naïveté was no comfort now. I had lost it.

Hillman thought I needed a change and sent me to Rochester, where the men's clothing industry was fully organized. My job was to develop activity and leadership in the women's local. Its membership was apathetic and meetings were poorly attended. I became friends with the girls, spotted the most likely new leaders, and planned interesting programs for the meetings. They became lively and well attended. In the next election a new leader was made chairman. The previous longtime chairman was chagrined and surprised. But she shook hands with me, remarking wryly, but in a tone of respect, that she had never expected to be defeated by a college girl. She was an astute and experienced politician. I seem to have played the game intuitively.

Then came a struggle between the "ins" and "outs" for control of the Rochester organization. The "ins" represented responsible administration, whom the General Office in New

---

[8] Hillman's prophecy of several campaigns before the factory would be successfully organized turned out to be true.

York wanted to keep in power. The "outs" were irresponsible, but avid for power. It was not, however, a left-right struggle. I fought on the side of the "ins." We lost. The "outs" took office and, to my surprise, once in power they were as responsible as the former "ins." I wondered what the fight had really been about, and why I had put so much energy into it.

The emotional wave on which I had entered the labor movement seemed to have spent itself. I still believed in the workers' cause and the necessity of union organization. My social values had not changed. But I shuddered as I looked at the middle-aged organizers—holding on to a job. I was considered a successful organizer, but where was I to go from there? Tired of trying to get people to do something or to change, of being in the labor movement but as an outsider, I wanted the more normal social life of a young woman and hungered both for gaiety and intellectual companionship. I was bored. It was time for me to step out of the labor movement.

I went to New York and saw Hillman. When I told him I was resigning, he was surprised and offered to change my locale, to raise my salary, or to do anything else within reason to make me content. I thanked him, but said I had to leave. To his question "why," I answered that the reasons were complex and that I wasn't sure I knew all of them, but I was convinced I should resign, adding as an afterthought, "while my heart is in the right place." Hillman seemed to understand and complimented me on my work. I told him that I had learned much and that I was glad that I had worked for his union. We shook hands. I left his office and the labor movement, far more aware of social realities than when I had entered it.

Before beginning to study anthropology, I had experienced stepping in and out of my own society—in the family, in college, and in the labor movement.

II

LONDON SCHOOL OF ECONOMICS
STUDYING WITH MALINOWSKI

I went to England partly because I wanted to go there and partly to put an ocean between me and many personal ties in the labor movement. After visiting London, Oxford, and Cambridge, I decided to stay in London. Oxford and Cambridge were beautiful, but too secluded for me; London I loved at sight.

I wanted to study, but had no thought of a graduate degree or of an academic career. I registered for two courses at the University of London, one in geology and the other in social anthropology, although I had done no previous work in either. Rocks and primitive peoples, I thought, would be pleasantly and totally unrelated to social causes and to my recent activities in the labor movement. The geology course turned out to be boring, and I soon dropped it. But anthropology happened to be taught by Bronislaw Malinowski, who was then—in the fall of 1925—a Reader at the London School of Economics. (Two years later he was appointed to the Chair of Anthropology.)

The anthropology course opened new doors. I had found a discipline which, more than any other I knew, provided an understanding of man and his society, about which I was so curious. Malinowski's functional theory was a sharp instrument for social analysis and I was attracted by the breadth of the discipline and by his stimulating teaching. Anthropology was what I had been looking for without knowing it.

A young anthropologist on the staff of the L.S.E. (as the School is called colloquially) referred, in a recent conversation, to the late twenties there as "the Golden Age." Perhaps it was. In this chapter I try only to recall the mood of that period, to give the flavor of Malinowski's personality, and to mention those theories and ideas which left their mark on my

33

thinking. His work has been discussed at length, evaluated, and criticized by many anthropologists and other social scientists.[1]

Malinowski was an exciting teacher and person, as well as a distinguished anthropologist. As is well known, he received a Ph.D. in physics and mathematics from the University of Cracow in 1908.[2] His health was bad and the doctor ordered him to discontinue his studies. While recuperating, he read Frazer's *The Golden Bough* and he told us that reading this many-volumed book made him decide to be an anthropologist. The explanation always sounded overly simple to me. Whatever the other influences may have been, when healthy enough to resume his studies, he went for a short time to Leipzig where he studied under Karl Bücher. In 1910 he came to London and worked with C. G. Seligmann, receiving a D.Sc. in 1916 with his publications on the Austrailian aborigines and the Mailu.

When I arrived at the L.S.E. in 1925, he had done his lengthy field work in the Trobriand Islands and had published the

---

[1] See, particularly:

Raymond Firth ed., *Man and Culture, An Evaluation of the Work of Bronislaw Malinowski,* (London: Routledge & Keegan Paul, 1957).

Max. Gluckman, "Malinowski's Analysis of Social Change," *African Studies,* Vol VI, 1947; "Malinowski's Contribution to Social Anthropology," *Africa,* Vol. XVII, 1947. (Reprinted together as "Malinowski's Sociological Theories," *The Rhodes-Livingstone Papers,* No. 16, Manchester University Press, 1949.)

E. A. Hoebel, "The Trobriand Islanders: Primitive Law as seen by Bronislaw Malinowski," in *The Law of Primitive Man,* (Cambridge, Mass.: Harvard University Press, 1954), pp. 177–210.

Clyde Kluckhohn, "Bronislaw Malinowski 1884–1942," *Journal American Folklore,* Vol. LVI, pp. 208–219.

Harold Lasswell, "A Hypothesis Rooted in the Preconceptions of a Single Civilization Tested by Bronislaw Malinowski," Analysis 34 in *Methods in Social Science: A Case Book,* ed. Stuart A. Rice (Chicago: University of Chicago Press, 1931) pp. 480–88.

E. R. Leach, "A Trobriand Medusa," *Man,* No. 158, 1954, London.

Dorothy Lee, "A Primitive System of Values," *Philosophy of Science,* Vol. VII (1940), pp. 355–78.

G. P. Murdock, "Malinowski, Bronislaw," *American Anthropologist,* Vol. XLV, pp. 441–51.

[2] Most of the "fathers" of cultural anthropology were trained originally in the natural sciences: Boas in physics and geography; Haddon in marine zoology; Rivers in physiology; Radcliffe-Brown in experimental psychology, although his degree was in the moral sciences.

Argonauts of the Western Pacific. He was passionately involved in anthropology, and his enthusiasm and earnestness were contagious. Nor was his thinking restricted to the "savages"; in lectures he often gave comparative examples from modern civilizations, and in conversations he made amusing allusions to contemporary British tribal rites and customs. He was a cultivated humanist as well as a scientist, and my impression is that he saw no conflict between the two views.

The lectures Malinowski gave in the classroom were not polished statements of a completed theory. He prepared them carefully—detailed charts and outlines on long yellow sheets of paper—but as he lectured, one could almost hear him continuing to think. In the small seminars he made *us* think. If any one of the students had only half an idea, he encouraged and almost forced him, with kindly persistence, to follow through with it. He was at his best in Socratic discussion, and better at it than anyone I have ever met. We had to pursue a point until it led somewhere, or abandon it. This was a new experience for me and a good antidote to intellectual laziness.

Although his health was not always good, he had great vitality and was deeply involved with life—the minutiae and the general, whether in the Trobriand Islands or in London. He was also a man of paradoxes: kind and helpful as well as cruel and sarcastic. Keen perception and sharp wit helped make his barbs effective. Belligerence characterized many arguments with his peers. Then, too, he delighted in shocking people, particularly those he considered bourgeois and conventional. He boasted about his ability to swear in seven languages and sometimes demonstrated his fluency in inappropriate situations. The showing-off characteristic of a "bad boy" irritated some of his students and colleagues and amused others. It was my impression that his relationships with women were easier than those with men. With women he was a continental gentleman, somewhat in the well-known gallant and flirtatious tradition, which, however, did not prevent him from being completely serious when it came to discussing their work. He tended to see men as rivals and I think there was, in general, more ambivalence on both sides in these relations than in those with women.

During my first year at the L.S.E. only three graduate students were in anthropology. The other two were E. E. Evans-Pritchard and Raymond Firth. Isaac Schapera came the second year and we were soon joined by Audrey Richards, Edith Clarke, the late Jack Driberg, Camilla Wedgwood, and Gordon and Elizabeth Brown. Strong personal bonds developed between us and with Malinowski; it was a sort of family with the usual ambivalences. The atmosphere was in the European tradition: a master and his students, some in accord and others in opposition. Many other students came later, and their relations with Malinowski may have differed from ours.

The School, known as a brain-child of Fabians such as Beatrice and Sidney Webb and Bernard Shaw, was still "pink" politically. This was a pleasant background, although we—the small group of anthropologists—were much too deeply involved in anthropology to be interested in politics. The total number of graduate students from all departments was small enough for us to know each other. We had good companionship: congenial, interesting, and often gay. Bureaucratic formalities were few: a thesis and an examination on it, a required period of residence, and a sufficient knowledge of foreign languages to read the anthropological literature in them. Required courses, written examinations, and grades did not exist. The attendance at some of Malinowski's lecture courses was mixed —undergraduates as well as graduate students. The first year his courses were my introduction to anthropology. Later I still went to some of the lectures, because I continued to learn from them and because Malinowski liked his graduate students to attend, partly, perhaps, because he was then surer of a response when he asked a Socratic type of question. The lectures were usually in the late afternoon, and most of my days were spent reading in the library of the British Museum.[3]

C. G. Seligmann, Hobhouse, Westermarck, Laski, and Ginsberg were among the distinguished faculty. I took a course from each one of them except Laski and I audited one of his. I remember an exciting seminar in which all of them (except Seligmann) participated, along with four graduate students. Radcliffe-Brown lectured at the School one semester. Only he

---

[3] Anthropology was limited to social anthropology; archaeology, physical anthropology, and linguistics (all part of the American curriculum) were absent.

and Malinowski really influenced me, and in this respect the latter was far more significant.

Malinowski was in a particularly creative mood during this period, as he worked out his concept of institutions and his functional theories as they applied to magic, kinship, and primitive law. It is difficult now when much of Functionalism is an accepted part of anthropological and social science thinking to convey the tone of that early period when we felt we were striding along intellectual frontiers. An enemy was the diffusionist theories of that era, particularly those of Elliot Smith and W. J. Perry at University College. Their theory that all of culture originated in Egypt and fanned out over the world has been forgotten and discarded. But in my student days the members of the two schools were belligerent and Malinowski and Elliot Smith publicly damned each other's work. The term "evolution" was a bad word, whether referring to the Elliot Smith and Perry concept or to the oversimplified social theories which had followed publication of Darwin's theory of biological evolution. The concept of evolution has long since come out of the realm of historical fantasy, and is a significant and powerful theory rooted in physical anthropology and archaeology, as well as in ethnology.

An anecdote recalls the feeling tone of the period. Elliot Smith and Perry had sent word, by one of their students who was attending Malinowski's lectures, that they would like to see me. I ignored the invitation or command, until one afternoon, finding it difficult to continue reading in the British Museum because of an infection in an eye-lid—covered with a black eye-shade—I decided to call on the two men. University College was only a short walk from the British Museum. Both men were free and greeted me cordially. Their first question was about my thesis. When I mentioned that it was concerned with the nature of leadership in primitive societies, Elliot Smith immediately asked: "And what is the origin of leadership?" I answered that I didn't know and intimated, rather impertinently, that I did not care. They began arguing vehemently that the origin of all leadership was in Egypt. I thought it unfair to have my embryonic ideas attacked by two professors, but stuck to my point of view. About four o'clock, they asked me to have tea with them, which I declined. Feeling indignant, I rushed back to the L.S.E. and into the common room, announcing to graduate students and staff that I had just come from a fight with Elliot Smith and Perry. The burst of laughter and the exclamation, "So, this is what anthropology has come to!" made me recall the black eye-shade.

Malinowski's ideas about the origin of culture were formulated in his well-known theory of the basic and derived needs of men.[4] Man, as a biological organism with both psychological and biological needs, was the pivot of culture; this was a meaningful theory to me. Even more important in my development was Malinowski's holistic functional frame of reference, which still remains a strong part of my thinking. No matter what institution he was describing and analyzing—the family, mortuary rites, a system of barter, or any other—he vividly demonstrated, with a mass of concrete details, the interrelations between all elements of the culture. Magic, rituals, kinship, economics, myth, folktales, and so forth, were not separate categories, but parts of the whole. Years later, I was equally sympathetic to a holistic frame of reference for the study of personality.

The anti-historical aspects of Malinowski's teaching were uncongenial to my way of thinking. There is, of course, no reason for a functional point of view to be unhistorical. But in the 1920's too little was known to reconstruct the history of Melanesia as was being done for the North American Indian tribes. On the other hand the traditional life of many of the Indian tribes had been so changed that it would have been difficult to do a purely functional study among them. Even as a student, I thought Malinowski much exaggerated the anti-historicism, but accepted it as part of his belligerent argumentative tendency and was unaffected by it. I agreed only that data for real historical reconstruction of tribal societies was often lacking. Today the situation is quite different because of the great advances in archaeology and its close ties with ethnology.

Of great influence in my training were Malinowski's sensitivity to the imponderabilia of daily life, his interest in the exceptions to the norm in behavior, his awareness of the "savages" as individual personalities, not much different from us,

---

[4] An early published statement is in the article "Culture," *Encyclopedia of Social Sciences*, Vol. IV (New York: Macmillan Co., 1931), pp. 621–46.

his grasp of the native point of view and his objective analysis of it, his method of observing real cases, as well as asking questions about hypothetical ones. I listened to many lectures on kinship systems, followed their intricacies as diagrams were put on the blackboard, and participated in theoretical discussions about the extension of kinship terms. Sometimes I thought I never wanted to hear the word "kinship" again. (But in my first field work, genealogies proved to be a valuable tool for many purposes; then I became excited about working out the kinship system of "my" people.)

Malinowski's reading was broad and he was ahead of his times in his interest in, and knowledge of, psychology and psychoanalysis.[5] A. F. Shand's *The Foundations of Character*, with its discussion of sentiments, impulses, and instincts was our "bible" in psychology. F. C. Flugel's *Psychoanalytical Study of the Family* was a close second in influence. We read Freud and Jung and argued about their theories. We knew the early work of Róheim, trained in both anthropology and psychoanalysis. Seligmann was interested in a comparative study of dreams, but I did not share or understand his concern.

Many years later I learned about psychoanalysis through direct experience, the surer way to understand it and the subterranean unconscious. For personal reasons I undertook two long analyses. The second one, much deeper and more profound than the first, contributed indirectly but significantly to my continuing development as an anthropologist. Although a cliché, the saying is true that insight into one's self inevitably deepens understanding of others. As I suffered on the tortuous paths along which the second analysis led me, I remembered Malinowski's frequent quotation of the Greek, "Know thyself," to his students. Nor was it all suffering. The moments of clarity, of understanding the rationality behind the seemingly irrational behavior, of moving from an impasse, of the eventual acceptance of one's life history and personality, and of an increasing sense of freedom and of growth—these added an-

---

[5] As early as 1923, he wrote a letter to the editor of *Nature* (Vol. III, pp. 658–62) on "Psychoanalysis and Anthropology." In the same year he published "The Psychology of Sex and the Foundations of Kinship in Primitive Societies," *Psyche*, Vol. IV, pp. 98–128. A year later (1924), *Psyche* (Vol. IV, pp. 293–332) published his article "Psychoanalysis and Anthropology." Many more studies relating anthropology, psychology, and psychoanalysis followed.

other dimension to life and enriched it. I continue to be glad that I live in that period of history when psychoanalysis, with all its limitations, has been available. Although no statistics exist, there is a strong impression that more anthropologists than other social scientists have been psychoanalyzed. Perhaps the former are more exploratory by temperament. Also, anthropologists have pioneered in the study of relationships between the individual and society.

To return to student days (when it never occurred to me that I would go through an analysis), other influences were the French sociologists, Durkheim and Mauss. One year I was a partisan follower of Durkheim, and accepted his theory of the coercive power of institutions on the individual. But I became dissatisfied with its sociological purity and the complete absence of psychological motivations. He proved his case for the sociological reasons for suicide, but how could individual motivations be ignored for such a personal act as suicide? My experience in the labor movement had probably strengthened a "natural" tendency to think psychologically and in terms of individuals. Although I had emphasized the values of the union as an institution in the leaflets I distributed in Cleveland and in talks to workers, yet I was aware of the many personal factors (including friendship with me) behind the decision of factory workers to join the union, and the equally personal motivations for not joining it. Sociological explanations are obviously important in explaining social phenomena, but it was (and still is) difficult for me to accept the Durkheimian point that a sociological fact can be completely and exclusively explained only by another sociological fact. The theory did not seem to take account of the irrationalities and passions of men as I had seen them, for instance, in the struggle for power within the union. I thought Durkheim's theories were too simple. Many years later I came across the statement by the distinguished economist Jacob Viner that "Theory is always simpler than reality. Even when it seems terribly complex, it is still *simpliste,* as compared to the range of factors, operating as conditions, as means, or as ends, in any actual concrete situation." [6] This point of view does not reduce the need

[6] Jacob Viner, *International Trade and Economic Development.* (Oxford: Clarendon Press, 1953), p. 1.

for theories or their significance. But it makes me cautious about using any one theory as a complete explanation.

The works of English anthropologists such as Rivers, Marett, and Haddon were, of course, a part of training at the L.S.E., and I found the first two meaningful. I had also to read German scholars, among whom were Graebner and Schmidt, but the only result was boredom, increased by the slowness with which I read scientific German. Thurnwald, hailed as a fellow Functionalist, was more readable. Lowie was Malinowski's favorite American anthropologist at that time, and so I knew well his *Primitive Society*. In reading for my thesis I became familiar with the work of other American anthropologists, such as Boas' among the Kwakiutl, and Lowie's and Wissler's among the Plains Indians.

Malinowski's area range (when I was a student) was not broad. His descriptive data and illustrations came mostly from the Trobriand Islanders, other Melanesians, and the Australian aborigines (the subject of his D.Sc. dissertation). I remember hearing an undergraduate student mutter during one of his lectures that she was tired of hearing about the Trobriand Islanders. But, for me, they remained a fascinating and an alive people, as Malinowski probed deeply into their social system, their ways of thinking and their lives. For a student who has not yet gone into the field, to know vicariously one tribal society in detail and depth is not unimportant. Some of Malinowski's theories have become part of anthropology, others have dropped by the wayside. But his early field work is still regarded by most anthropologists as superb and having set new standards. No student of his could be uninfluenced by them.

Although Radcliffe-Brown lectured at the School for only one semester, he influenced all of us. I listened spellbound on the front seat as, tall and handsome, he gave a beautiful, polished performance. His book, *The Andaman Islanders*,[7] was one of our bibles and even Malinowski, his rival, admitted that the analysis of rituals was superb. Although both men were Functionalists and used the same theory of sentiments, their concepts differed and a lively controversy went on between them. Radcliffe-Brown was far more a true Durkheimian

---

[7] Cambridge University Press, 1922.

than was Malinowski. The social systems described by the former, whether in his writings or lectures, were in perfect and harmonious balance. Equilibrium was thought to be the desired and normal condition of society. We never heard of Andaman Islanders who broke the rules, nor did they ever come alive as people. The analysis of their ritual dances was brilliant, but we knew little about the dancers. I was fascinated by his theories for a while and they remain with me, but I never became his disciple, as did others.

My hunch is that at least some of the difference between the work of Malinowski and that of Radcliffe-Brown could be correlated with their personalities. Radcliffe-Brown, in sharp contrast to Malinowski, seemed to be more aloof from life, modern or tribal, and without close family ties. He spent many of his adult years alone and away from England.[8] I saw him rather frequently during the six weeks I spent in Sydney enroute to Lesu, when he was chairman of the Australian National Research Council (which was financing my field work), and professor at the University of Sydney. He gave the impression of enjoying being an English gentleman in voluntary exile, but he also seemed lonely. His long cape and high hat, which he wore on social evenings, his level of sophistication, as well as his brilliance, set him off from his Sydney colleagues.

In his books and lectures, he was apparently interested in people primarily as cogs in a social system. It is difficult to imagine that he had any but superficial personal relations with the Andaman Islanders. The exceptions to the rule, their loves and hates, their idiosyncracies of behavior seemed outside the range of his interests and observations.

Again, compared to Malinowski, his relations with men seemed to be easier than those with women. Also, Radcliffe-Brown had disciples in the real sense of the word. Malinowski's students learned from him, but they also argued, talked back, and made jokes about him. He wanted loyalty (you had to be on his side) but not reverence. In fact, he enjoyed irreverence. No Malinowski cult ever developed among his students. I was profoundly grateful for the basic training he gave me and I

---

[8] He was professor of anthropology at the University of Cape Town between 1921 and 1925; the University of Sydney, 1925–31; University of Chicago, 1931–37; Farouk I University, Alexandria, 1947–49.

think others were, too, even those in opposition. But it was a taking-off point, from which we went in different directions. Radcliffe-Brown, on the other hand, gathered about him a group of worshiping young disciples. I never heard any of them snipe or ridicule him. Today, some of these British anthropologists, now middle-aged, seem to belong to an ancestor cult. I see no point in the old argument about which of these two distinguished anthropologists—Malinowski and Radcliffe-Brown—was the greatest. Each, in his own way, was great.

I learned much from my fellow students, particularly Evans-Pritchard, Raymond Firth, and Isaac Schapera. We spent long hours in pubs or in the inexpensive restaurants of Little Soho, discussing and arguing. I felt decidedly inferior to them, and was also envious. Each had "a people" while I had none. Evans-Pritchard would hold forth about the Azande, among whom he did field work while still a student. Firth told us about the Maori, whom he knew before he came to London. Schapera already had an extensive knowledge of the Bushmen and other South African tribes. Theories were argued back and forth. Gossip about our teachers was told and retold gleefully. We talked of the need to keep the natives pure and undefiled by missionaries and civil servants. Missionaries were an enemy, except for Edwin Smith and H. A. Junod, who apparently were more interested in learning about the tribal peoples than in converting them.[9] British civil servants on leave came to Malinowski's lectures, and we accepted his point that training could make them more respectful and less disruptive of native life. Now, with the sociological interest in social change and with the knowledge of the significant roles played by missionaries and civil servants in it, our hostile attitude seems indeed biased.

The summer vacations were spent in Oberbozen (Soprabolzano) in the South Tyrol, where the Malinowski family had a villa. This part of the Dolomites remains one of the most beautiful places in the world for me. I remember one summer when Firth, Schapera, and I stayed in a priest's house in Maria

---

[9] The books of these two men are still highly regarded: Edwin W. Smith, *The Golden Stool* (London: Holborn Publishing House, 2nd ed., 1927) and H. A. Junod, *Life of a South African Tribe* (London: MacMillan Co., 2nd ed., 1927)

Himmelfarb, about ten or fifteen minutes' walk from the Malinowski villa. Frau Eula, the housekeeper, was a famed Tyrolese cook, and our meals, at a long table covered with oil cloth, were bountiful. With us at meals were also two student priests and the "Father"; the atmosphere was informal and relaxed. During the day my fellow students and I worked on our respective theses. Tea time, we walked over to the Malinowski villa and Elsie Malinowska served tea on the lawn, from which we could see the snow-covered mountains of Rosengarten, Latemer, and Schlern. Their three young daughters were usually playing in the immediate vicinity. After tea, Malinowski often walked, or rather climbed up a hill, with one of us, discussing our thesis. He talked continuously as he walked; I was often breathless, but not he. After dinner we were at the Malinowski villa again. Elsie, in her pleasant clear voice, read aloud from one of her husband's manuscripts or from another anthropologist's book. Radcliffe-Brown's *Andaman Islanders* was read in this manner. Malinowski or one of us would raise points for discussion. About ten o'clock, the two young men and I said "good-night" and went to a near-by café where we drank vermouth and enjoyed looking at local life.

Life in London outside the anthropological circle was also amusing. With the exception of one winter in Hampstead, I lived in Bloomsbury, and had friends in the Bloomsbury circle as well as among the anthropologists and other L.S.E. people; some overlapping occurred between the two groups. I went to gay parties, was interested in contemporary art and frequented the galleries, had one season of intense interest in the ballet, and, in general, enjoyed London life. But most days I could be found at my desk in the reading room of the British Museum. This vast vaulted room, with its strange combination of readers—distinguished scholars, students, and "cranks"—was home to me. To return to my desk and to the uninterrupted hours of reading on a Monday morning after a gay weekend was steadying. Life during these student days had its ups and downs; but happy or unhappy, I felt as if I belonged. There was no stepping in and out of this society. I was an indigenous part of it.

After three years I was awarded a Ph.D. degree. This had not been my reason for coming to London and I originally planned to stay only one year. Towards the end of the first semester, Malinowski had suggested that I pick a subject for my Ph.D. thesis. He was shocked when I told him I did not plan to take a degree, and that I was studying for "fun." I had "principles" against higher degrees, and seriously argued what higher goal could there be than studying merely for enjoyment. I seem to have been without ambition for a career or the drive to make practical plans for the future. (Marriage was a possibility.) Malinowski was irritated and said he was not giving his time and energy to training students for their "fun." I walked along the Thames, debating whether or not to give up my "principles" and take a degree. Anthropology fascinated me. I wanted to continue studying and to be part of the L.S.E. group. I would be excommunicated if I did not work toward a degree. By the end of the first semester I registered retroactively for it and went on to become an anthropologist. I have never regretted the decision.[10]

---

[10] After returning to the United States, I was influenced by a number of anthropologists. The most significant for me was Edward Sapir, in whose department at Yale University I was a research associate. Others included Clark Wissler, Ralph Linton, Alfred Kroeber, and Ruth Benedict. Later I came to Robert Redfield's work, which strengthened my humanistic point of view. The work of A. I. Hallowell and of Abraham Kardiner and, of course, of Edward Sapir, helped make a bridge between anthropological and psychoanalytic thinking. Analysis and, later, Erik Erikson's writings were major influences in that no-man's land. Twenty-five years of teaching have also been part of the learning process.

PART II

LESU

INTRODUCTION

Lesu is a village on the east coast of New Ireland, an island in the southwest Pacific. About two degrees from the equator and part of the Bismarck Archipelago (southeast of New Guinea), it is under an Australian mandate.[1] The island is about two hundred miles long with an average width of twenty miles; a low range of mountains, three thousand feet at the highest altitude, runs through the center. Lesu, approximately eighty miles from the northern end of the island, had a population of 232 at the time of my field work, April 1929 to February 1930.[2] The village was part of a linguistic unit of four other villages (Ambwa, Langania, Libba, and Tandis) which I visited to attend rites and secure ethnographic information. Occasionally I went to a village in an adjacent linguistic unit for a special ceremony. The people were Melanesian—tall, black, with bushy hair—members of the Oceanic Negroid race. Their homogeneous society belonged to a late Stone Age culture.

I was the first anthropologist to study this society, then relatively uninfluenced by modern civilization. German Catholic missionaries had been in the southern part of New Ireland, as well as in other parts of the archipelago, and had written about the religion and the *Malanggans*, ritual carvings connected with mortuary rites. But no missionary had lived in the linguistic unit where I worked. A few people in the village were technically members of a Methodist mission (Australian in origin), but appeared unaffected by its teachings in any significant way. A "mission boy" in his teens held services on Sundays, but was without influence. Writing was unknown;

---

[1] Before World War I, New Ireland was called Neu Mecklenburg and belonged to Germany. The spelling of the village name on old government maps and publications is Lossu. Lesu approximates the native pronunciation of the word more phonetically.

[2] The field work was financed by the Australian National Research Council.

49

no one had been to school and pidgin English, spoken mainly by young men and children, was the only language other than Melanesian. Technological influence from outside was slight and implements were primitive—stone axes, wooden digging sticks and spears, sharp sea shells for scraping taro (a tuber vegetable). Rituals were performed in traditional manner and native customs were followed. The exceptions to the latter were cannibalism and murder, both forbidden by the Australian Mandated Government. Occasionally a few men left their villages to "sign on" for three years of work on a coconut plantation on New Ireland or a nearby island, but they brought little cultural innovation back with them. At the time of my study, none of the men were away from Lesu. Government patrols made infrequent brief visits to the villages. In general, native life was traditional and had a coherence and logic of its own. I was able to participate rather fully in it.

III

FIRST NIGHT ALONE

This was my first night in Lesu alone. As I sat on the veranda of my thatched-roofed, two-room house in the early evening, I felt uncertain and scared, not of anything in particular, but just of being alone in a native village. I asked myself, "What on earth am I doing here, all alone and at the edge of the world?"

I had arrived two weeks earlier, accompanied by the Australian government anthropologist and a young English anthropologist (working on another island), who had met my boat in Rabaul, the capital of the Mandated Territory of New Guinea; they had generously offered to help me get settled in Lesu. When we met, the expression on their faces was, "Oh, my God!" I was a young woman, essentially urban, and obviously knew nothing about how to live in a primitive village. Their help in setting up my housekeeping was invaluable. The introduction by the government anthropologist was good because he was known to the natives through his occasional patrols, and he was well liked. The Englishman, an expert in pidgin English, gave me daily lessons in it. Pidgin is not bad English, but is a limited combination of English and native words, with a construction of its own. In this area a few German words were also in the vocabulary. My teacher was good, and I was able to practice immediately.

Both men supervised the finishing of my house (begun before my arrival for visiting government patrols), the building of a privy, the making of a primitive shower, adding a room to the cook-house for a servant's bedroom, and all the other details of settling in. Compared to the one-room village huts whose floor was the ground, my house seemed luxurious. It was raised from the ground and had two windowless rooms with a wide veranda between them and a narrow one around

51

the sides of the house. One room was for sleeping and the other for keeping supplies. I worked, received company, and ate on the wide section of the veranda. The thatched roof was an advantage in the tropics.

Ongus, the *luluai*, an Australian-appointed chief, was a well-built, intelligent-looking man, obviously in command as he directed the unloading of my boxes and bales and the finishing of my house. I was lucky that he was well respected by the Lesu people. I knew that in the past there had been no chiefs and that authority had rested with the important elders. The Australian Mandated Government had appointed a chief in each village, in order to have a representative with whom to deal when they made patrols.

During these first days I was busy unpacking and settling in. Almost everyone in the village was in and around the house gazing with wonder, admiration, or amusement at my folding army cot, kitchen equipment, sewing basket, a ring of safety pins which particularly fascinated two old men, an oil lamp with a gas mantle, a portable typewriter, and all the other odds and ends which I thought necessary to existence. When I unrolled a thin mattress for the army cot, the English anthropologist was scornful. I replied serenely that I belonged to the comfort school of anthropology. I could see no reason for being more uncomfortable than necessary. He seemed to believe that discomforts were essential. During this time I made no real contacts with the native peoples, although I had a feeling that they were friendly. We smiled at each other, exchanged greetings in pidgin English, and I played a little with two babies. One responded with delighted coos; the other wailed loudly.

I had two servants, selected in Rabaul by the government anthropologist to accompany me to Lesu. The man, nick-named Pau, was a short, middle-aged Papuan with an unusual characteristic of extensive baldness. He came highly recommended as a cook and his experience included cooking for the Germans before World War I, as well as recently for Australians. He was responsible for the kitchen and for the shooting of birds for dinner. Taiti, the woman, a Melanesian, about thirty-five years old, had lived and worked in Rabaul for many years. She took care of my house, did the laundry, mending, and other such chores. Their wages, fixed by the Mandated Government, were, by Western standards, ridiculously little: two dollars a month plus a blanket and rations. Taiti had appeared willing to leave her half-caste Chinese husband in Rabaul. I knew nothing about Pau's marital life, but he seemed not to have any wife at this time. Both servants were still strangers to me.

My real contacts were limited to the two anthropologists; we talked about anthropology and gossiped about anthropologists. I was still primarily in my own modern world. In a couple of weeks, when my house was finished, Ongus, the *luluai,* and my anthropologist friends knew that a feast must be held to mark the occasion. The people in each hamlet of the village contributed piles of yams, taro, and bananas which they placed on the ground in front of the house. I noted that the women and small children sat together on one side and the men on the other side. Ongus made a speech about how the house was "finished good" and then distributed the food and my contribution of Virginia Emu Twist tobacco to the men. Fortunately, an anthropologist in Sydney had told me tobacco would be my best currency, and I had purchased a hundred dollars worth of it.

A day or two later, my anthropologist friends left me to return to their own work. As I waved good-bye, I felt like Robinson Crusoe, but without a man Friday. That evening as I ate my dinner, I felt very low. I took a quinine pill to ward off malaria. Suddenly I saw myself at the edge of the world, and *alone.* I was scared and close to panic. When I arrived I had thought the place was lovely. Everything seemed in harmonious accord: the black natives, the vividness of the sea and of the wild flowers, the brightly plumed birds, the tall areca palm and coconut trees, the delicate bamboo, the low thatched-roofed huts, the beauty of the nights with the moon shining on the palm trees. But now the same scene seemed ominous. I was not scared of the people, but I had a feeling of panic. Why was I here, I asked myself repeatedly.

There seemed to be no adequate reason: anthropology, curiosity, career—all seemed totally unimportant. *Why* had I come? I began to think of all the events which had preceded my arrival here. I had been envious of fellow students in London

who had done field work, who had their people, while I had
none. Towards the end of my studies, I had selected the Mafulu who lived on top of a mountain in New Guinea to become
"my" people, partly because I liked the idea of being perched
on a mountain top and partly because an adventurous solicitor,
Robert Williamson, had published in 1912 a grammar of their
language and some ethnographic data, both superficial but
of potential usefulness to a beginning field worker. Malinowski
had then arranged that the Australian National Research Council invite me to make the study. Their grant included the payment of all expenses, plus £100 (then the equivalent of about
$500) as a personal stipend, for such items as cigarettes, tooth-
paste, and so forth.

Many months of preparation followed. First, I made a long,
detailed outline—forty odd pages—of all I wanted to find out,
and this was discussed in a small graduate seminar. I went to
see a doctor at the School of Tropical Medicine (to whom Seligmann gave me an introduction) to learn a few simple rules about
how to maintain good health in the tropics; the important ones
were to see *always* that water was boiled, to sleep under a
mosquito net and to take the nightly quinine pill as a prophy-
lactic against malaria. I shopped for mosquito boots and other
appropriate clothes. Farewell parties were given. I had gone
home the preceding summer to say "good-by" to the family.
Finally in December, 1928, I boarded a P. and O. ship.

Just before leaving I had received a cable from Radcliffe-
Brown, chairman of the Australian National Research Council,
to postpone my arrival in Sydney for a month because he would
not be back from the field until then. Having kissed everyone
good-by, I felt it would be an anticlimax to wait in London,
and decided to sail as planned and stop over in Ceylon for a
month. India seemed too vast for a month's visit.

I remembered the ship's dull English passengers who took
their bridge and deck tennis with religious seriousness, while
I studied the Mafulu grammar with equal seriousness. Some
evenings I danced. I was pleased to learn that Géza Róheim,
the Hungarian anthropologist and psychoanalyst, and his wife
were in first class on their way to Australia. I was in cabin
class, but saw them frequently. I enjoyed their company, but
wondered that Róheim seemed to know exactly what he would

find among the Australian aborigines. I left the ship at Colombo and was met by a Singalese prince, a former student at the London School of Economics, who drove me in great style— a string of chauffered cars—to the Y.W.C.A., the only place I could afford. It was fortunately attractive, surrounded by spacious lawns and tall trees. Ceylon was interesting, but I had a sense of marking time until I should board a ship again and bo on my way to Sydney.

When I arrived there, I went immediately to the anthropology department at the university to see Radcliffe-Brown, the chairman, and pick up mail. I found a letter from the government anthropologist advising (which meant commanding) me not to go to the Mafulu, because of the difficulties of securing porters to carry boxes and other luggage to the mountain top. Later I learned that the Mandated Government also feared the isolation of the Mafulu and was anxious about its responsibility for the first woman to work alone in its Territory. The government anthropologist suggested in his letter that I go to Lesu, a village in New Ireland, and I duly accepted his suggestion.

Lesu sounded like a good place and actually, I had no alternative, since I knew I should be dependent on the Government for practical help in transportation after I reached the islands. The next boat did not leave Sydney for a month and I settled in a one-room apartment, with an efficiency kitchen which looked very American. Much of my time was spent in the university library reading everything I could find on the Bismarck Archipelago, all written in German by missionaries.

A daily tea in Radcliffe-Brown's office brought me in touch with him and the other members of his department. I had great respect and admiration for him, but could not play the worshiping role which he seemed to need. Ian Hogbin, who had returned from his first field work in the Solomons, taught me how to use a Graflex camera that the department was lending me, and helped me shop, mostly at Woolworth's, for a year's supply of gifts for the Melanesians, whose pattern of reciprocal gift-giving was well known. Camilla Wedgwood, whom I had known in London, Lloyd Warner, and a few others were in the small anthropology group at the university. Some one in Baltimore had written to distant cousins in Sydney who were most hospitable. I enjoyed the company of my new friends, but, again, I was marking time. Occasionally, I had a horrible feeling that I might go on traveling forever, arriving places, meeting pleasant people, and shopping for equipment. Field work seemed to recede further and further away. I was truly glad when the S.S. *Montoro* of the Burns Philip Line was ready to sail. It was a small cargo boat carrying supplies to the islands and copra (dried coconuts) from them, and a few passengers.

I shall never forget the day the *Montoro* sailed from Sydney. It was supposed to leave at 9:00 A.M.; three friends who had come to see me off stayed until it actually left at four in the afternoon. The waiting was exhausting; I begged my friends to leave, but they insisted on staying. Radcliffe-Brown sent roses, and a note cautioning me not to forget to type my notes in duplicate and to send the extra copies to him as often as possible, just in case anything happened to me. One of the Australian Council's field workers had died in the field and another anthropologist was then writing up his notes.

I shared an inside cabin with two women. One was Mrs. O'Hara, weighing about two hundred pounds, good-natured, not too bright, amusingly vulgar, and taking the round-trip of the islands. Mrs. Bacon, my other cabin-mate, was the young, pretty wife of a government official on her way to Rabaul to rejoin her husband. Mrs. O'Hara regaled us with funny tales of the late Mr. O'Hara and confided her hopes of finding another husband on this trip. The three of us managed to get along fairly well in our small hot cabin, as the boat sailed up the east coast of Australia and crossed the equator, stopping frequently at islands to load and unload cargo. Other passengers included a few planters, traders, missionaries, gold miners (gold had been discovered in New Guinea), and a few minor government officials. Everyone was curious about me. As I sat on the deck putting finishing touches on cotton dresses that I was expecting to wear in the field, I answered their questions facetiously and said I was a modiste, interested in studying the latest style in straw skirts. It was obvious that none of the questioners had any interest in, or curiosity about, the Melanesians. Much of the time I had to escape from the women's never-ending tales about the danger of being raped by native men.

Finally, after eight days, came Rabaul, situated in a cove and hemmed in by mountains. The heat was oppressive. When I complained, the English anthropologist, who had met my boat, said sternly that people there did not talk about the heat. He took me shopping and I bought oil lamps, gallons of kerosene, tinned butter, jars of marmalade, many other grocery staples, a dutch oven, and a few cooking utensils. Shopping was sociable, as if I had met the store keepers on a big picnic, but had not been formally introduced. Tea parties, drinks, and dinners with government officials and their wives were more formal. Everyone gave me advice, and I tried to conceal that I was falling asleep and not hearing all of it. I had started taking quinine daily and it had the usual first effect of causing sleepiness and partial deafness. The Melanesians I saw were most disappointing. The servants looked sullen and furtive. The police boys with white caps perched on top of their bushy hair seemed slightly ridiculous.

After four days of Rabaul I was glad to go back to the S.S. *Montoro,* which had finished its unloading and loading and was ready to proceed to Kavieng, the capital of New Ireland. Soon we were there and for the first time I felt that I might be approaching the end of my traveling. Kavieng was small, not hemmed in as Rabaul was, and cool breezes were blowing. We were met by the District Officer, who invited us to stay at his home for a few days while we arranged for transportation by lorry over the rough road to Lesu. I spent much time in a hot warehouse, collecting my many bales, boxes, trunks, and so forth, and added to them by doing still more shopping. The small group of Australians in Kavieng were hospitable, but I had the feeling of being inspected. The worst crime I could be accused of was snobbishness. I had to be a friendly young woman, as well as an anthropologist with a new Ph.D., and I had to listen carefully to all advice and give an impression that I could handle any practical situation that might arise with the "savages."

Finally we were off. The road followed the winding curves of the east coast, up hill and down hill. Miles without any sign of human habitation, and then suddenly we would pass through a village and I would have a glimpse of tall black men in their loin cloths at a feast, and a group of women sitting on the ground chatting and playing with their babies. They looked attractive and quite different from the Melanesians I had seen in Rabaul. Sometimes the road passed through a plantation with its orderly rows of coconut trees, owned by an Australian. Always there was the sea on one side and the bush on the other. After eighty miles, we arrived at Lesu. About four months had passed since I had left England.

Now I was sitting on my veranda, presumably ready to begin work, yet in a panic. I asked myself again, why am I here alone? I had to admit that no one had compelled me to come, that the expedition was not only voluntary but intensely desired. There could be only one explanation: I must have been mad. I quickly decided that although I may have been mad, I did not have to remain so. I would go home on the next boat which would leave Kavieng in six weeks. This brought some relief and I felt I could stick it out for that short time. The newspapers had publicized my being the first woman to go alone into the field in this area, and I now saw future headlines, "Anthropologist Leaves Field After Six Weeks Because She Is Scared!" But even that was better than being mad.

While I was immersed in gloom, visitors arrived: Ongus, the *luluai,* who had competently directed the finishing of my home, with his wife, Pulong, and their adolescent daughter Batu. With Pulong and Batu I had only previously exchanged greetings. They presented me with a baked taro, and I asked them to sit down. Ongus and his daughter spoke pidgin English but Pulong did not. As we talked, Ongus gave me some words of the native language which I wrote down, and he told me a few stories about the former German administration (before World War I), which had been hated. He also told me a little about himself—how, when young, he had gone away to work for a few years on a plantation in New Guinea, where he had learned his pidgin English. He added that now he would never leave Lesu again. At the end of a few hours he said that he would soon call all the people together so that I could explain to them what I planned to do. He mentioned that they were very curious. At the end of the evening I felt at home not only with Ongus, but also with Pulong and Batu, who had said very little. When they were leaving Ongus said that I should "sing out" if I needed anything and he would come immediately. Their house was directly opposite mine.

I was no longer alone. I had friends. I went to bed and fell asleep almost immediately. No more thoughts of madness or leaving entered my mind. Several years later I learned that a definition of panic is a state of unrelatedness.

IV

GETTING STARTED

Then came the day when Ongus called all the people to as-
semble in front of my house. They stood or squatted on the
ground, men separately from women, as I told them why I was
there in newly learned pidgin interspersed with a few native
words I had picked up. My people at home, I said, knew nothing about Lesu or New Ireland and had sent me to find out
about their customs. When I went home, I would tell them
all I had learned and write it in a book. The audience had
never seen books, and I passed around a few anthropology
monographs with pictures of dark-skinned people. These
aroused much interest. The Lesu people had not known so
many other black people were in different parts of the world,
which for them consisted of the islands, Australia, and a vague
unlocated place called Germany.

To explain where the United States was, I traced a map on
the ground and told them how long it took for me to come in
a big ship. The Melanesians were impressed and flattered that
I had come such a long distance to find out about their customs.
I told them quite truly that my prestige (using the native term
for it) when I returned home depended on how much I knew
and how accurate it was, and this, I added, depended on how
well they helped me. In a sense, I threw much of the burden
on them, and they were apparently pleased to accept it.

The next day I began, with Ongus's help, to make a diagram
and census of the village. I started at one end and worked
gradually to the other end, three or four miles away. On the
diagram I marked every house with a number and wrote the
names of the people who lived in it, their sex and kinship to
each other, and if they were related to next-door neighbors.
The diagram also contained the position of the men's house
(where they gathered to discuss and make decisions), the

cemetery, the cook houses, a mission church, bush which had not been cut down, and the boundaries and names of the fifteen small hamlets into which the village was divided. I described also the interior of the thatched-roofed huts, and noted their cleanliness and the fact that they were, apparently, used only at night for sleeping and during the rains.

Some mornings when I was making the census, the women were in their gardens, about three-quarters of an hour's walk along a narrow footpath through the bush. But the men and children were at home, the father often playing with his baby as he sat outside of his hut. In the afternoons, the women were back from the gardens. Most activities, except, of course, sexual relations, were carried on outdoors, a boon indeed for a field worker who lived in the middle of the village. Nothing was too small to escape my notebook: how women held their babies; the way two adolescent boys walked with the arm of one thrown casually around the shoulders of the other; a man putting powdered white lime on his hair to cleanse and beautify it, and so on ad infinitum. The census (suggested by Malinowski) was a useful way of starting, particularly as I was diffident about beginning. Taking the initial plunge is never easy. Why bother people with impertinent questions, was my first unanthropological reaction. But the census was relatively impersonal, easily understood, and very specific.

Malinowski had also told us to note down everything we saw and heard, since in the beginning it is not possible to know what may or may not be significant. I faithfully tried to carry out this injunction but, of course, all observation is selective. Later I found that some of the first impressions were keen and important, while others were incorrect or insignificant. In response to my question about garden magic, a woman told me there was none. This seemed impossible in Melanesia, and so I thought it was secret. Later I learned that every step in gardening was openly accompanied with magical rites made by a man. Either the woman misunderstood my question and perhaps thought I was asking about woman's magic, or she did not feel sufficiently in rapport with me to talk about it. In any case, it would have been better to have waited and asked the question when it was in the proper context of gardening. I made a similar mistake in inquiring too early about beliefs in life after death, and was told that there were no such beliefs. In this case I think the question was phrased poorly and misunderstood because later I received full information on this topic from some of the same people I had asked originally. I recorded not only what was said or done, but also the shrug of the shoulder, the lowering of the voice, or an evasion of a question, hoping I should learn later what they meant.

From the beginning, people were friendly. They wanted to know about my family: parents, brothers and sisters, uncles, aunts, cousins, and other relatives of my "clan." One night as I sat around a fire with a group, they repeated after me, in chorus fashion, the names of each member of my family. The moon was full and the coconut palms shone in its light; the sea murmured along the shore and my Melanesian friends uttered in unison after me: Louis, Minnie, Florence, Theresa, Morris. There was difficulty with the "fl" of Florence, an unfamiliar sound to them. They asked for details about the marriages and the children and this interest remained throughout my stay in Lesu. When I was getting some information from the men, I sometimes said that my father or uncle would be particularly interested in it. On the arrival of the occasional mail, my Lesu friends listened with interest to the news that a cousin had been recently married, that my mother and father were well, and that my brother had gone on a long trip. My parents sent a message of thanks to Ongus for taking good care of me; he and other friends sent greetings to them. However, they were not curious about my culture and asked no questions even when I showed them pictures in newspapers or magazines which arrived in the mail.

Where was my husband was the big question. I realized that in a society where literally every one was, or had been, married, and where all girls were wed shortly after puberty, it was not possible for people to understand how a young woman, such as myself, could be unmarried. The functioning of this Melanesian social system, with its sharp and complementary division of labor between the sexes and their social and ritual separation, made it necessary for every adult to be married and part of a family household. The only exceptions were a few elderly widows and widowers, living with one of their children or a maternal nephew, and an occasional divorcee, who had not yet remarried. So I told my Lesu friends that I had been married and divorced, adding that my ex-husband had not worked well, one of the reasons for native divorce. My friends murmured, "just like us."

The village was a sociable place and I often had company in the evenings, unless I was busy typing or developing photographs. One night when a number of people were on the veranda, an elder demonstrated his skill at cat's cradle, and told a folk tale that went with it. The tale was amusing and accompanied with much laughter. I was pleased that I understood the reason for the latter. Singing supplemented another cat's cradle. On a leisurely afternoon, Pulong, Batu, and my servant, Taiti, sat on my veranda, smoking—Pulong with her pipe, Taiti and I with cigarettes—all of us eating a baked yam and talking about my clothes. The two women commented freely on them. Some they liked and thought appropriate; others, they did not fancy.

From the beginning I fitted, as far as possible, into the native economic system. In this society, no one did anything for nothing. Equality was the ideal in reciprocal gift giving, but if there was a difference, prestige belonged to the person who gave the most. Quite early I began a pattern of distributing gifts on Sunday morning to those who had been particularly helpful to me during the week. The most popular gifts were the useful ones: knives of all sizes (from pen knives to twenty-four-inch butcher knives), spades, and hatchets, which enabled the people to fell trees, cut away the tangled bush, plant taro, and do many other jobs more easily and quickly than with their stone and wooden tools. Gaily colored cotton material was well liked for loin cloths. Toy balloons were popular with the children, and young men liked jew's harps. There was a native version of this instrument, but my commercial ones were much enjoyed. Tinsel trimming, the kind used on Christmas trees, was a novelty. Men and women used it to decorate their hair, usually ornamented with flowers and leaves. The tinsel trimming was in much demand for ritual dancing, but unfortunately I did not bring enough with me and my supply did not last long. Small mirrors delighted the people and were the first they had ever seen.

Trade was also based on the principle of reciprocity. The native medium of exchange was *tsera*, one unit of which was an arm's length of tiny flat shell discs strung together. It was made under ritual conditions on Lawongai, a nearby island. Objects which were sold—breast ornaments, arm bands, spears, canoes, fishing nets, drums, pigs, and so forth—were evaluated in *tsera*, and a man who paid more than the set price gained in prestige. The concept of a bargain was unknown. Services, such as the performance of magic, the carving of a *malanggan* or dancing mask, or the teaching of a dance were likewise paid for with *tsera*. It was also used in marriage payments. My currency was Virginia Emu Twist tobacco and I used no money at all. After a morning's work with one person, he received a few sticks of tobacco. I gave it also to those who brought me food such as fresh fish, a turtle, a branch of a banana tree with several dozen bananas on it. Everyone—men, women and children—much preferred the Virginia Emu Twist to their own native-grown tobacco. They smoked pipes, although a few young people rolled cigarettes in a piece of paper from my household. (My cigarettes were too mild for their taste.)

It is difficult to evaluate the exact effect of these gifts on the culture. Probably most important were the iron tools, giving the people a concept of efficiency not known before. Since my gift-giving and payments of tobacco were in the context of native customs, I doubt if the reciprocal nature of the social system was altered in any significant manner. No one ever asked me for anything, and I never gave anything for which there was not either a return service or a gift.

I once manipulated the system of reciprocal gifts to get data. At ritual feasts I had observed that sometimes a man was reluctant to take a large gift of roast pig if he could not see his way to returning it in the near future. I was finding it difficult to get rain magic, although it had been relatively easy to learn the magic to make the gardens grow, to catch wild pigs and fish, to woo a woman or a man, to wage a war successfully, to make an ill person well; I even managed to get some data on black magic, the practice of which had been forbidden by the Mandated Government. Only one quite old man knew the rain magic. His health was not good and he stayed in his hut most of the time, participating only rarely in village life. On one of these rare occasions when I met him, I saw that, unlike the other Lesu people, he did not understand why I wanted his esoteric knowledge and that he was reluctant to give it to me. I decided on an indirect approach. I was on good terms with his son and daughter-in-law and at discreet intervals I sent small gifts to the old man through them. Months went by without any acknowledgment from him. Then one morning, the son came to my house and said that his father was ready to give me the rain magic. A number of Lesu people were on my veranda at the time, and their comment was, "It's about time." Everyone knew why I had been sending gifts to the old man and if he had not given me the magical spells in return, his prestige would have fallen.

Another time a gift had an unexpected result. I gave a ring with a large stone (purchased in Sydney's Woolworth) to a man who had done some service for me. He put the ring on a finger, clenched his hand as a fist and remarked, "something belong fight." I insisted that the ring was only an ornament, but he was equally certain that it was a weapon. I was puzzled. After we talked for a while, I learned that the Germans, the first white people to appear in New Ireland, had knocked the natives on the head with their fists and that the blows were extremely painful because of the rings the men often wore. I gave no more rings away, as it was impossible to convince people that they were not for fighting; somehow, I felt that I should not encourage that.

The incident, however, led to further discussion about fighting. Two men might fight over a woman, or two women over a man, with the rest of the village as spectators. Warfare, usually caused by the men of one group stealing the women and pigs of another, had been abolished by the Australian Mandated Government. By our standards, the traditional wars had been exceedingly small. Spears were the weapons, and perhaps two or three men might be killed or wounded. An enemy who had been killed was eaten by the victors. The men who had eaten human flesh smacked their lips as they talked about it. As far as I could make out, this was another meat dish in a diet which did not have much meat (only roast pig at feasts), as well as a way of imbibing the strength of the dead warrior. With all my alleged objectivity, I felt a bit squeamish during the conversation. However, I was assured that only enemies taken in war had been consumed—never friends.

Returning to the days of getting started, I began quite early to work regularly on the language. Collecting a vocabulary was relatively easy. Radcliffe-Brown had given me small sheets of colored paper, about six by three inches, with different colors for nouns, verbs, adjectives, and so forth. A rubber band and cardboard covers bound each group of papers together. These were always in one of my large pockets ready for notation, as I constantly asked the names of this or that. But this method gave me no grammar. For that I recorded texts of folk tales and myths. Fortunately, I had taken a year's course in phonetics in London, which had sharpened my ears and enabled me to record the language phonetically.

A middle-aged man, with a clear enunciation and much patience, dictated the tales to me and then helped me translate them into pidgin English. Working out the syntax was difficult. I had Codrington's book on Melanesian languages with me and it was of valuable help, although often it seemed that the Lesu Melanesian language was quite different from those he had recorded. I am not a good linguist and learning the Melanesian dialect was my hardest job. I literally sweated over it, but the work was worth while, even from the beginning. An important elder became interested in helping me when I first managed to use a few phrases and sentences in the native language. After a while, I could understand enough of the casual conversation to know what was going on and to ask further questions. Although my competence in the language increased, I never became expert in it. But my friends were so pleased at my trying to learn their language that they exaggerated my ability to use it. I always understood better than I could talk. I knew my limitations and even after many months in Lesu I went over the speeches I recorded phonetically at feasts and other rituals with my teacher and he helped me translate them into pidgin English.

Eventually, I managed to get along moderately well in conversation. But one day I made an amusing linguistic mistake—not the first, but the most diverting. Without meaning to, I used a native obscene term, the sound of which was close to that of the word I meant. Everyone laughed and my mistake was repeated as a good joke all around the village. I thought it was funny, too, but not so my teacher. Annoyed, he came to see me and said he wished I would do better, because my mistakes reflected on him. Everyone, he continued, knew he was my teacher. I felt properly chastised.

I think it would probably have been better if I had concentrated almost exclusively on learning the language the first three months. But I was too much in a hurry, too curious about the native society, to have the patience to spend all of my time on the language. If no particular event was occurring in the village, I worked at home with informants, taking down their genealogies or discussing some feast I had attended, as well as learning the language. Late afternoons I often strolled casually through the village, noting what was going on, and one day I happened to come upon men practicing a dance. I knew it was taboo for a woman to watch men rehearse a dance, although women would be in the audience when the dances were performed. The men had seen me emerge from a thicket of trees and bushes, and it was too late to turn back. No rule existed for this situation, because a native woman would have known (as I did a bit later) exactly when and where the men were rehearsing. I merely followed the ordinary canons of good manners and walked past the dancers with head averted, so that I did not see them, and on to the next hamlet.

This first month I walked warily. Friendly contacts were made more easily than I had expected, but I wondered if I might not do something inadvertently to disturb the cordiality and friendliness. Gradually I began to feel more secure. I was not such a curious phenomenon as I had been at first, and people seemed to take me more for granted. Equally important, I was getting over some of my self-consciousness and losing the feeling of butting in.

At the end of a month, or "moon" as the Lesu people would say, Ongus came to see me and said that the important men had held a meeting in the men's house and discussed whether or not they would continue to work with me. Fortunately, for my peace of mind, I had not known in advance of the meeting. Ongus reported that they had decided to keep on helping me, and had commented favorably on my walking with head averted past their dance rehearsal. I was naturally pleased. I knew that the decision of the men on another island had been negative about working with an anthropologist, who had then left.

Although pleased with the friendliness of the Lesu people and their cooperation in giving me data, yet I was a bit disappointed that some had had contact with white people. I yearned romantically for an "untouched" people and I began wondering about the possibility of going to another island where contacts were almost non-existent. I wrote to Radcliffe-Brown about this, but before I could receive his answer telling me he was pleased with the data I was getting in Lesu and urging me to stay there, I had already decided that my fantasies about other islands were probably a matter of "greener pastures" and that I was lucky to be in a functioning tribal society. As I continued working in Lesu and the nearby villages, I realized how superficial the contacts with modern society had been.

About this time I wrote to Malinowski and, among other things, thanked him for the training he had given me. I mentioned that I had been able to begin working immediately, without the trial and error period through which some young anthropologists suffered. But, I added, in spite of the excellence of his teaching and the vivid emphasis on his own field work (also among a Melanesian people), yet, life in Lesu was different from what I had expected. His answer was, "It always is!"

V

SERVANTS

The organization of my household was part of getting settled. Servants are a necessity in field situations where living conditions are primitive. Wood has to be chopped, birds and game shot, water often carried from a distance, cooking done over an open fire, clothes washed on rocks and ironed with a charcoal iron, and other chores done in an equally primitive way. Frequently, servants in the field have other important functions: as trusted friends, as informants about native culture, and, in some circumstances, as entrées into it.

The government anthropologist had told me in Rabaul that no one in Lesu would have any experience in cooking or doing household chores for Europeans; he had found Pau and Taiti —experienced servants—to accompany me. It was soon obvious that Pau, trained cook, was not suitable for Lesu. He complained about my primitive kitchen equipment—a grate over an open fire, a dutch oven, a few pots and pans—and about my simple menu. Ecstatically, he talked of large meals he had cooked for former employers, and he was scornful of my simple lunch and unelaborate dinner. Nor did he and Taiti get along. She and all the women of the village made fun of his baldness and rejected his advances. He did not make friends with the men, either. Nor was I able to make any real contact with him, since his many years of service had conditioned him not to go beyond the formal relationship of servant and mistress. Most of the day he sat forlornly on a bamboo bench outside the kitchen, playing a doleful tune on a pan pipe.

Taiti was different. She and I became friends. If I was not busy, she would talk and gossip with me. She was friendly, too, with the other women, often joining them when they came to see me. But she did not like Pau and slept in the house belonging to Pulong and Ongus, instead of in the cook house.

Soon she began to complain about missing her half-caste
Chinese husband who worked in Rabaul.

I grew weary of Pau's constant grumbling and of the tensions between him and Taiti. I knew the best servants for me
would be a married couple and I wrote the government anthropologist to find out if any were available. Fortunately, a
couple working for a government official about to go on leave
were free to come in three weeks. They sounded good because
they came originally from a New Ireland village some fifty
miles north of Lesu, had not been away too long, and were
young. Pau went back to Rabaul, and Taiti said she would
remain until the new couple arrived. During this time I did
the cooking, as Taiti knew nothing about it and was not interested in learning. Besides, it took less time for me to prepare
the meals than to teach her. One of the local young men
chopped the necessary wood for the fire, but none of them
knew how to handle a gun and neither did I. During this period
all my meats came out of cans.

I was glad to see Sinbanimous and Kuserek, the new servants, when they arrived. Attractive-looking, young, obviously
at home in the village, they were at ease in my simple household, although a bit shy with me. After they arrived, Taiti
showed no inclination to leave, although the day before she
had remarked that she wished they would hurry and come, so
she could return to Rabaul. She became ostentatiously friendly
with me, and was critical of the way Kuserek made my bed
and did other household chores. Taiti was really not a very
good servant herself, but I did not want to tell her to go. I
liked her and she had helped me in many ways when I was
feeling "new."

At the end of a week Kuserek became jealous of Taiti in
relation to her husband and the two women quarreled. Taiti
told me about it and said that now she would have to go, as
there would be no peace if she stayed. I said I was sorry, but
agreed that the situation would be impossible. I had a feeling
that she wanted me to urge her to stay, and that she would
then not have left. But I did not want a household in which
there was constant jealous fighting, and besides, there was not
enough work to keep three servants even half busy. I knew
that Mr. Grosse, the nearest planter, was going to Kavieng the

next day, and that Taiti could go up with him in his lorry. She left very early to walk to the Grosse's plantation. As she said good-bye to me, she wept. I felt badly, too. She had been with me since my first day in Lesu and I had learned much—some of it intangible—from her. Her protective attitude had been amusing, but also helpful.

As soon as Taiti had gone, Sinbanimous and Kuserek lost their shyness. We became friends. The evening after Taiti left, Kuserek came up after dinner to chat and we were later joined by Pulong. She sprawled lengthwise on the floor as was her custom, puffing at her pipe; Kuserek sat on an empty box and I on the one chair and we smoked cigarettes. The latter was a sign of Kuserek's sophistication from having lived in Rabaul. However, she was pleased to be back in a village not too different from her own. She described in detail the rites at the time of the first menses and Pulong commented on the differences in the Lesu rites on the same occasion. The three of us sat smoking and talking until quite late. Finally we all became sleepy. Pulong went home, Kuserek joined her husband in their room next to the kitchen, and I turned in.

Sinbanimous was just right as a cook. He did not aspire to doing fancy dishes, but he knew the basic facts about cooking and he baked an excellent loaf of bread. When we occasionally had eggs, he made a delicious creme caramel. He was always solicitous and protective about my interests. When I gave a boy a stick of tobacco for a papaya which I had not noticed was overripe, Sinbanimous was indignant and asked whether I wanted to throw my tobacco away. He told the boy in no uncertain language what he thought of him, and, of course, got another papaya from him. Sinbanimous' sense of justice was somewhat different when we found in a box of groceries from Kavieng an article I had not ordered and which was not on the bill. I remarked that I would send this item back. Sinbanimous thought this was foolish and wanted to know why I could not keep it. His argument was that I had spent plenty of money at the grocery store and that it was time they gave me something. From a Melanesian point of view he was quite right.

He was a tall, attractive young man and the little boys in the village adored him. They carried water, chopped wood, and did many other small chores for him. He was skilled in making pan-pipes and small toy canoes, which he gave to them. Both he and Kuserek were popular with adults, too, and participated fully in village social life—the dances, feasts, and more casual social activities. They came from a different linguistic unit and while the social organization was basically the same, there were differences in some customs. The discussion of the similarities and the differences naturally interested me.

One difference was in totemic birds. When Sinbanimous was looking for a bird for my dinner one day, he saw one whose feathers he thought would make an attractive dancing head-dress. He shot it, evidently unaware that the bird represented a totem in Lesu. I knew nothing about the incident until a large crowd led by an angry old man appeared suddenly in front of my house. Everyone was talking so excitedly and shrilly that I could not understand what they were saying. Finally they quieted down, and I was able to find out what the excitement was about.

The old man had seen the dead bird and was in a terrible rage. (Killing the bird was a major crime.) Sinbanimous had dropped the bird and fled into the bush. I was in a delicate position. I did not want to desert my servant, and it was with my gun that he had killed the bird. On the other hand, if I took too much responsibility for his act, I feared it might weaken the good will of the Lesu people. I did not say much, but pointed out that Sinbanimous had shot the bird in ignorance and had not known what he was doing. Many in the crowd, particularly the younger men, agreed with this point. Sinbanimous was genuinely liked and his popularity helped him now. But, scared by the old man's threats to kill him, he stayed away three days. In the meantime, the old man quieted down, and when Sinbanimous returned nothing more was said about the incident.

My relationship with both Sinbanimous and Kuserek was easy-going. They knew what I expected them to do, and I rarely had to instruct them on any specific task. Their work took only a small part of their time, and they participated fully in the activities of the village. We became a ménage of three, each with our own responsibilities. I was not supposed to do household chores of any type, or to carry anything—

even a light native basket. But I accidentally discovered that I had a reputation as a hard worker. Sinbanimous brought a message one day from an old man whom I had asked to come and work with me, that he was then too busy making dancing masks; Sinbanimous added that the old man was as hard a worker as I, who was always taking notes and working with informants from the time I got up until night.

The relationship with my servants was unusual on these islands, where the tempers of white men (and women, too) were short. Irritated by the heat, the rains, the ever-present malaria, they often lashed out at their servants on the slightest pretext. Contributing to this situation was the lack of under-standing between Australian and Melanesian and the absence of a code of *noblesse oblige*, which tends to keep a person from losing his temper with some one not in a position to fight back. I prided myself on being different, until I fell from grace. I had been away for a day and a night attending rites in Libba (about ten miles from Lesu) and had returned, exhausted from lack of sleep. To my dismay, I found a roll of photographs, which I had taken just before going to Libba, lying exposed, damp, and ruined on the bamboo table in the kitchen. I had put them, as usual, in a can of unused tea leaves, to keep dry until there was time to develop them. Sinbanimous had mis-taken this tin for another one, and had dumped the film on the table, where it had been rained on. I was angry and exploded with exasperation. Later, I was chagrined over my loss of temper. But Sinbanimous took it in his stride. This was the only eruption in our even relationship.

The domestic life of Sinbanimous and Kuserek was not nearly as calm as their relationship with me. They often quar-reled, the fights usually provoked by Kuserek's nagging sus-picion of Sinbanimous' intentions towards other women. In the beginning, the quarrels interested me as data, but since they were quite uniform, they soon lost that function and were only a disruption in the household. When we were at Logagon (twenty-five miles away) for some important rites, they had a big fight, and Kuserek ran away to relatives in that neighbor-hood. We returned to Lesu without her. I announced to the world in general, i.e. to this native world, that I was grieved that she had run away. A few days later a boy came with a

message from Kuserek: her "cross" had not been with me, but
with her husband; now the "cross" was finished and she would
return if he would come and get her. He went immediately.
They arrived a few days later at night, wet, tired, and miser-
able after walking since before daybreak in the rain. They
seemed feverish and I gave them aspirin before they went
to bed.

Just when I was feeling pleased with the long period of
peace which followed this episode, Kuserek dashed up to my
house, saying that Sinbanimous was going to beat her. I strolled
over to the cook house; Sinbanimous was breathing fire and
brimstone against his spouse and obviously about to beat her.
Wife-beating was customary in this society, and I could not
tell Sinbanimous to refrain from exercising his rights. However,
I mentioned the last fight and how upset the household had
been, his long walk to bring Kuserek back, and I ended with
the remark that this time she might run even farther away. He
muttered to himself and said nothing. I went back to my house.
Kuserek was sitting on the steps and announced that she would
sleep at my house that night. When night came, I asked her if
she had brought up her blanket. She giggled, and said that the
"cross" was over, and that she was sleeping in her own house.

A more dramatic and more ambiguous episode happened
later. Sinbanimous and a number of Lesu people had spent the
evening on my veranda recording songs and hearing them
played back. The evening was pleasant and normal. After
everyone had gone home and I was getting ready for bed, I
heard a commotion outside. I went out and saw Sinbanimous
with a long knife (which I had given him) running after Ladawin, a young buck of Lesu, his constant companion. Kuserek
explained hastily that her husband had gone "mad," that it had
happened before and was caused by his dead brother's spirit
entering him, and that Sinbanimous at these times was quite
unaware of what he was doing. Accompanied by Malalis, a
boy of about twelve years (one of Sinbanimous' admirers), she
ran after him. The other Lesu people were afraid of a "mad"
man and did not join the pursuit. It continued with Ladawin
in advance, Sinbanimous running after him, and Kuserek and
Malalis trying to catch up with Sinbanimous. I sat on my veranda, wondering what I would do if he came back raving and

belligerent. No lectures in anthropology and no books had included information on how to handle a "mad" native; nor were there any native rules. While waiting for Sinbanimous to return, I thought of the triangular relationship between him and Ladawin and Kuserek. Ladawin was constantly around the cook house and was attentive to Kuserek. I had often wondered that Sinbanimous never appeared to be jealous.

After an hour Sinbanimous returned and without a word went to his bed and fell sound asleep. Ladawin had secured the knife and returned it to me. The next morning, Sinbanimous said he remembered nothing of what had happened the preceding evening, except running up the road. He did not remember why he had done so. He was embarrassed and did not want to talk. Kuserek talked more freely, but not in her husband's presence. She said that he had been subject, at irregular intervals since he was a boy, to these "seizures" which she described as a kind of illusion, caused by his dead brother's spirit. A day later, Ladawin resumed his former practice of being constantly around the cook house as Sinbanimous' best friend. This relationship continued without any further interruption, as long as we were in Lesu. Sinbanimous did not ask me to return his knife, but I gave it back to him a month later.

I thought vaguely about the psychological overtones of this incident, but was not sufficiently interested or skilled to explore the matter further. The household returned to its normal, pleasant routine.

Sinbanimous and Kuserek were not only important in freeing me from all domestic responsibilities and in making me comfortable; we were also friends and often participated together in village life. With them the household had its niche in local society.

VI

THE LONG HAUL—
SYSTEMATIC WORK

The days were long and full. I arose with the sun, which was always at six o'clock. Since the island was about two degrees from the equator, there was almost no change in the time of sunrise and sunset. It was impossible to sleep late because the whole village was up at sunrise and I could hear the people chattering outside my house. (The only exception occurred after all-night rites when everyone slept through the next day.)

After breakfast I frequently worked on the veranda of my house with a male informant; genealogies, language, magical spells, speeches made the previous day at a feast, and other aspects of native life were the topics. A short nap followed a light lunch. In the afternoons I often strolled through the village and joined a group of women as they sat on the ground preparing the taro to be baked. Other times, several of my women friends came to see me. They sprawled on the floor of the veranda, telling jokes, talking about themselves, or gossiping about others. An elderly woman told of her youthful sexual episodes and how she led one man on for quite a time before surrendering. These intimate tales of extra-marital sex life were told without embarrassment and to the accompaniment of much laughter. Much of the data about the women's private lives came in this casual manner and I had a sense of real understanding, when unaided, I saw the point of their jokes. During these gay, friendly visits, I generally did not take out my notebook, but wrote after they went home what the women had told me.

Some days were spent away from home, going with the women to their gardens, fishing with the men, or attending one of the many feasts and other rituals. When I was away from Lesu, the milk of a coconut was my lunch, and I had to forego my nap.

In the late afternoon I went swimming. The water between the Lesu beach and a reef further out was relatively shallow, and I had been told that sharks were not apt to come there. After the swim, I changed from shorts and shirt or jacket to a cotton dress, amused at my "dressing for dinner." But the change was refreshing. I usually read while I ate dinner, or, occasionally, daydreamed about life away from Lesu. After dinner I typed notes, or developed photographs, or, weary from these tasks, sat with my Lesu friends around their fire or on my veranda for sociability. But I could not keep from making mental notes, when something was said, to follow up the next day. When the evening was over, I went to my cot, and was asleep within a few minutes. I did not wake up until I heard noise outside at sunrise. Day after day went by in this way. I adopted the native method of telling time by the position of the sun in the sky. When making an appointment for the next day, a man pointed to the place in the sky where the sun would be when he planned to visit me. If a number of people were involved, nothing happened until everyone arrived. I liked this leisurely pace. At home I had tended to be unpunctual, often failing to get to a class or appointment on time. If I were taking a train which ran every hour or so, I rarely tried to make a specific one, but went to the station, book in hand, and read until the next train arrived. The second day in Lesu, I went swimming with my watch on my wrist! Sun time suited me perfectly.

I managed to keep track of the days by marking them off on a calendar and varied the week by doing different things on Sunday. In the morning, I held a "clinic" on my veranda. Many of the Lesu people had open sores—yaws—which I washed with a solution of potassium permanganate; and I dispensed quinine to those who had malaria. Sunday afternoons I often recorded native songs. The University of Sydney had lent me an Edison recording machine, the old-fashioned type with a large horn. The first time I used it there was much excitement among the group of fifteen or so people on my veranda. To show how the machine worked, I sang into the horn and then played the record back. Astonishment and laughter was the initial reaction of the Lesu people. They were too scared to sing into it at first. Then Ongus stepped forward and spoke briefly—somewhat in the form of a magical spell—admonishing the machine to sing well. It occured to me that if the machine had become part of their culture, the words of Ongus might have become a spell, uttered each time before the machine was used. After speaking, he sang into it, and I played the record back. Everyone was delighted. The fear was gone, and the only problem was to get my friends to stop singing and go home. I finally got them to leave by promising that we would have another "concert" soon.

The first systematic work (after the census, and outside of learning the language) was with genealogies. As a graduate student I had taken a year's course in kinship and had become bored with the intricate classificatory systems written on the blackboard and discussed for many hours. Intellectually I had known their significance, but it was not until I saw one actually functioning in Lesu that I understood how it was the very basis of tribal social structure. The explanation of why so and so is doing this or that, or refraining, was almost always in terms of kinship. When one man refused to mention a woman's name because she was in a taboo relationship, I tried to get the relationship but failed. I did his genealogy but the taboo woman did not appear in it. It was only after I did his wife's genealogy that I learned the taboo woman was his wife's mother's sister's daughter.

Many mornings I worked on my veranda with an informant on his genealogy. I had special large notebooks for this; one genealogy spread over several pages and often took a few days to complete. It was not that the genealogies were so long; at the most I got only four generations and, more usually, three complete ones. But the interesting digressions which I encouraged took the time. W. H. R. Rivers had written that genealogies were an excellent way of getting much information other than kinship, and I seemed to be proving it again. My informants gave me significant information about people of their parents' and grandparents' generations, as well as of their own. I also had two definite lines of inquiry, one related to the possibility of a system of clan intermarriage and the other to population statistics. It was easy to secure the clan name for each person in a genealogy. Clan membership was too significant—for determining position, inheritance, and duties—to be forgotten. Records of birth and deaths did not exist in this pre-literate society. No one even knew how old he or anyone else was, although who was older and younger was known. It was, however, possible to get relevant data through genealogies. The number of children born to each woman was always remembered. For the people who had died, my informants could tell me whether the death was shortly after birth, in infancy and before weaning (between two and three years), in early childhood, in late childhood and before puberty, in adolescence and after puberty, young manhood and womanhood, middle age or old age. (The last two terms were, of course, by native standards.) I noted on the genealogy the approximate time of death for each member who had died.

The Australian Mandated Government was concerned with the question of why the population in the islands was declining, i.e. whether births were decreasing or deaths increasing. They had asked me to try to find out; since I was financed by them, I regarded the inquiry as an obligation. Also, I was curious to investigate a theory advanced in a book I had read as a student, *The Clash of Cultures*, by G. H. L.-F. Pitt-Rivers.

He was an amateur anthropologist who after making a tour of the islands had expounded a theory that the population was declining because the people had lost their *joie de vivre*. He assumed some mystical connection between the latter and fertility. Even a short time in Lesu had convinced me that Pitt-Rivers' theory did not apply here. Marital and extramarital relations were obviously enjoyed. My woman friends had mentioned that while the missions were responsible for their having to wear a Mother Hubbard blouse, their teachings had no effect on their sex life, whether in the huts with their husbands or with lovers in the bush. The people were gay and apparently living well-functioning and normal lives, i.e. normal in Melanesia. I could see no absence of *joie de vivre*, rather the opposite. But what were the reasons for the decline in population, as indicated in censuses made by the government anthropologist for the whole area?

As I worked, I had an impression that the birth rate was stable and that deaths among babies and children were increasing. The government anthropologist at my request sent me the official medical reports on introduced diseases, and my theory was that they, particularly tuberculosis and yaws, were the cause of the increase. I saw adults who looked as if they might be tubercular depositing sputum on the beaten ground that was the floor of the house, and crawling babies in contact with it. One baby, a few months old, had a badly infected yaw on his thigh and his parents asked me for medicine. Even to my inexperienced medical observation, the baby appeared to be on the point of death. I said I could give no help. I really did not know what to do, and if I had done some simple thing such as wash the infected sore with a potassium permanganate solution and the baby had then died, I should probably have been held responsible. I was uneasy about the matter, but felt quite strongly that, given my medical ignorance, I should do nothing. Several hours after the request, the baby died. These and other observations seemed to confirm my hypothesis. However, I had too much to do to stop and analyze the genealogical data on births and deaths.[1]

I continued working on genealogies until everyone in the village was represented. Colored pencils were helpful in differentiating categories of data. When all the village genealogies were finished, I sat on the floor and, working on large pieces of brown wrapping paper pasted together, made a chart showing all the relationships in the village. Everyone in it was related through consanguinity or through marriage. I was proud of my chart and of my extensive list of all possible relationships associated with each kinship term. The chart was useful. But the excessively detailed list of kinship terms was a tour de force and later I wondered if some of the details were superfluous.

Working with genealogies had an advantage other than the rich data they yielded. The adults in Lesu not only knew their genealogies but were much interested in talking about them.

---

[1] This was a tedious job after I returned from the field. My impressions turned out to be correct, and the results were published in an article, "Vital Statistics of New Ireland As Revealed in Genealogies," *Human Biology*, Vol. III, No. 3 (September 1931).

They knew, even if they did not formulate it in sociological terms, that kinship was the underlying motif of their society. When a topic is interesting both to the anthropologist and to his informants, the data on it are usually full.

After I had been in Lesu for about three months, I was given a place in the kinship system. It happened at a large gathering of women—about sixty or seventy from several clans—who had just finished their communal preparations for a big feast. The taro had been scraped and wrapped in leaves and placed between hot stones—the native oven. The women were sitting at ease on the ground and chatting. An elderly woman from my hamlet, Pulong's maternal aunt, suddenly stood up and announced that I was her daughter. Earlier that day, her grandchild was being taught to call me *Nangga* (Mother). She was an attractive baby, perhaps two years old, and I had often played with her. The next day my "mother" sent me a large bunch of bananas, and a day or so later I reciprocated with a small gift. I was pleased with having a native "mother" and "child," but did not fool myself that I was really part of a Melanesian clan. It was rather that my Melanesian friends liked me and this was their symbolic way of expressing it— not too different from a child calling a close friend of his family "uncle" or "aunt." My impression is that when an anthropologist is "adopted," it is usually done simply and informally.[2]

Relations with the men were a bit more formal. I did not sit in the men's house or on the beach listening to them talk and gossip. But there was no problem in getting good male informants. Anyone I asked was glad to come and work with me (with the exception of the old rain magician, already described). Only one man took the initiative in asking to be an informant. He was Sevok, the Luluai of Ambwa, the next village. I had met him at several feasts and had intuitively disliked him on sight. He seemed weak and untrustworthy. I did not like his shifty eyes. But he was persistent in asking to work with me. I kept putting him off with one excuse or another because I surmised that he would not be a good informant and that he wanted only the tobacco that came after a

---

[2] Cf. Alice Marriott's *Greener Fields, Experiences Among the American Indians*, Dolphin Books (New York: Doubleday & Co., 1962), pp. 72–3.

morning's work. But I ran out of excuses, and so at last I told
him to come the next morning. I asked two of my most trusted
men informants to be present at the same time. Sevok started
on his genealogy, then branched off on some other topics, and
I wrote down everything he said as was my custom. When he
left, an appointment was made for him to return the next
morning. The two old men, who had sat quietly listening during the session with Sevok, then told me of his various "lies"
or "mistakes." They mentioned that, in general, he was considered "no good" and had the reputation of being a liar. No
one would tell me this until I found it out myself.

The next morning, Sevok, unaware of my knowledge, returned to work with me. The two elders, who were present the
day before, had evidently spread the news of that session
around the village. A large group of people appeared in front
of my house when Sevok arrived, as if they were expecting
something unusual to happen. I stood on the top step of the
house and held up the notebook, open at the pages where I
had written what Sevok had told me. Then, with a broad gesture and a bright red crayon pencil, I crossed out the writing
many times, saying that it was no good, that Sevok had lied
and that now I had made what he told me die. He slunk away
from the house and never returned. The Lesu people were
pleased. It then became customary for informants, if they did
not know the answer to a question I asked, to say, "Do you
want me to lie like Sevok?" It interested me that the small clues
by which I knew intuitively that Ongus was honest and that
Sevok was untrustworthy were cross-cultural.

Living in the village and participating in its life made it
easy to perceive these Melanesians as human beings, alike in
their cultural roles but differing in personality much as people
at home did. One woman was a jester, another a scolding nag;
one man told taboo jokes to the wrong people and got away
with it, while another was always punctiliously correct. I had
come to the end of the world to study a Stone-Age people and
found people who, although they were quite different, yet reminded me in some ways of relatives and friends! I mused
about whether there were universal personality types.

These Melanesians were likewise well aware of individual
differences between white people, even though they did not

see many whites. After I had been in Lesu about six months, Beatrice Blackwood, an English anthropologist from Cambridge, suddenly appeared on my doorstep. She was on her way to the Buka passage, had been told of my being in Lesu, and decided to visit me instead of waiting two weeks in Rabaul for her boat. We had not met before, but I was glad to see her. It was wonderful to have some one to talk to about data, and I talked myself hoarse the first few days. It also made me feel good to be able to give her lessons in pidgin and tell her some of the practical things I had learned about living in this part of the world. After she left, my Lesu friends objectively discussed the differences between us. They pointed out many things, such as the way she walked—much faster than I did —the differences between her British and my American accent, even our gestures, and many other quite subtle personality traits.

Another visitor came—a minor government official—whom I did not like and whom the natives did not like, either. He only stayed overnight and I had to be formally polite to him. But without my saying a word about it, the natives knew exactly how I felt.

It is my impression that pre-literate peoples are often more perceptive and intuitive in their human relations than modern ones. The psychological responses of the former tend to be more direct and less overlaid with intellectualizing and rationalizing. Being with people of this type was a sort of bonus in the long days of continuous work.

VII

MORTUARY RITES

During the second month in Lesu, I was awakened one day before dawn by the sound of mortuary wailing. No one could mistake the meaning of the sounds. I dressed quickly and was much excited—my first mortuary rite. I thought of the lectures I had heard and the books and papers I had read about their significance. I particularly remembered Camilla Wedgwood's paper in a graduate seminar and Radcliffe-Brown's description and discussion of the functions of these rites in the Andaman Islands. Through the rites I expected to get beliefs and attitudes towards life, as well as towards death.

My neighbors, who were up and waiting for me, said that a man had died at the far end of the village, in a hamlet where I had only a superficial acquaintance. We walked up together and found a large number of people already there. The wife was inside the hut wailing beside the body of the dead man. Others, whom I did not know, were outside and doing different things. I quickly decided that it would be best to record what each one was doing, getting the names of participants from one of my friends. Later I could work out the relationships with the dead man. (I had not yet done the genealogies of the people in this hamlet.) I took my notebook out of a pocket and was about to begin to write. But suddenly I said to myself, "How can you take notes in the midst of human sorrow? Have you no feelings for the mourners?" I had a quick vision of a stranger with a notebook walking into the living room of my Baltimore home at the time of a death. The notebook went back into my pocket. But I continued, "Are you not an anthropologist? This may be the only mortuary rite you will witness. Think of what you will miss, if you do not record it. A knowledge of these rites is absolutely essential." The notebook came out of my pocket. Before I could begin writing, the dialogue with myself began all over again and continued as the notebook went in and out of my pocket. This uncomfortable ambivalence was finally resolved. I took the notebook out and wrote what was happening.

An hour or so later while I was sitting on a bamboo bench in front of the hut busily writing, the widow came out and cheerfully greeted me. She sat down beside me, composed and untearful, and remarked that she was glad I was present and writing everything in my book. Even before she spoke, I had realized how mistaken I was in projecting on to a pre-literate people my attitude about taking notes at the time of death. I had already explained that I would write down everything because my memory was not good enough to recall it all accurately when I went home. The Lesu people understood this, and since they did not have writing, they had none of my associations with it. Moreover, in this particular situation, the widow's wailing was purely ritual. She had two husbands; the dead one had been old and she much preferred the younger one.

I need not have feared that I should not witness other mortuary rites. The next month an important old woman in the neighboring village of Libba died and I knew in advance that the rites for her would be more elaborate than usual. I walked the ten miles to Libba, accompanied by some of my Lesu friends and by my servants. We arrived at night and came upon a group of about a hundred men, bodies painted with white lime and hair decorated with leaves, doing a war dance around a fire. Their shouts, the brandishing of dangerous-looking spears, the naked gleaming bodies, the beating of the drums—all had a wild, exciting quality. The night was dark with no moon and the fires threw strange shadows on the hundreds of natives sitting in the compound and watching the dances.

I quickly found a place among the women and began immediately the inevitable recording in my notebook. The singing and dancing lasted all night, and about three o'clock in the morning I could no longer keep my eyes open. I knew that other important ceremonies would take place just before daybreak, and I wanted to be wide enough awake to observe them intelligently. I had a blanket with me and had learned that leaves of a coconut tree laid on the ground make quite a good resting place. I went away from the dancing, rolled up in my blanket, and slept soundly until an hour or so before sunrise. I awoke refreshed and ready for the new round of ceremonies, culminating in the burial late in the morning. Then came the feast, with the distribution of bundles of baked taro and roasted pig, and many speeches.

Finally it was all over and my Lesu friends and I trudged wearily home. I wondered why no one in Australia had suggested that I buy a bicycle. It would have been far more functional than the tent which I never used. Kuserek, carrying my blanket and other things, walked beside me, holding a large blue Chinese umbrella over both of us for protection from the hot sun. Since she was heavily loaded, I suggested that I'd carry the umbrella. She was hurt at my suggestion and asked if she was not holding the umbrella at the proper angle. I assured her that no one could hold an umbrella better and the matter was dropped. She then began telling me in great detail about her past life. On and on she droned as we walked in the tropical heat. My mind was almost blank from weariness and the heat. It was impossible for me to listen intelligently. However, I hoped I'd remember enough to reopen the conversation another day.

Just before we reached Lesu, I began fantasying a tall glass of icy cold lemonade. But I knew that on reaching my house I'd have a cup of hot tea! It was late afternoon when we arrived and I was glad to shed the clothes which I had not been out of for three days, take a brief swim, eat, go to bed and sleep until the next morning. Then came the work of going over my notes, getting the kinship of the participants to the dead woman, and discussing details of the ritual with two good informants who had witnessed it.

Many more mortuary rites, from those for young children to those for elders, occurred. I had to go to all of them, long after they brought in diminishing returns in data. When I knew the patterns and variations according to age, I wanted to skip some of the rites. I had so much to do and was always behind in typing my notes. But it was not possible to follow my inclination; I had to be at every mortuary rite. The custom of being present and recording in my notebook had been established and if I did not follow it, the people involved would be offended and think that I did not regard the rite as important. On one occasion I appeared without a notebook and seeing that the people present were disappointed and hurt, I sent a young boy back for it. My notes on mortuary rites and customs were far more voluminous than was necessary for an understanding of them. But, perhaps, the very repetition of the observations was one of the ways in which the culture became part of me—entered my bones as well as my intellect.

In rite after rite, I saw the functioning of the kinship system and the clan in the assignment of responsibility for the preparation of the feast and for the dances. The rituals likewise provided a demonstration of the theories I had studied. The magnitude of the ceremonies was obviously symbolic of the dead person's social importance. For the young children the rites were brief; for the middle-aged and the elders, elaborate feasts and dances were part of a lengthy ritual. As I listened to the speeches, they seemed to embody Radcliffe-Brown's theory of the social function of mortuary rites. Individuals told of their sorrow over the loss of a good worker to their clan and to the community. There would be one less person to assist in the preparations for feasts and participate in the rites. The coming together of the group at this time, in the cooking, at the feasts and the dances, was an expression of group solidarity to offset its loss, and I was grateful to Radcliffe-Brown for having provided a theoretical frame of reference for my observations. I suppose that no matter how logical a theory may be, real understanding of it comes only with seeing it demonstrated in behavior. In this first field trip I did not go much beyond the theories I had learned as a graduate student. But seeing the theories work out, confirming in life that they were really true, was part of my initiation into anthropology. It is also possible that a too great adherence to the theory, together with my lack of experience, may have prevented me from seeing other aspects of these rites.

Malanggans, elaborate carvings for which New Ireland is famous, were part of the ritual for the dead. Making these carvings and preparing for the rites took so much time and wealth that they often occurred long after the individual in whose honor they were made had died. The carvings were also used on occasions not directly connected with death, such as the initiation of boys. Sometimes *Malanggan* rites were held whenever one man, or several men, had collected the necessary wealth.

I went to every ritual of which *Malanggans* were a part, often walking to distant villages for them. I photographed the carvings and drew them on paper, learned the names of the birds, fishes, and snakes represented on them, and worked out the relationships of the dead ancestors to the man who was responsible for the rites. I listened to myths about the origin of the *Malanggans*. They followed the same pattern: a *gas*, the spirit counterpart of every individual, appeared in a dream and gave the design for the carvings. The right to make it was vested in one man, acting as a custodian for his clan, and this privilege could be bought and sold. I interviewed owners and carvers. *Malanggans* were made for dead women as well as men, but those responsible for the rites were always men; women were not supposed to see the carvings and their role was limited to preparing food for the feasts and performing some of the dances. I was able to classify fifty-seven *Malanggans* into five groups and knew which ritual was common to all and which was peculiar to an individual carving.

The sale of the right to make one *Malanggan*, its making, and the final rites took three months, and I observed most of the details. Pombi, a man from Logagon, about twenty-five miles away, came to Lesu to buy a *Malanggan* and its associated ritual from Palou, a leading elder of the Sinpop clan. Palou agreed to have the carving made and to relinquish his "ownership" of it; payments would be made when the *Malanggan* was displayed and rites held for Pombi's dead maternal uncle. (I was so impressed with the economic ramifications of this undertaking, that in *Life in Lesu*, it is described in a chapter on work, with cross references to the section on religion.) The project began when the men of Palou's hamlet (the home of his clan) went into the bush, singing and in festive mood, to cut down a tree trunk from which the carving would be made. When they returned, Palou paid them with tobacco and coconuts. Upon the completion of a little house in which the *Malanggan* would be made, the men were given a small feast. Palou and a skilled carver spent their days in this house, as the former gave instructions. During this time the sexes were even more separate socially than usual: the men ate together every evening and a feast was held for them each week.

The carving took two months, longer than usual because the carver had to interrupt his work to execute a rush order to make a small *Malanggan* in another village. When the carving for Pombi was finally finished but not painted, the men carried it, wrapped in leaves, to Logagon. They started their long walk gayly and with an air of importance. The women carrying baskets of uncooked taro went to Logagon a week later, and I went with them. During the next week the men rehearsed the dances, made costumes and masks; the women prepared the food for the preliminary rites. I was busy, as usual, taking notes.

The rites were the most beautiful I had seen. Two men, representing *gas* or spirits, wearing feather headdresses and carrying shell rattles in their hands, led the men into the enclosure. In it, still unpainted, the *Malanggan* was displayed in a handsome formal setting. Dancers were already in their place. Representing small birds, they wore feather headdresses, and in their mouths were carved imitations of the bird's beak. The dancers knelt with hands clasped behind their back and swayed gracefully in unison, dramatizing the birds sitting on a reef. The effect was lovely, and appreciated by the audience.

After the dance a feast was held for the men inside the enclosure, and for the women outside. At the men's feast speeches were made and payments of *tsera* (shell currency) were given to Palou, the former owner of the *Malanggan*. The final rites began four days later when the clan relatives of Pombi (the man who was buying the *Malanggan*) arrived from Tabar, a neighboring island. They came bringing many pigs, but, as was usual, their leader made a speech deprecating their contribution, saying that the pigs were few in number and small in size. At a feast, later in the day, more *tsera* was given to Pombi who handed it over to Palou. Pombi spoke with pride of how much *tsera* had been paid and how many pigs had been contributed and, with the same pride, of how poor they now were. The only mention of the dead relative was that this was Watlau's day and that he and Pombi were each important men.

Three days later, the *Malanggan*, now painted, was placed

in a special house within the enclosure and the final feast was
held at which still more *tsera* was paid. In the evening the
dances began, one of them unusual in that both men and
women participated. The dancing was supposed to go on all
night, as it did on similar occasions in Lesu and other villages.
But Logagon was the home of a Catholic mission and at ten
o'clock the "Father" blew loudly on a horn from the veranda
of his house; the dancing stopped and everyone went to their
homes. All-night dancing in other villages was often followed
by sexual promiscuity; the Father's curfew was presumably
to prevent this. The dancing continued the next day, followed
by a distribution of piles of food. The Lesu people indicated
that they did not want any, because they did not wish to be
burdened carrying bundles on the long walk home.

We left at sunset and after walking all night, arrived at Lesu
by noon the next day. Everyone was exhausted and went right
to bed and slept.

The total payment for this *Malanggan* and its rites had been
one hundred eighty *tsera*. At the native rate of exchange one
tsera was worth five shillings; the costs had therefore been
forty-five pounds in Australian currency, or two hundred
twenty-five dollars as the then current American value of
Australian shillings. Palou received one hundred forty *tsera*,
which he distributed among the members of his clan, keeping
a large share for himself; Pombi gave the remainder to the
relatives from Tabar, who had contributed pigs and helped in
other ways.

The ritual had set a large amount of wealth—native currency, taro, and pigs—into circulation and had brought prestige to those who initiated it. I was much impressed with these
economic functions. I probably stressed them because of Malinowski's study of the *Kula* exchange among the Trobriand
Islanders. I was also fascinated by the conspicuous distribution of wealth as a prestige motif in a society with a subsistence
standard of living. I knew, of course, from Boas' studies, that
this was a major theme among the Kwakiutl Indians, a much
richer people of Alaska. It is true for many other tribal peoples, but no detailed cross-cultural study has yet been made
to determine the prevalence of this theme.

What was the meaning of the *Malanggans* and the elaborate
masks worn by the dancers? The representations of animals,

birds, and men were easy to understand. However, on one mask, I noted an abstract design which I had not seen before. The owner could not tell me what it meant and I began to speculate on its possible symbolic significance. At the same time I was trying to find the carver. Finally, I found him in another village, and he said that he had copied the strange design from a piece of cotton material imported from Manchester for loin cloths! I was amused at my earlier speculations on the symbolism of the design.

The problem of the underlying and symbolic significance of the elaborate carvings was far more difficult. The ideas of German missionaries who had written about them did not satisfy me. I could see no foundation for their elaborate theories of a sun and moon cult. They interpreted every circle—no matter what the context—as the sun or moon. It was comparable to the interpretation of every church spire or other elongated object as a phallic symbol. Obviously the carvings were made to honor the dead; yet, I could get but little data about their specific connection with the dead, their ghosts, or their spirit doubles, the *gas*. Some magical spells (particularly those for success in war and in fishing) appealed to the ghosts of dead ancestors for their assistance. But there appeared to be no coherent theory about life after death in relation to the *Malanggans*. Speeches at the rites and discussions with informants stressed the prestige that the making of them brought to the living. When I asked what would happen if a man did not make a *Malanggan* for a dead clan relative, my informants found it difficult to imagine such a possibility. When pressed, they said such a man would be scorned by everyone because he did not have sufficient wealth to honor the dead. Before leaving Lesu I purchased two *Malanggans*, explaining that they would be carefully housed in a museum, and that "my people" would come to look at them. Two old men, watching my servants pack the carvings, urged me to tell "my people" that these were not just carved, painted pieces of wood and to emphasize all the wealth that had gone into their making.

When in Lesu I was much aware of the gaps in my knowledge about the religious meaning of the *Malanggans*. A possible earlier mystical significance may have been lost. In reading over my notes, I see a few inconsistencies, which I apparently did not notice in the field. I wonder now if I could have pursued the problem further. It would have been helpful if at the time I had been more comparatively oriented and had had access to studies of similar ceremonies in other cultures. While in Lesu, I played with the idea of going to Tabar (a neighboring island) where, according to the myths, *Malanggans* originated. The culture and the language of the two islands were quite similar and I kept thinking about going to Tabar and taking two or three of my Lesu friends with me to help make contacts. But how could I leave Lesu, when there was still so much to get there? Then the rainy season came and the trip was impossible. But the idea of what I might have learned in Tabar still tantalizes me, as does the larger problem of the meaning of the *Malanggans*.

Today, I think about the similarities and differences between the Melanesian mortuary rites and those in contemporary United States. Satirists such as Evelyn Waugh and Jessica Mitford have shown how undertakers work hard and unscrupulously to sell their costly ritual to the families of the dead. The clergy, traditional custodians of the ritual, are on the side of the satirists and oppose the modern funerals as a "lot of paganism," not in keeping with Christian attitudes.[1] Neither the satirists nor the clergy mention that the "hard sell" of the undertakers, their large profits, and the vulgarity of their advertisements are hardly unique in our society. They are not too different from the *mores* of the larger business community. Vulgarity is only intensified because it is displayed at the time of death, traditionally surrounded by religious customs rather than by those of the market place, and because the "hard sell" is directed to people who are emotionally upset. Modern society has its separate establishments: religious, business, political, academic, art, and so forth. At the time of death some are in conflict with each other. In Lesu each segment of life was an integral part of the whole; mortuary rites were harmoniously interwoven with what we call economics, religion, art, and kinship.

Then, too, in Lesu, no satirists or non-believers existed, as contrasted to our society where men question religious, business, and other mores. In tribal life, as in medieval Christianity,

---

[1] *New York Times*, September 3, 1963.

belief in life after death was not questioned, whereas in this scientific age, skeptics are present. But even for many of them, death without such a belief is apparently difficult to accept; hence the attempt to make the dead look life-like and the glossing over of the fact that death is the end, an absurd or tragic event, or both. In this period of American culture the undertakers profit. In Lesu, control of the ritual was vested in the relatives of the dead; the payment to the carvers of the *Malanggans* was set; the considerable wealth associated with the elaborate rites was an expression of basic and unquestioned cultural themes: honor to the dead, prestige to the living, and a continuing relationship between them.

VIII

MONOTONY

My life and native life seemed to consist mainly of endless repetition: rising with the sun every day; going to little feasts and big ones, to mortuary rites and other ceremonies; working with individual informants on genealogies, language, magical spells, economic and other aspects of the social structure; listening to folk tales and myths; strolling through the village; chatting with the women when they were at leisure; writing notes continuously and typing them later; taking photographs and developing them; and so on and on.

The lack of seasons contributed to the monotony. There were only two—the rainy and the dry—and it rained briefly during many days of the dry season. The rainy season was sometimes quite uncomfortable. Fortunately, I had a strong raincoat and boots with me. One evening when the rains had been particularly heavy, tiny insects, which came with them, were attracted by the light of my lamp and swarmed all over the place. As I ate dinner, they crawled down my back, entered my mouth when I opened it, and drowned in the coffee cup. They did not sting or bite, but were most uncomfortable pests. Only one escape was possible: to crawl into bed under the mosquito canopy. Other times, wearing my last piece of clean underwear, I wondered if the sun would ever shine again and permit washing and drying. It always did and was so strong and hot that everything—the ground as well as my clothes—dried quickly and I forgot the inconvenience of the last torrential downpour.

During the rainy or the dry season, whether working with an informant on my veranda or attending a feast or other event in the village, I was continuously writing down everything in my notebook. I used a hard lead pencil and hard-cover unlined notebooks, about four and one-half by seven and one-half

inches, suggested by Malinowski because they were convenient for recording away from home. I could sit on the ground
or on the stump of a tree, with notebook on knee, and write.
Everything (except genealogies and linguistics which had their
special books) went into these notebooks in chronological order. This had the advantage of a diary of everything as it
occurred. When a book was filled, I indexed it according to
the topics in the detailed outline made before I left London.
On every page I marked with a red pencil the appropriate
number and letter for each topic and sub-topic, such as childhood (birth, nursing, weaning, play) economics, mortuary rites,
and so on. On the last pages of each notebook was an index
with topic headings and the pages which had the relevant data.
The notes were written in a strange combination of English,
pidgin English, and the Melanesian dialect.

The typing—two copies—was done, of course, in English
under the topics and subheadings, which had cross references
to each other. For instance, magical spells had cross references
to economics, love, weather, fishing, and so on. The struggle
to find the time to type was constant and I was rarely caught
up. With new data available, it was difficult for me to stop
and type the old. But I forced myself to do it, and about once
a month took stock of where I was in the process. As Radcliffe-
Brown had suggested, one copy of the typed notes was mailed
to him. There was thus a preliminary organization of data
while in the field, and I could see some of the gaps while reading the typed notes.

Sometimes I was discouraged. How could I ever get data on
all the topics in my long outline and in the much fuller *Notes
and Queries,* published by the Royal Anthropological Institute
of Great Britain, which I also consulted. Common sense told
me that I could not possibly find out about everything, that
my outline and the *Notes and Queries* were only guides, useful
in directing attention to subjects I might overlook. But now
and then I felt overwhelmed by all I did not know, by the
number of things still to find out, and by the awareness that
there was much I could never learn. To "crack" a strange culture, never taking anything for granted, to ferret out relationships between customs, to dig out the system of kinship from
many genealogies, to understand the social structure, to learn

a language which had never been recorded, was decidedly not easy. Less than halfway through my stay in Lesu, I conveyed some of my impatience and discouragement to Ongus. Looking at me quizzically, he asked if I expected to know everything in four or five moons?

As I worked out the details of the social system, I kept thinking about the future presentation of the material. The people in Lesu were so alive to me that I did not want to lose them in a dull monograph with chapters on kinship, economic structure, religion, and so on. I was continuously getting ideas, and changing them, about how to write about life in Lesu. I was also involved in theoretical speculation. Durkheim's rather metaphysical theories had a certain fascination for me, but they seemed to lead me around in circles. I longed for an anthropologist to talk to. But there was no one. So my thoughts went on paper.

Developing photographs was more of a chore than writing. This was my first experience in both taking and developing pictures, except for practicing in Sydney. Fortunately, the Graflex camera which the university had lent me was an exceptional one, and after a period of trial and error, my pictures were not too bad. But developing them got me down. I had to wait until several hours after sunset before the water was cool enough; midnight saw me with a tin cup in hand leaning over a bucket of water, washing the negatives. When I finished, I fell exhausted on my cot, wishing that photography had never been invented. The next day when the negatives were dry, I carefully put them in an empty tea tin and hoped they would stay dry. Eventually they would all be printed, but I sometimes ran off a few temporary prints to see how they turned out and for the pleasure of my Lesu friends. Having no real interest in photography, I took pictures primarily because it was necessary to my work.

For the same reason I collected specimens of leaves, herbs, and roots used in native medicine and preserved them in a botanical press. I also dutifully recorded dreams, because Professor Seligmann had asked me to record them for him. This request had made little sense to me. If I had been more aware of the significance of dreams, I could have found out much more about them and their associations, for the Melanesians

took their dreams seriously and talked freely about most of
them. Some of my best friends even told me dreams of incest
or of copulation with a pig, topics not usually discussed among
themselves. Now I wish I had explored attitudes to dreams
and other problems connected with them. However, given my
lack of psychological training and of sophistication about this
kind of symbolism, it was, perhaps, just as well that I did not
work on dreams. In recent years I have been struck by the
naïveté of some anthropologists who have attempted to work
with material from the unconscious. If an anthropologist, or
anyone else, has not explored his own unconscious rather intensively, his ideas about the unconscious processes of others
may be quite misleading.

I neglected some of the things I was supposed to do, and
others could not be done because of the situation. The University of Sydney gave me a pair of calipers to take head measure-
ments. I had never taken a course in physical anthropology
and then had no knowledge of or interest in it. Besides, I thought
the Lesu people might not like to have their heads measured.
I decided to "lose" the calipers.

Arnold Gesell, the distinguished child psychologist, had
heard about my expedition and written to ask me to make
observations on the activities of young children which would
be comparable with his studies on American children. I had
carefully read his book on the long voyage to Sydney and
looked forward hopefully to making a contribution to his work.
But in Lesu there was no record of ages and since Gesell's
observations were correlated with an exact age, I had to give
up the idea of securing cross-cultural data. Other people wrote
and asked me to give tests which involved writing. Since these
Melanesians had never held a pencil in their hands, I did not
see how the results of such tests could be comparable with
those given to literate people.[1]

Probably the most monotonous part of my life in Lesu was
the food. Breakfast consisted of a papaya, bacon (a whole side
of it was in the kitchen), fried sweet potatoes, bread, marmalade, and coffee. Once in a while I had an egg. Chickens

---

[1] Projective tests, such as the Rorschach, were not yet used by social
scientists.

had been introduced in the area, but were few; occasionally there were delicious turtle eggs. Lunch was light: tea and cheese with bread or baked taro. The cheese in tins and jars was not bad, but I found the tinned butter uneatable. For dinner there was usually fresh fish or a bird the cook had shot. The fish, broiled over a fire, tasted very good, as did a bird, roasted or made into a stew. Once in a while I was lucky enough to have a lobster fresh from the sea. This menu was varied with tinned frankfurters, the only canned meat I had with me which I liked. The canned vegetables were so tasteless that I ate them only rarely. Dessert was a papaya, pineapple, or banana, all available in abundance. On a special occasion, such as my birthday, I opened a bottle of olives for dinner.

What I missed most were salads, fresh vegetables, and good drinking water. I could easily have had a vegetable garden if I had brought seeds with me and been willing to give the necessary time to gardening or supervising it. Water, coming from a little spring which burbled up through the sand on the beach, was horribly brackish in taste and I could drink it only when made into strong tea, coffee, or lemonade, of course without ice. Some boys reported a pond off in the bush which they said had better water; for a number of days they brought me water from it in long, hollow bamboo stems. The water did not taste good. After a while it occurred to me that maybe I should have a look at the pond and so I went with the boys over the narrow footpath through the bush. In the pond, to my horror, a pig was wallowing. I went back to the spring on the beach. Fortunately, one of my few strict rules was that water had to be boiled—to tremble as the ground did in an earthquake, I explained to my cook. If I had known enough, I could have rigged up some way of catching rain water. I had no fresh milk, except an occasional gift of goat's milk from a planter who was passing by. It tasted better than champagne.

I had one bottle of whiskey with me, from which I drank only rarely on some special occasion like my birthday or Christmas, or if I had a chill. (After walking home one day in the tropical midday heat, I had first mistakenly welcomed a cool breeze, sweeping through my thatched-roofed house; the result was a chill.) Although accustomed to normal drinking, I had been strongly warned by several people not to drink in the field. The warnings were many: drinkers suffered from malaria more than non-drinkers; drinking was not conducive to general good health in the tropics; drinking to excess when alone and if depressed was dangerous. The characters in Somerset Maugham's novels set in the tropics were held up as examples not to follow. I seem to have taken these warnings seriously, for my bottle of whiskey was almost half full when I left Lesu.

Any quite small change in food or domestic life was significant. Using a new toothbrush, different in color from the past one, gave me a feeling of diversity. One day when I was feeling a bit low, I came, unexpectedly, upon a box of Yardley's soap given by a friend when I left Sydney. My spirits were lifted.

The steady deterioration of my household goods was depressing. Much of the enamel had worn off my table ware after six months. The inside of each of the two cups was horribly discolored with large rough black spots. Feeling desperate, I began drinking tea and coffee from a glass which had formerly held peanut butter. It had never occurred to me during shopping expeditions to bring unbreakable "china" instead of enamel ware. The canvas seat of my one chair had to be regularly mended, and the collapsible wood table was in danger of collapsing forever. A pair of Japanese straw bedroom slippers were in shreds and there was no possibility of new ones. These irritations were small but they loomed large, even though I was amused at their seeming importance.

My health remained good, although I lost considerable weight. I enjoyed being almost continuously outdoors and became acclimatized more quickly to the tropical heat than I had to the damp coldness of London winters. I took my five grains of quinine every night and never suffered from malaria, even though it was all around me. But sometimes, in spite of good health and the steady accumulation of data, the monotony, which I could not change, was very oppressive.

IX

ESCAPES FROM LESU

There were, indeed, times when, totally fed up with my life and with native life, I longed to be only a participant, to stop taking notes, and to communicate freely with a few close friends who had the same basic assumptions. I felt then that I had to escape.

Books which I had brought with me and the mail which came every six weeks were among the few forms of escape. Because I had been overwhelmed by the large number of necessary things to take with me and was uncertain about whether carriers would be needed for the last part of the trip, I had not taken many books. While still in London I had selected sixteen, about equally divided between anthropology and novels. In addition, I had Whittaker's Almanac (1928), the Bible, and two anthologies of poetry which together covered the period from Shakespeare to modern times. With the exception of the almanac and the Bible, I knew the books well before leaving London.

In Lesu I reread the anthropological monographs—mostly about other Melanesian peoples—and read a few new ones that were sent me. It seemed that I was reading critically for the first time. My judgment was now based on more than book knowledge of tribal peoples. However, these monographs were hardly an escape, since inevitably I compared my data with them.

Among my novels were the *Brothers Karamazov, The Red and the Black, The Growth of the Soil, Ulysses, Jean Christophe,* and *The Tales of Genji.* I had selected well. I could escape from the endless details of life in Lesu into the multiplicity of details in another culture. On an occasional day off, I was able to lose myself in one of the novels and be refreshed. Someone sent me a collection of short stories and they seemed all wrong, with their emphasis on one episode and a quick climax. They offered no relief. A devoted friend regularly sent detective stories. I could not abide these before I went into the field and I found them just as unreadable there. So also were contemporary, light, second-rate novels which occasionally came my way. I kept wishing that I had brought with me more novels of the type I enjoyed.

I had looked forward to reading both the Old and New Testaments from beginning to end. But this plan was never carried out. The Bible seemed to be one genealogy after another and it read like a description of other tribes. I was constantly making comparisons with the Melanesians. Decidedly, the Bible was no escape, and I soon stopped reading it.

The poetry, after the novels, was my wisest choice. I read and reread my favorites, often as I ate dinner, and memorized some of them.

The almanac unexpectedly provided amusement. During a particularly heavy rain storm, it cheered me to read almanac stories about storms and floods in other parts of the world. A terrific thunderstorm accompanied by vivid flashes of lightning occurred at the commencement of a balloon race at Pittsburgh on May 2. In New York on January 1 the temperature dropped thirty-five degrees and wind gales were forty-five miles an hour. At Wada Musa, near Petra, there had been great swarms of locusts on February 2. I hoped that in the next almanac the heavy tropical rains in Lesu on October 18 would be mentioned. Facts about the stellar system, the British peerage, the Indian empire, had a soothing effect on me. Perhaps it was because they were presented free of ideas and I did not have to think about them.

The arrival of mail about every six weeks was a red-letter day. There was no air mail at this time and it took at least two months for a letter to come from the United States or England. It was, accordingly, difficult to follow the courses of minor events in the lives of family and close friends, because they often changed during the intervals between letters. But I was always interested in knowing whether my correspondents were happy or unhappy and their general state of being. My writing to them was a major form of escape. Whatever I was feeling went into my letters, and I was less lonely after writing them.

A member of my family sent newspapers which arrived at
least four months late. I could not have been less interested
in most of the news: a strike, an election, the unemployment
problem, and all the other perennial "news" which appeared
not to have changed since I left home. But I was deeply sad-
dened when I read that Serge Diaghilev had died. His dancing
had always seemed like poetry in motion. I had never seen
any dancer who could compare to him and during one season
in London, I had gone to every ballet in which he had performed. Now he was dead, and I had a sense of loss.

The New Yorker and *Punch* were sent to me by two friends.
It was now my fifth year away from the United States, and I
could not always follow *The New Yorker*'s topical wit. Because
of my recent residence in London, I was somewhat more in
touch with the topics on which *Punch* commented. But the
cleverness of both magazines generally left me unmoved. What
really interested me was their advertisements, which lifted me
right out of Lesu. A picture of a diamond brooch for a thousand dollars somehow comforted me when I was in need of
safety pins. Pictures of beautiful cut glass goblets permitted
me to forget temporarily my worn enamel cup. I was torn
between the "car of cars," a Cadillac, and a small sport car,
"so easy to handle in Picadilly traffic," and was oblivious to
the fact that the next day I had to walk five miles to another
village. From the advertisements I conjured up a society to
which I had never belonged, and it provided a fantasy escape
from Lesu.

Another possible escape was sporadic visits with Australian
planters. But a few visits with the handful of those whose
coconut plantations were scattered along the two hundred miles
of the east coast of the island soon proved that they were no
escape. When I saw people from my own culture I wanted to
discuss my anthropological findings, or talk about literature,
and even more I longed to be gay. But the planters were decidedly not gay, and they had only one interest—copra, the
dried coconuts which they marketed. They saw the natives
solely as a source of plantation labor and we could not have
been more different in our attitudes towards them.

I went to one small dinner party on a plantation about thirty
miles away. The food was excellent, a welcome change from

my simple menu. After dinner, the women sat conventionally separate from the men (just as in Lesu!). A dominating elderly woman sternly looked me over and inquired rather fiercely if it was true that I lived in a native hut. In my most soothing tone, I told her about the comforts of my home, stressing its difference from native huts. She interrupted, "How do you take a bath?", implying that this was impossible for anyone who lived in a native village. I replied that I had a portable bath tub, a wash basin, even a primitive shower, soap, towels, and added, that, besides, I went swimming every day. But she was not satisfied. "Well," she said, "I think it is perfectly horrible for you to live in that village." "But I find it pleasant," was my rejoinder. She countered with, "Have you had the fever?" When I answered, "No, I've been enjoying good health," she turned away in disgust.

Another quite different woman, middle-aged, sweet, and timid, inquired in an apologetic tone, "Don't you think that the natives are just like human beings?" I replied in the affirmative. She continued, "Have you noticed that they really appreciate kindness?" Again, I nodded affirmatively. "Oh, I think it is so good of you, so kind, to live among the natives," she said, and pressed my hand.

A young woman, quite new to the Territory, asked me if I did not find it just "too thrilling" to live among the "wild savages." Instead of answering, I quickly turned the conversation to another topic.

The more general conversation among the women was about a new pattern for making their husbands' pajamas. There I was with people from my own civilization, talking my language, and with little communication between us. I appreciated my host's driving thirty miles on a rough road to bring me to the party, and driving me back to Lesu the next day, but I politely declined the second invitation, and then had no more. However, he and the other planters who lived south of Lesu continued to be kind to me, stopping by when they went to Kavieng to inquire if I needed anything from the store there, and to take my mail. On the return trip they brought my mail if a boat had been in and any small supplies I wanted.

Fortunately, the nicest of the planters, Mr. and Mrs. Grosse, lived the closest to me. Mrs. Grosse differed from many plant-

ers' wives, who lounged around all day reading women's magazines and wishing they were back in Australia while their
native servants did all the domestic work. She was a pioneer
type, making all the clothes that she, her husband, and their
children wore, keeping chickens and goats, doing some cooking,
tending a vegetable garden, teaching her young children the
three "R's," and, in general, enjoying and surmounting the
difficulties of island life. She and her husband did not mingle
much socially with the other planters. They left me alone, but
it was understood that when I felt like it I could walk the
three and a half miles to their plantation, have tea, and walk
back. I enjoyed the occasional tea with her—about once a
month—and the eggs and goat's milk which she generously
gave me.

However, she had no more interest in the native peoples
than any of the other island Australians, and I never discussed
my work with her. Mostly we talked about clothes. On my
return to Sydney, I sent her a pair of long dangling earrings,
the most impractical gift I could think of. She was a most
practical person, and occasionally yearned to be different.

I met only one missionary on the island. He lived in Logagon
(twenty-five miles from Lesu), which I visited for *Malanggan*
rites. This Father, late middle-aged, rotund, and red-faced,
invited me to dinner. I was not too familiar with the mores
of missionaries, but I thought it wise to leave my cigarettes at
home. To my astonishment, when I arrived for dinner, he
offered me a cigar and was surprised when I refused it. I was
the first white woman he had entertained during his thirty
years of residence here and he assumed that by this time women
were smoking cigars. Over the dinner, accompanied by red
wine, he began talking about a moon cult which he thought
existed here. Any circle, whether in a dance formation or a
design on a *Malanggan,* he assumed represented the moon. His
theories became more far-fetched the more eloquent he became. His voice became louder and louder and I thought the
monologue might go on forever. About midnight, I abruptly
stood up and broke into the flow of words and wine, saying
I must return to the village. I did not see him again during
my stay at Logagon.

The government anthropologist, E. W. P. Chinnery, a delightful person, visited me whenever he made a patrol on the island, and I always enjoyed his visits. Except for them, and an occasional tea with Mrs. Grosse, white people usually offered me no escape. There was no way out of loneliness, except through letter-writing, rereading a novel or poetry, or composing limericks (a minor addiction) and then becoming busily absorbed again in Lesu society—participating and taking notes. The price I paid for my one-woman expedition was loneliness. I do not think the price was too high; after all, loneliness is quite bearable and is not restricted to field work.

Into the sameness of life in Lesu came an exciting invitation which promised to offer something different. The District Officer and his wife in Kavieng invited me to attend the festivities to honor Lord Stonehaven, the Governor General from Australia, and his wife, who were making an official tour of the Mandated Territory. The invitation included transportation and hospitality at the D.O.'s home. I accepted the invitation with pleasurable anticipation, particularly as I remembered that in the small trunk of clothes which I had left at the D.O.'s house (since I would have no need for them in Lesu) was a beautiful white taffeta evening dress—with a tight bodice and wide bouffant skirt—bought in Paris and worn on the long trip from England to Australia.

Never had I so looked forward to any party. It would take me out of this Stone Age culture, out of my shorts, jackets, and simple cotton dresses, into a pleasant ritual of my own society. I was sure that with my relatively recent Paris evening dress I would, for the first time, be the best dressed woman at the party, an exhilarating thought. The white residents of Kavieng were all Australians, and women's clothes from Australia at that time were rather drab.

Finally the important day came. Lord Stonehaven and his entourage had left the man-of-war at the southern end of the island and were to pick me up when they drove through Lesu. Although they were not expected until midmorning, Kuserek was so excited that as soon as I had finished my breakfast, she ran up to my house every ten minutes to tell me that "the king" was almost here and that I should hurry. I knew that the party would not arrive for several hours, but to calm her I finished my dressing and sat waiting on the veranda. I then looked at my nails, and brought out my manicure kit, used up to now only to keep nails clean and short. But on this day I polished them, to the interest of native friends waiting eagerly around my house to see "the king." Excitement increased when five airplanes, accompanying the man-of-war which carried the royal party from Australia, flew over the village. The natives had never before seen an airplane. When they first heard the whirr of the engine, they thought it was a boat. Then they saw the planes. Bewildered and amazed, they shouted at them and then asked me why they did not fall down. I found it difficult to explain, since I had never really understood the mechanism of planes, or for that matter, of many other instruments of our machine age.

Finally, "the king" and his party came and I joined them. On the way to Kavieng we stopped for a picnic lunch, and I was seated next to Lord Stonehaven. He was a serious man and plied me with questions about the natives. Some of the questions seemed foolish to me; with difficulty I restrained the impulse to answer facetiously.

Upon arriving in Kavieng, I went to the D.O.'s house to dress for the dinner, which preceded a dance at the Club. In the not-too-bright light of oil lamps, I unpacked the trunk and my white taffeta dress looked as beautiful as ever. A few drinks, the attentions of an attractive, flirtatious young doctor in the Governor General's entourage, a quick scanning of the costumes of the other women, and the general excitement of the occasion, all contributed to my mounting sense of gaiety and well-being. I was sure I was the best-dressed woman. All evening long I danced on the veranda of the Club. About midnight I happened to stand directly under the light of one of the Japanese lanterns that hung from the roof. I looked down and saw that my full white taffeta skirt was in shreds and tatters. It looked like a native straw skirt. How long it had looked like this I did not know. The disintegrating process might have been happening all evening, or it might have occurred as soon as I lifted the dress from the trunk. I learned later that taffeta rots in the wet tropics. But by the time I discovered that my skirt was in tatters, I had reached such a peak of enjoyment that it was totally unimportant. I assumed that the Australians thought this, too, was the latest style from Paris. As far as I was concerned, I was still the best-dressed woman at the party.

I had no desire to linger in Kavieng. The Governor General's party was sailing on to the next port of its grand tour, and I much preferred daily life in Lesu to that in Kavieng, which usually gave me a curious feeling of imprisonment. Then, too, white people on the island seemed extraneous and foreign to it. The place belonged to the blacks.

I returned to Lesu, sleepy but feeling good. The party had given me a "lift," and yet I was glad to be at home in Lesu. The whole village turned out to greet me. However, they were disappointed that I arrived in a lorry, rather than flying back in a plane. They wanted to hear everything about the rites for the "king." I described them in considerable detail, but omitted the splitting of my white taffeta skirt. Finally my friends left and I took a much-needed nap. I awoke refreshed, dressed in my usual shorts and shirt, and, with notebook and pencil, went eagerly to a small feast in the next hamlet.

About two weeks later, the luluai from a village eight miles away visited me to find out what Lord Stonehaven had told me. The luluai thought Lord Stonehaven was my mother's brother.

X

A WOMAN ALONE
IN THE FIELD

In casual daily life I was much more with the women than with the men; the sexes were quite separate in their social and economic life. I often sat with the women of my hamlet and of neighboring ones, watching them scrape the taro, the staple of their diet, and prepare it for baking between hot stones. Notes on the different ways of preparing taro became so voluminous that I sometimes thought of writing a Melanesian cook book. I was apparently compulsive about writing everything down, but I justified the fullness of the cooking notes by saying that they illustrated Melanesian ingenuity and diversity with limited resources. More important than the cooking notes were my observations on the relationships of the women with their daughters and with each other; listening to the good-humored gossip provided many clues for further questions and added subtlety to my understanding.

Pulong, whom I saw daily, was in the middle stage of her pregnancy, and I could observe her customs such as not eating a certain fish believed to "fight" an embryo in the stomach. Full details about pregnancy customs and taboos came later and gradually. When I first asked Pulong if there was any way of preventing pregnancy, she said she did not understand and looked vague. It seemed evident that she did not want to talk about the subject. Somewhat later, she and my adopted "mother" and a clan "sister" brought me leaves that they said would produce an abortion if chewed in the early stages of pregnancy. I put them carefully in a botanical press for identification when I returned home.

It was taken for granted that I should go to all the women's feasts in or near Lesu. The morning of a feast was usually

spent in preparing the food; then came the dances, distribution
of food, and speeches. At one such feast in a nearby village to
celebrate the birth of a baby, the hundred or so women were
in a particularly gay mood, which I enjoyed. One woman, a
born jester, who was not dancing because her relationship to
the newborn baby precluded it, grabbed the drum and began
doing amusing antics. It was like an impromptu skit and all the
onlookers laughed loudly. Encouraged, she continued. Then
came the distribution of bundles of baked taro, most of it to be
carried home, and the women's speeches praising the ability
of their respective husbands as providers of food. However,
one complained that her husband was lazy and did not bring
her fish often enough. In the late afternoon, my Lesu friends
and I trudged home. A basket of food and sometimes a baby
was on each woman's back (except mine), and although we
were all tired after a long day, a pleasant, relaxed feeling pervaded the small group.

As I ate my dinner that night and thought about the day's
events. I felt happy to be working in a functioning traditional
culture rather than one in which the anthropologist has to get
most of his data about tribal life from the reminiscences of the
elders. Sometimes I asked for details of a ritual in advance of
its performance; when it took place, some differences usually
showed up, even though the customary pattern was followed.
After one rather important ceremony, I made this point to an
informant who had given me particularly full details in advance. He looked at me as if I was either stupid or naïve (or
both), and asked if I didn't know that nothing ever took place
exactly as it was supposed to. Nor can generalizations by Melanesians, or anyone else, include all the specific details of actual
happenings.

Although it would not have been considered appropriate for
me to be with the men in their casual social life as I was with
the women, it was understood that I must observe and learn
about men's economic and ritual life, which was apart from
the women's. I worked on my veranda with individual men as
informants and as teachers of the native language. I did not
go to men's feasts and other rites unless I was invited, but I
was invited to everything. When the men were having a feast,
usually in the cemetery, two elders called for me and escorted

me there. I sat on one side, apart from the men, and munched a banana as I recorded what was said or done. Later I went over the notes with one or two of the men who had been present. One morning, although I arose very early—before dawn—to go to a men's feast in a neighboring village, I was still eating my breakfast when the Lesu men were ready to leave. Without saying anything to me, they detailed one man to wait. The sun was just rising when he and I started our walk to Ambwa, about three miles away.

I had to go to all feasts for the same reason that my presence was required at every mortuary rite. But no law of diminishing returns operated for the feasts, since the events they cele-brated were so varied: birth, bestowal of name on a newborn baby, appearance of his first tooth, early betrothal, first men-struation, initiation of boys, marriage, completion of any work, death, and practically every other event—small or big—in life. Through these feasts I gained not only a knowledge of the normal round of life, but I saw also the economic system functioning. It was evident from the speeches and from my informants that the exchange of bundles of baked food was by no means casual, but followed a rather rigid system of recipro-cal gifts. I heard praise for those who were generous and gos-sip about those who were slow to make gifts in return for those taken. As I typed my notes and mulled over them, I thought that perhaps I would organize all my data around feasts. An article on them, rather than a book, did eventually emerge after I left the field. There, I found it difficult to think in terms of articles, because I was always trying to relate one aspect of the culture to everything else.

I was more selective in going to other activities. I could not afford the time to go regularly with the women to their gardens. They left in the early morning and did not return until midafternoon. But I did go often enough to observe the various stages of their work. Fortunately, there was no feeling that my presence was necessary at all gardening activities. It was the same situation with the men's fishing. I waded into the shallow water by the beach and watched the different forms of fishing: with spears, nets, traps, and hooks. But I was con-tent with seeing each kind of operation once or twice and discussing details of it afterwards with informants. Later, I wrote down the magical spells connected with gardening and with fishing.

I was lucky that during my stay the initiation rites for eight boys from Lesu and from two neighboring villages took place. (They did not occur every year, but only when the number of boys reaching puberty was sufficient to justify the elaborate rites.) Less than a month after I settled in Lesu, the women began practicing a dance each evening. An elderly man was teaching them, but it was taboo for other men to see the rehearsals, although they would see the dance at the ritual.

I sat watching the women practice. The moon was new and delicate, the sea dark and noisy, and the singing women moved in a circle around a fire with slow dancing steps. They asked me to join them, but I was too self-conscious. I sat watching and held one of the babies. But each night, as the music and formal steps became more and more monotonous, lasting until midnight, I became increasingly bored. I had to force myself to stay awake.

Finally, one evening, I gathered my courage and began dancing. My place in the circle was between Pulong and an important old woman in her clan. The old women danced with more vivacity than the young ones; the gayest woman of the village was a grandmother. Good-natured laughter greeted my mistakes, which were carefully corrected. The steps were not difficult and I soon caught on to them. No longer were the evenings monotonous. Every night, as the moon became fuller, I danced. But, somehow, I did not think ahead to the night of the big rites.

Finally it came. That morning, Pulong and several other women came over and presented me with a shell arm band and a *kepkep*, a tortoise-shell breast ornament, and asked that I wear their favorite dress—a pink and white striped cotton. I gulped, and said I was not going to dance; I would just observe. But why, they asked in astonishment, had I been practicing every night? I could not explain that I had started because I was bored and that now I felt too self-conscious to participate in rites which I knew would be attended by thousands of natives from all over the island and nearby islands. Soon I saw that I had to dance. A refusal now would be a rejection.

All day there was an increasing "before the ball" excitement. Hair was colored with bright dyes and bodies of men were ornamented. The tinsel trimming which I had brought with me was in demand by the women dancers, who wound it around their hair. At sunset my dancing companions assembled at my house and we walked together up to the far end of the village. Like the other women, I had a yellow flower behind my ear; the *kepkep* strung on a piece of vine hung from my neck; shell bracelets were on my left arm just above the elbow. I wore the pink and white striped dress. I was excited and nervous.

When we arrived, about two thousand Melanesians from all over New Ireland and neighboring islands were sitting around the fires. We took our places and watched the dances, which went on continuously all night long in an open clearing before an intently absorbed audience. Most of the men's dances were dramatic, often acting out a story such as the killing of a crocodile. Masks were elaborate; dancing was strenuous and the drums beat vigorously. The women wore no masks and their dances, which alternated with the men's, were far less elaborate and formed abstract patterns of lines, squares, and circles. Young men held burning torches near the dancers, so that all could see them.

I was unable to pay much attention. Consumed with self-consciousness, I imagined my family and friends sitting in the background and muttering in disapproving tone, "Hortense, dancing with the savages!" How could I get up before all these people of the Stone Age and dance with them? I prayed for an earthquake—the island was volcanic. But the earth was still, and all too soon it was our turn to dance. I wondered if I would not collapse on my way to the open clearing which served as the stage. But there I was in my proper place in the circle; the drums began; I danced. Something happened. I forgot myself and was one with the dancers. Under the full moon and for the brief time of the dance, I ceased to be an anthropologist from a modern society. I danced. When it was over I realized that, for this short period, I had been emotionally part of the rite. Then out came my notebook.

In the early morning the boys were circumcised inside the enclosure. I was invited to watch the operation, but decided not to. Nor had I gone into the enclosure during the preceding

few weeks when the boys were confined there. The normal
social separation between the men and women was intensified
during the initiation of the boys. The mothers (real and classificatory) openly expressed their sorrow at losing their sons who
would now join the adult men. The women wept (not ritual
wailing) when the boys went into the enclosure for the operation, and began a dance which expressed their feelings. Men
ran out from the enclosure and engaged in a spirited fight with
the women. They threw stones and coconut shells at each other
and exchanged jeering talk. Since I had been identified with
the women, even to the extent of dancing with them, it seemed
unwise in the hostile atmosphere between the sexes to swerve
suddenly from the women's group to the men's. Or, perhaps,
I was unable to switch my identifications so quickly.

Later in the morning the piles of food (contributed by the
clans of boys who had been circumcised) were given to the
dancers. A particularly large pile was put in front of me and
a speech was made praising my dancing and expressing appre-
ciation. From then on the quality of my relationships with the
women was different. I had their confidence as I had not had it
before. They came of their own accord to visit me and talked
intimately about their lives. I secured eight quite long detailed
life histories. My relationships with the men were also subtly
strengthened. The formal escort to their feasts continued as
before, but there was a greater sense of ease between us and
they gave me freely any data I asked for. I was glad for many
reasons that I had not given in to my self-consciousness. Thinking about it, I was amused to realize that all the things white
people had tried to make me fear—snakes, sharks, crocodiles,
rape—had not caused me anxiety. Nor had the expedition
taken any particular courage. As one of my friends remarked, I had the courage of a fool who did not know what
she was getting into. But to dance with the women at the initiation rites—that had taken courage.

A woman alone in the field has certain advantages. Social
separation between the sexes is strict in all tribal societies.
Male anthropologists say it is difficult for them to be alone
with native women, because the men (and the women, too)
suspect their intentions. When traders and other white men
have had contact with native peoples, they frequently have

had sexual relations with the women, with or without their consent. No precedent existed, at least in Melanesia when I was there, for a white woman to live alone in a native village. We could establish our own patterns, and obviously these large strong Melanesians could not be afraid of me. (The gun which Radcliffe-Brown had insisted I take with me for protection remained hidden in the bottom of a trunk.) My relations with the women were more chummy than with the men, and data from the former were more intimate. But the men completely understood that I had to find out as much as possible about all sides of life and, very definitely, did not want the masculine side omitted. It was the men, not I, who suggested escorting me to all their feasts. My impression is that field work may be a bit easier for a woman anthropologist alone than for a man alone.

Being alone for a male or female anthropologist gives a greater intensity to the whole field experience than living with company, and frequently provides more intimate data because the field worker is thrown upon the natives for companionship. On the other hand, it has the disadvantage of loneliness, and, perhaps, getting "fed-up" more often. A mate and children reduce the loneliness, and they may be of help in securing data from their own sex and age groups. Children are often an entering wedge into the study of family life. A team of colleagues, particularly from different disciplines, makes possible a many-sided approach to complex problems and offers the stimulation of exchange of ideas while in the field. A disadvantage of the family and team is that they may make relationships with natives more difficult. One member may be quickly accepted and the other disliked. It is usually easier for people to relate to one stranger than to several. The initial pattern in participant observation was the lone anthropologist. Today the family and team are becoming more common.

XI

"GOING NATIVE?"

Although I had enjoyed those brief moments of feeling at one with the women dancers at the initiation rites and although I was fairly involved in this Stone-Age society, I never fooled myself that I had "gone native." I participated rather freely, but remained an anthropologist.

While I did fit, to a considerable degree, within the Melanesian social system, small incidents sometimes brought out a sense of my difference. When I admired the beauty of the night, my friends looked at me as if I were quite strange. They appeared to take the scenery for granted, and I never heard them comment on its beauty. When I was trying to find out about the inheritance of personal property, I naturally asked everyone the same question: who would inherit upon death their *tsera* (native shell currency), their *kepkep* (tortoise-shell breast ornament), and other small personal possessions. My informants apparently compared notes, for after a while one man wanted to know why I asked everyone the same question. Did I not know, he asked, that there was only one custom of inheritance? His question came at the end of a long day's work and I was too tired to explain the concept of a sample. I contented myself (and presumably him) with saying that asking the same question of many persons was one of the strange customs of my people, thinking to myself of social scientists. On the other hand, it was I who thought it a strange custom when an old man told me while I was doing his genealogy that he had strangled his father and mother when both of them were old, ill, and wanting to die. I looked at the man's kindly face and wondered how he could have done it. I realized in a few minutes that his attitude might be called realistic and mine sentimental, and I did not like the latter label.

Sometimes a crisis brought out a latent conflict between the roles of being in and being out of the society. My good friend Pulong was ill and no one knew whether she would live or die. In the early morning, before daybreak, she gave birth prematurely to her baby, born dead, and her own life appeared to be in danger. All day women of her clan were in her mother's house (where she had gone when the birth pains had started), giving her native medicine, performing magic to cure, and tending her. Ongus, her husband, sat on a log outside the house. (Because the illness was connected with childbirth, he could not go into the house.) He sat, with his back to the house, his shoulders bowed—a lonely, tragic figure. His large, beautifully proportioned body and its attitude of tragedy made me think of a Rodin statue and of one of Michaelangelo's figures on the ceiling of the Sistine Chapel.

Psychologically, I was not at ease. I walked in and out of the house where Pulong lay, but I could do nothing. Obviously I knew too little of medicine to administer anything from my kit. Pulong was my best friend among the women and a very good informant; personal sorrow was mingled with fear of scientific loss. My sense of helplessness was difficult to take. Inanely I remarked to Ongus that I hoped Pulong would be better soon; he replied gravely that he did not know. Even before he answered, I knew my remark was silly. I sat around the bed with the women, went back to my house, wrote up everything, wandered back to Pulong's bed again. The fact that I was getting good data did not take away my restlessness. I felt all wrong during this crisis: outside it, though emotionally involved.

Living in a culture not my own suddenly seemed unnatural. It was as if the group had withdrawn into itself, and I was left outside. Pulong recovered; the normal daily life was resumed and I lost this feeling. But during Pulong's illness and in similar emergencies, I knew that no matter how intimate and friendly I was with the natives, I was never truly a part of their lives.

Another crisis occurred when I was in Logagon for *Malanggan* rites. On the afternoon of the second day there, my Lesu friends, a large number of whom were at Logagon, were extremely cool to me; they were polite, but the easy friendliness had disappeared. I was puzzled and concerned. I tried to think of something I might have done to offend them, but could recall nothing. Then the rites began and, as usual, I took notes; but I worried about what had caused the strange unfriendliness. That night, Kuserek told me the reason. The Lesu people felt that I had betrayed their confidence by reporting a case of sickness to a government medical patrol.

Earlier that day, two Lesu men, arriving for the rites, had stopped at my house to chat. Giving me news from Lesu, they mentioned that Mimis, a young girl, had been afflicted with the "big sickness." An epidemic causing the death or paralysis of natives had begun to sweep the island. The people called it the "big sickness." [1] Seven people had died of it in a village six miles from Lesu. Before I left for Logagon there were no cases in Lesu. Naturally, I was worried about its spread to Lesu. While I wondered what to do, a medical patrol from Kavieng drove down the road in a lorry. I dashed out of the house, yelling at them to stop. Finally they heard me and I told them about the sick girl in Lesu. They said they were going all the way to the southern end of the island, and would stop in Lesu on their way back and take the girl to the Kavieng hospital, if she were still alive. I walked back to the house, relieved that I had been able to report the sick girl to a medical patrol.

But my Lesu friends had a very different impression of this incident, which they had witnessed. For them, the Kavieng hospital was only a place in which death occurred, and if they were going to die, they preferred to do so in their own home. (Ill people were so far advanced in their sickness when they entered the hospital that they usually did die there.) By reporting the sick girl to the patrol, I was sending her to die in Kavieng, far from relatives.

Stunned by this version of the affair, I immediately went over to where a group of Lesu men, many of them trusted friends and informants, were sitting, and began to explain. They listened politely, said nothing, and turned the conversation to a different topic. Feeling helpless, I decided to let the matter drop for a few days. Everyone was busy with the rites, and I went about taking notes, wondering when I should try to

---

[1] Unfortunately, I neglected to get its technical name and in my notes used the pidgin English, "big sickness." It seemed similar to polio.

reopen the subject. Then one evening when I was with Ongus and a few people whom I thought had trusted me, I began again. I gave the facts simply and clearly: the horrors of the "big sickness" and the seven deaths in a nearby village, all of which they knew. I said that I was concerned that the people of Lesu did not die in the same manner; that I did not know whether Mimis would live or die in the Kavieng hospital, but her absence from the village would at least prevent other Lesu people from catching the "big sickness" from her. I explained as well as I could the meaning of contagion. All this I repeated several times. The men listened and apparently understood the general point. The former friendliness returned.

The climax came several months later. Mimis returned from the Kavieng hospital, well, except for a slight limp. At a small feast to honor her homecoming I smiled inwardly when speeches were made stressing that I was responsible for her being alive.

An incident which might have been interpreted by outsiders to mean that the Lesu people thought I was one of them occurred when I was feeling a bit indisposed and tired, although not sick. I decided to take the day off. Kuserek dragged my cot out to the veranda and I lay on it, alternating reading with sleeping. In the late afternoon, Ongus came over and said that he was very sorry to hear of my illness and my approaching death. Startled, I hastily told him that I was not going to die. But he insisted the end was near. The cry of a certain bird, believed to be an omen of death, had been heard in the village, and the meaning was evident. Ongus then assured me that I did not have to worry. Since my own relatives were far away, "my" clan would take the responsibility for providing the proper mortuary rites. I got up immediately and walked about the village so that everyone could see that I was decidedly alive, and not begin preparation for my mortuary ritual. The attitudes of Ongus and of "my" clan did not mean that they regarded me as one of them, but rather that to them it was unthinkable for any human being not to have the proper rites after death. My new friends liked me, knew that my real relatives were far away, and therefore planned to do the "honors."

It never occurred to me or to the Melanesians that I was going "native." Understanding between people is, usually, a two-way process. I had told my Melanesian friends something about my family and explained my customs as those of my society; and they knew the function of my living in Lesu—to understand their society. Beyond our differences in culture, they seemed to perceive and understand me as a human being in much the same way that I perceived them as human beings. Preliterate people are usually able to size up an anthropologist as a person, understand his role, and become his friends if they like him, though his skin is of a different color and he comes from a strange culture. Likewise, they quickly spot the phoniness of an anthropologist who thinks or pretends that he is really one of them.

Long after I left Lesu, I was told about a couple—both anthropologists—who had worked among an Indian tribe in South America. The wife decided she wanted to "go native" and left her husband for a short time to live with an Indian family. She slept in their house, dressed as they did, ate the same food, and, in general, tried to live the native life. At the end of an agreed-upon period, her husband and his colleague called for her. As she climbed into their truck with a sigh of relief, her Indian host winked broadly at her husband. He and his family had been humoring her play-acting.

XII

LEAVING LESU
AND RETURNING HOME

After nine months in Lesu, I began to read the shipping news in a Sydney paper which a friend sent me. I noted the dates of sailings from Sydney to San Francisco, and from Kavieng to Sydney, and figured out possible connections. I knew I could hold out for another month or so, but had doubts whether I could last much longer than that, and continue working. I was tired of the enervating weather, of cutting my own hair, of the clothes I wore, of working from sunrise to midnight; fed up with life in Lesu. I felt I had been there nine years instead of nine months. After I had booked passage and knew I was leaving in about six weeks, I felt better. I realized that after I left, I would probably want to return. But now I wanted to go home.

However, the people of Lesu and the neighboring villages seemed to think I was staying forever. By this time my presence and participation in village life was taken for granted, accepted as a matter of course—an ideal situation for a field worker. But I was still a phenomenon for people in distant villages who had only heard of me. During my last month in Lesu a man from the southern part of the island was passing through and he and Ongus were talking, not far from my veranda. The wind carried their voices to me, and when I heard my name mentioned, I unashamedly listened. Ongus was saying: "You know when she came here, she was so dumb. She did not even know how to speak. She was like an infant. She knew nothing. But now, ah, all is changed. She speaks and she understands us; she knows our magic; she can dance with the women; she has learned our folk tales; she knows how we garden and the different ways we fish; she has been to all our feasts; she knows about the *Malanggans* . . . Ah, she knows much. Who is responsible? I am." I wished I knew as much as he thought I did. Ongus seemed to be expressing the attitude of many of the Lesu adults towards me. I was a sort of daughter to whom they had taught the ways of their society.

My Lesu friends must have known I would leave sooner or later, but they were shocked when I told them I was going after another "moon" had passed. Pulong came over and urged me to marry and settle with a husband in Lesu. She had even thought of a mate: a young Australian schoolmaster who had come down from Kavieng to see me occasionally. Interested in linguistics, he was learning the native language and he lacked the usual prejudices towards natives. Pulong talked about how fine it would be if we three couples—she and Ongus, Kuserek and Sinbanimous, and I and a husband—would spend the rest of our lives together in Lesu. Ongus came a bit later to tell me that several of the important men of the community had discussed my impending departure and suggested that he ask "the government" (the Mandated Government) to intercede and get me to stay. He had replied quite simply that I could not be forced to stay against my will, and that I wanted to go home and see my family. They understood.

My friends continued to instruct me to the end. They were in the house, supervising Sinbanimous as he wrapped the carvings I had bought in burlap bags, and telling me not to omit anything they had told me when I talked to my family. Ongus kept insisting that I must be sure to tell my people just how I had lived—not in Kavieng or on a plantation, but in their village, Lesu, and how I had been part of life there. One of the jokes of the village, repeated many times, was that when I returned home, I would continue to talk in the Lesu language, and no one would understand me. Other times, my friends remarked sadly that I would soon forget their language, since I would have no one to talk to in it. They also expressed their regret about my departure by saying how empty and lonely my house would be; sometimes they said that the house would be no good after I left.

During the last month, I was too busy checking data, typing final notes, packing, and so forth, to think much about the actual departure. I mused about having my hair cut by the finest hairdresser in Sydney and about clothes I would like to have. Mrs. Grosse had decided to make a dress for me and, on a visit to Rabaul, bought the material—red organdie. I happily designed it. I wondered whether my former high color would return; a daily dose of quinine and the tropical sun had taken away most of it.

A week before I left, a big feast was given in my honor. Everyone in Lesu came. Speeches expressing sorrow at my departure were made and presents were given me.

Later I distributed some of my belongings. Most of my household possessions (the kitchen equipment and my folding cot, mattress, and sheets) went to Kuserek and Sinbanimous. They had asked me to hold their wages, since money could not be spent in Lesu. With their accumulated wages and my household goods, they planned to settle down in their own village. They would probably be the richest native people on the island. My blanket and other small possessions I gave to different friends. I wondered what to do with an old heavy wool coat, which I had thought would be useful on the New Guinea mountain top where I had originally planned to live among the Mafulu people. Naturally, I had never worn it in Lesu. Ladawin (Sinbanimous' friend) was eager to have it. Tall and husky, he could not even get his arms into the sleeves. But wearing the coat as a cape swinging from his shoulders, he strutted happily in the tropical heat of Lesu.

The morning of my departure came. Mr. Grosse's lorry, which I had hired to take me to Kavieng, and a driver were waiting as I finished breakfast. My Lesu friends stood without speaking in a circle around the truck. They wept openly; tears rolled down their cheeks. I felt terrible, torn by ambivalent feelings. I was truly fond of my Lesu friends and was much upset at the severing of ties with them; yet I was desperately eager to leave the island and go home. I wanted to cry, but I didn't. I stood silent, and then told my friends that I would never forget them. Hastily, I climbed into the truck and was off.

At Kavieng, I said good-bye to the D.O. and his wife before boarding the same S.S. *Montoro* which had brought me there. Tired and depressed, I lay in my bunk and could think of nothing I knew about Lesu. It did not help me to look at a metal trunk filled with field notes, which was in my cabin because I would not trust it to the ship's hold. In desperation,

I began to recite Melanesian kinship terms, to prove that I had learned something. A bit later, I worried about returning home. Did I really want the close ties awaiting me?

Eating with ten strangers, after months of solitary meals, was horrible. But there were compensations during the trip. I ate huge quantities of salad, drank gallons of water, and slept a lot. I had drinks with the purser, half French and half British, the nicest man on the boat. My mind was a blank. After a week, I began to feel better.

The voyage was rough, as we cruised along the coast of New Guinea. But the harbor of Madang was beautiful. In two weeks we landed in Sydney. I saw my anthropologist friends, but found it difficult to talk about field work. I wanted to forget it for a time. Fortunately, they had had similar experiences and understood. My hair was cut, as I had planned. I had pictures of my Lesu friends enlarged and framed, and sent them to the D.O. in Kavieng. He had promised to see that they were delivered in Lesu.

After a couple of weeks I boarded a Matson Line ship to cross the Pacific, and it seemed like the essence of luxury. The food was wonderful and I could afford to gorge since I had lost twenty-five pounds. An interesting, attractive man provided companionship and a sense of being taken care of. He had a cultivated voice, talked well, and did not expect me to say much. This suited me. I still felt detached; much of the time I thought about how my Lesu friends would regard ship life.

Then came San Francisco, and a visit for a few days with old friends. After buying a ticket to Baltimore and putting aside something for incidentals, I had exactly one hundred dollars left. I spent it all on clothes; it was spring and I, literally, had nothing suitable to wear.

In my new suit and hat, I went to meet the anthropologists at Berkeley. Although I knew Malinowski had sent a letter of introduction to Lowie, I was a bit scared before my first meeting with American anthropologists. But I lost my fear at the departmental lunch when everyone was so cordial. Kroeber was particularly nice to me. He asked me my plans. I told him I wanted a fellowship in order to be free to write about life in Lesu and that I would like to be on the Atlantic seaboard. He mentioned that all the fellowships, except those of the National Research Council, had already been awarded, and that the application date for that had passed a couple of months ago. However, he thought it worthwhile for me to go to Washington and meet the chairman, Fay-Cooper Cole, to whom he would send a note of introduction.

I phoned for an appointment as soon as I reached Baltimore and received one for the next day. Cole was sympathetic to my need for time to write, and understanding about the lateness of my application. As he said, I could not have applied while on the high seas. He told me that I must have a sponsor at a university where I could be in residence, and that the meeting of the Council was in a week's time.

I knew that Radcliffe-Brown had sent a note of introduction to Clark Wissler at the American Museum of Natural History, and that Wissler was a part-time professor at the Yale Institute of Human Relations. It sounded like a good place for me. After sending cables to Malinowski and Radcliffe-Brown asking for recommendations to the National Research Council, I went to New York to see Wissler. He kindly consented to sponsor me and even offered temporary office space at the Museum. I stayed up most of one night writing the application, and sent it special-delivery to Cole. Then in good Melanesian style, I made a magical rite to insure its success. Within several days, I heard from Cole that a fellowship had been awarded to me.

I relaxed with the family, even visiting various relatives in the hope of finding a clan. I soon gave up that idea. The family, thinking I looked badly (thin and yellow), sent me to a physician for a check-up. After a thorough examination, he said that I was in excellent condition and that all I needed was a good time. I knew this was easier to have in New York than in Baltimore.

New York was just what I needed. Friends were there to provide the good time. I loved the city and found it exhilarating. Riding up Fifth Avenue on the top of the old double-decker bus was exciting. As I looked at the beautiful skyline, I wondered what my Melanesian friends would say about it. Late one afternoon, I went to a friend's wedding in an Episcopal church. The service was unfamiliar to me and, without thinking, I reached into my pocket for a pencil and paper to take notes on a strange wedding ritual. It took a minute or less for me to realize that I did not have to take notes at a friend's wedding. A watch was on my wrist, but I kept looking at the sky to see the position of the sun, and I was casually late for most appointments. People looked so pale to me; a dark skin had become natural looking. I should have written an article, "New York Through a Melanesian's Eyes," but I was in no mood for writing then.

I was glad that I was going to Yale in September to write. In the meantime I wanted neither to think nor to talk about life in Lesu. I needed frivolity and time to become detached from it. Detachment did come after a few months. Then I was ready to think and write about the Melanesians.

PART III

MISSISSIPPI

INTRODUCTION

My field work in Mississippi was done under the auspices of the Social Science Research Council between September 1932 and May 1933, and for three months in the summer of 1934. The interval between the two trips was spent at the Institute of Human Relations, Yale University, organizing field notes and writing them up. The second visit to Mississippi was to fill in gaps and to study activities, such as religious revival meetings, which occurred only in the summer.

XIII

CHOOSING A COMMUNITY

Life in Lesu was completed. What next? I discussed this with
Edward Sapir, chairman of the anthropology department at
Yale University, where I had a research post at the Institute
of Human Relations. He suggested a North American Indian
group, and I shook my head. Because of my British training
I knew little about American Indians, and furthermore, was
not interested in them. Sapir then mentioned the possibility of
studying a group of Hassidic Jews in New York City, who he
thought posed interesting problems. Again, my reaction was
negative: lack of interest, no knowledge of Hebrew or Yiddish,
and a feeling that I lacked the necessary objectivity to study
orthodox Jews. His next question: "Well, whom do you want
to study?" My answer was prompt: "American Negroes." Sapir
said, "Fine. Draw up a project and submit it to the Social
Science Research Council."[1]

I went back to my office and, to my surprise, within a few
hours I had made a detailed plan to study a community in the
deep South. I must have been thinking, consciously and unconsciously, for a long time about this type of research problem. I had, of course, been aware of Negroes in Baltimore.
Our family had had a succession of Negro "girls," as day-time
servants were called. I seem to have taken them for granted
and none made any particular impression on me. But I remember liking a Negro dressmaker who came to our house to sew
and also made clothes for us at her home. She was a slight,
graceful, brown colored woman, a skilled seamstress, with good

---

[1] Now I am surprised that it never even occurred to me to return to the
southwest Pacific and work again among Melanesians. Apparently, I was
interested in learning about a broad range of cultures rather than in a
narrow but more intensive knowledge of one. Each approach has its advantages and disadvantages.

taste and intelligence. I remember, too, my pleasure in walking down Druid Hill Avenue, where houses had been converted into apartments for Negroes. Negro children were often looking out of the windows; in summertime the families were sitting on the white steps so familiar in Baltimore.

One incident relating to Negroes stands out vividly from my years at home. I was coming home on a streetcar late one hot August afternoon from the playground where I taught during some summer vacations while a college student. White and Negro men who had obviously been digging and working in the sun boarded the car. They were all dirty and sweaty. The car was crowded and people had to stand close to each other. A white woman standing by me complained about the smell of the Negroes; they did smell. I wondered about the white workers and moved next to them; they smelled, too. The blue cotton uniform which I wore as a playground teacher was wet with perspiration from my strenuous day. I then became aware that I smelled. The streetcar incident stood out as a discovery.

I knew no Negroes as friends in Baltimore. The high school was all white, as was the playground where I taught. I do not remember any Negro students attending Goucher during my time. The first Negro I met socially was a woman student at the University of London when I was studying there. She was reading at the British Museum, where I spent much of my time. A mutual friend introduced us and we all went to tea at the usual four o'clock break. I was enormously curious about this young Negro woman, but also exceedingly self-conscious. She knew I came from Baltimore, and I felt myself being watched. We became friends, although never close. Actually, we did not have too much in common; but my curiosity (and probably hers too) promoted a friendly casual relationship for a couple of years. I learned that she was not much different from anyone else I knew. Her experiences as a Negro seemed only to give her personality a certain slant.

Many years after my Mississippi study I learned during a period of psychoanalysis that my interest in Negroes was no accident. However, the desire to go south and study the Negroes (and the whites there) sprang not only from deep and unconscious interests, but also from an intuitive return to my

involvement with society. When I had left the labor movement, I had naïvely thought that I should and could separate
my concern about society from research. But, as James Coleman has noted, research can be rooted in a deep concern with
society.[2]

Sapir liked my plan for study and backed the application to
the Social Science Research Council for a fellowship, which
was awarded me. The stipend was $1800, plus an additional
$225—the cost of a second-hand Ford, purchased after my
arrival in Mississippi. In the mid-thirties, the stipend was adequate, at least, for my way of living and method of work.

I had never been in the South, and my knowledge of it was
casual. After considerable reading and thinking, I tentatively
chose Mississippi; it seemed to represent the deep South, and
no social studies had yet been done there. I left the selection
of the exact community until I knew more about the local
situation.

The Lynds' famous Middletown had given an impetus to
community studies. While their goal—an objective and holistic
study of a community—was anthropological, they and their
large staff were sociologists and not too much outside the
traditions of their discipline. I was interested in seeing how
far I could work as I (and other contemporary anthropologists)
did in tribal societies, i.e. alone, without elaborate techniques,
participating as fully as possible. As far as I know, I was the
first anthropologist to study a modern community in the United
States. When Robert Lowie, who had reviewed and liked
Life in Lesu, heard of my plans, he wrote me that although a
study in Mississippi might be interesting, I should not go too
far in the direction of modern communities. After all, anthropologists were then supposed to limit their studies to primitive
peoples. However, Clark Wissler made me feel better about
the project by saying that "anthropology is what the anthropologist does." Many years later Lowie studied contemporary
Germany. By that time Wissler's definition was more or less
accepted.

---

[2] James S. Coleman, "Research Chronicle: The Adolescent Society," in
Philip E. Hammond ed., Sociologists at Work: The Craft of Social Research (New York: Basic Books, Inc., 1964), p. 184.

Perhaps more important than the wish to do a modern community study was my strong curiosity about Negro life and my desire to understand it. I was still a Functionalist, and assumed that the biracial situation would be related to and affect all other aspects of the society. A few of Sapir's seminars which I had sat in on and many conversations with him had stimulated my psychological interests, which were later reflected in an emphasis on attitudes in the Mississippi study. But I had no hypotheses to prove or disprove.

Field work was to begin in September of 1932, and the preceding summer I spent in New Hampshire with the Sapir family. Much of the time I read rather generally about the history of the South and of Mississippi, and about slavery; I thought about the project and discussed it occasionally with Sapir. The leisurely summer was distinguished by a deepening friendship with all of the Sapir family and by the stimulating quality of Edward Sapir's mind and conversation.

One particularly long weekend was memorable when Harry Stack Sullivan, the distinguished psychoanalyst, was a guest and the two men discussed their ideas (still embryonic) about the relationship between culture and personality. The thoughts of one man kindled those of the other. My impression was that the remarkable flow of conversation between them was due not only to the high quality of their minds and to their mutual interest in the relationship between the individual and his society, but also to their personalities—each man seemed to combine within himself something of the scientist and of the poet. I was excited by listening and participating even slightly in this creative communication.

When the summer was over, I went to Fisk University to consult with Charles S. Johnson, chairman of the social sciences department, and Franklin E. Frazier, professor of sociology in the same department. Both men were distinguished sociologists and Negroes who had chosen to study their own people. They agreed that Mississippi was a good choice for a study, but said that I could not go there, "pitch my tent," and say, "I've come to study you," as I had done in Lesu. They thought I should enter the community through some easily understandable role in the state's education department, and Johnson suggested that I see the state superintendent of education in Jackson and ask for a title without duties or salary attached to it. Both men said the field situation would not be easy. Johnson was optimistic that I could handle it, but Frazier was pessimistic because he did not think white people would permit me to move around freely with Negroes.

For several weeks I lived on the Fisk campus, talking informally and getting to know the sociology faculty, research fellows, and graduate students, all of whom were hospitable and friendly. I had a sense of being in an ebony tower. One evening I went to a Negro night club in Nashville with three of the younger members of the department, and, to my surprise, no one at the club seemed taken aback at a white person's being with Negroes and a white woman's dancing with a Negro man. One of my friends explained that everyone thought I was a Negro "high yellow." My skin was quite fair, with considerable pinkish tone, my hair and eyes brown, and my features were in no way Negroid. This was my first experience with unconsciously "passing."

About the time I was ready to leave Fisk, one of Johnson's research assistants was driving to her home near Oxford, Mississippi, and he suggested I go with her as far as Oxford. I was pleased with the suggestion. Entering the deep South with a Negro woman and seeing it, to some degree, through her eyes, was an excellent beginning; we became friends and she talked freely. I was mistaken for a Negro by colored and white people. Aware of this whenever we were in a Negro restaurant or hotel, I was amazed that my physical appearance did not count at all. My companion was quite dark but I met other Negroes lighter than I. In a few days I acquired some of the feeling tone of what it meant to be an educated Negro young woman in Mississippi.[3]

At Oxford my companion left me and I went to a white hotel. I had sent, in advance, a note of introduction from a Yale sociologist to a professor of sociology at the state university there and, when I phoned, he cordially invited me to dinner, saying apologetically that it would be very simple.

[3] The situation would be different at this writing, when white people from the North have joined with southern Negroes in their revolt. But in the mid-thirties, any white person seen socially with Negroes would be considered Negro by members of both races.

Later, he explained that the state had run out of educational funds and that he and his colleagues had not been paid salaries for several months. They were living on credit and the dinner was simple: spaghetti without meat. The state fiscal system seemed to operate casually and the sociologist gave me the feeling of having been beaten down by the whole social system. It was my good luck that he happened to be a cousin of the state superintendent of education, to whom he kindly gave me a letter of introduction.

I presented the note in Jackson and quickly got an appointment with the superintendent. He was genial and talked for almost an hour about the interracial situation in Hawaii, where he had never been, and where I had visited for one afternoon when my ship stopped there on the way back from Australia. I listened, nodded my head in seeming agreement to everything, and said practically nothing. After the monologue, he remarked, "My cousin says you are a nice girl from Baltimore. What can I do for you?" I told him I'd like a title in his department without a job or salary. His answer was to pick any title I liked. I chose "visiting teacher," and he gave me a formal letter of introduction to education officials in the state, requesting that they cooperate with me in my research. The letter was to serve as an entering wedge in a community.

Next, I looked up Mr. Green,[4] the Rockefeller Foundation Representative for Negro education. The Foundation had a local man in each southern state, whose function was to try to raise the standards of Negro education. My main problem at this point was the choice of locale. I desired a county in which the old single-crop cotton plantation system still functioned, along with recent developments such as the New Deal program for diversification of crops. My premise was that new economic patterns would probably influence social life and attitudes; I wanted to study the past and the contemporary. It amused me to see how quickly my early historical interests asserted themselves. A further condition for choosing a site would be the presence of county education officials, white and Negro, on whose cooperation I might count.

---

[4] The names of Mississippians are all pseudonyms, with the exception of Mr. Will Percy from whose book I quote.

After some discussion, Mr. Green narrowed my choice to three counties. He then suggested that I go with him to a statewide meeting of Jeanes supervisors, in session that day in Jackson. These were Negro men and women paid by the private Jeanes Fund to work for the improvement of Negro schools. Mr. Green indicated the supervisors from the three counties he had suggested. One of the three supervisors, Mrs. Wilson from Sunflower County, seemed decidedly superior. Her participation in the discussion was intelligent and vigorous. Mr. Green introduced me to her after the meeting was over. We liked each other immediately; I felt there would be no problem in working with her and she was eager to have me come to Indianola, the seat of Sunflower County, where she lived. Mr. Green told me that Mr. Smith, the white superintendent of education in that county, was moderately liberal by Mississippi standards. He had been to a northern university for a year on a Rosenwald fellowship, while most of the other superintendents had never been outside of Mississippi. So, it was settled. I would live and work in Indianola and the surrounding rural area, part of the delta region formed by the Yazoo and Mississippi rivers. Indianola was a couple of hundred miles northwest of Jackson and Mr. Green said he would drive me there the next morning.

I had no way of knowing then that in 1954 Sunflower County would become the birthplace of the White Citizens' Council. My impression is that this institutionalized form of bigotry might have originated in almost any one of the surrounding counties and that relations between the Negroes and whites were about the same in all of them.

XIV

ENTRÉE INTO INDIANOLA

Mr. Green and I arrived in Indianola just before lunch time and went immediately to the court house to see Mr. Smith, the county superintendent of education. I presented the letter from the state superintendent. Mr. Smith seemed noncommittal and said he would have to call a meeting of the leading members of the community that afternoon so that they could discuss my proposed research. Apparently I could not be there for one day without being accounted for.

After a greasy lunch in a small restaurant, I left Mr. Green and went around looking for a place to live. I looked first at the town's one hotel. The bedroom doors had no locks, the guests were mostly traveling salesmen, and, quite obviously, the only women who might stay there would probably be prostitutes. The town had no apartment house, and I inquired about boarding houses. I went to a couple of them, and they had no room for me. I did not know if the houses were literally full or if they had no room for an unidentified Yankee.

As I walked around, the physical appearance of the town depressed me. It and the surrounding country side were completely flat; I am always more at home in a hilly or mountainous region. The orderly rows of snug little bungalows with an occasional larger and more pretentious home, all with well-kept gardens, interrupted here and there by a church, gave me a sense of middle-class uniformity. The business district was four blocks grouped in a square. Its outstanding building was a red brick court house, which dominated the commonplace smaller buildings: post office, a few drug, dry goods, and grocery stores, a bank, newspaper office, barber shop, a beauty parlor, two restaurants, a few other small businesses, a jail, hotel, bowling alley, offices of the Federal Farm Bureau, the FERA, the Red Cross, and of a few lawyers and doctors. From the cotton gins, off one side of the business section, came a

pleasing deep, rich odor. A swampy bayou, with dark cypress
trees rising from the muddy waters, lay across one corner of
the town and conveyed a melancholy feeling. I knew that the
Negroes lived across the railroad tracks, but that afternoon
provided no time to explore there.

It was almost 2:30 and time to return to the court house for
the meeting of leading citizens which Mr. Smith had called.
Present were the mayor, the heads of the Chamber of Com
merce and of the Rotary Club, the principal of the white high
school, several Protestant ministers, the woman president of
the Parent-Teachers Association, the women heads of two
church societies, and several other people considered important. We all sat around a long table; Mr. Smith, Mr. Green, and
I were at the head of it. Mr. Smith introduced Mr. Green. Mr.
Green then began a lengthy introduction of me, in the dramatic manner of a southern minister or politician. I listened
with amazement as somehow I became a Baltimore belle, because I had gone to Goucher College (attended by many
upper-class southern girls) and my family lived in that city.
Then, according to Mr. Green, Yale University and the entire
Rockefeller Foundation were behind my research project. He
ended his oration: "She might have gone to Georgia, but no,
she did not go to Georgia; she might have gone to Alabama,
but no, she did not go to Alabama; she came to Mississippi.
She might have gone to Isaqueena County, but no, she came
to Sunflower County. Ladies and gentlemen, she is yours!" I
was then expected to say something. Not wanting to spoil the
effect of Mr. Green's flowery introduction, I decided that the
less I said, the better. I talked for only five or six minutes about
my interest in studying the Negro family, an innocuous subject, I thought.

The leading citizens of Indianola were completely uncon-
vinced by Mr. Green's oration or by my few words. They were
suspicious of a Yankee and did not want their "niggers" studied
by anyone. Their questions, the expressions on their faces, and
the tone of their voices indicated both fear and hostility.

The first question: "Are you interested in changing the status
quo?"

My answer: "I am here to study it," which happened to be
the truth.

"Are you going to publish newspaper articles when you

leave?", accompanied by statements about Yankee journalists who spent a few days in the South and then wrote lurid articles about it.

I answered quite truthfully that I would not write newspaper articles.

"What are you going to write?"

"A scientific book."

So the questions went, some less pointed, but all fearful. After an hour or so, the meeting was over. Mr. Green, saying, "God be with you!" left immediately for Jackson.

I was thoroughly depressed. I knew that I could not work with Negroes if everything had to be sieved through this group of white citizens and approved by them. Moreover, I had no place in Indianola to live, or even spend the night. Where was southern hospitality? No one at the meeting had inquired where I was planning to stay, and I sensed it was hopeless to ask any of them for help on this problem. I remembered Franklin Frazier's point that white people would not let me work with Negroes, and decided that he had known what he was talking about. It was not pleasant to admit defeat, even before I had begun. I could think of only one thing to do: return to Yale and give back the fellowship to the Social Science Research Council. At the time, I was so depressed that the possibility of changing the area of research did not occur to me. To get out of Mississippi was my only idea. But the one local train a day had left; there were no buses; I had no car; I had no place to stay overnight.

I was feeling desperate. Suddenly I remembered that Will Percy, the poet, lived in Greenville, and upon inquiry was told that it was only forty miles away. I had read his lyric poetry and liked it.[1] An acquaintance of mine (who knew I liked Percy's poetry) at Yale University Press, his publisher, had given me an introduction to him which I had mailed a few days ago. From Mr. Smith's office I phoned him. His attractive, cultivated voice cheered me, and he said he had been waiting for me to arrive. He suggested that I come right over; he could not know how very glad I was to do just that. I immediately hired a local white man who ran an informal taxi

[1] William Alexander Percy, *Selected Poems* (New Haven: Yale University Press, 1930).

service to drive me to Mr. Percy's office. Both the taxi driver
and the county superintendent knew who Mr. Percy was and
seemed impressed that I was going to see him. From them I
learned that he was a lawyer and a planter.

Will Percy's office was small and dingy. But he had a kind
of beauty: a sensitive face, soft gray hair, a slight graceful
body, an interesting, sophisticated voice. He really looked like
a poet. He welcomed me and we began talking about poetry,
the only context in which I knew him. I have always loved
poetry, and our tastes in it were traditional and not too different. After a while, he asked how I was getting along in Indianola. I told him about the meeting with their leading
citizens, omitting none of the grim details, and also that I had
been unable to find a place to live. When I finished, he threw
back his head and laughed and laughed, saying, "Now you
have seen the flower of our Southland!" His laughter and irony
were just what I needed for a perspective on Indianola. I felt
better. He picked up the phone and called the mayor of that
town. After the usual polite words of greeting, he said casually,
"Miss Powdermaker, an old friend of the family, is here with
me in my office. I understand she will be living in Indianola
for a while, and I do hope you will make her comfortable."
Such was the magic of his voice, that I was sure everything
would be all right. I was to learn soon that Will Percy was
one of the few remaining aristocrats in Mississippi. As he later
told me, most all the others were either dead, in the poor
house, or in New York.

Mr. Percy, a bachelor, suggested that I stay overnight with
a friend of his, in Greenville, Mrs. Branton. He would not hear
of my going to a hotel. Mrs. Branton turned out to be widowed,
charming, aristocratic, and lonely. She wrote books for children, and was a cultivated person, interested in literature.

The next morning she and I went back together to Indianola
in Mr. Percy's shabby old car, driven by his Negro chauffeur.
As an aristocrat he could "afford" to drive such a car. In Indianola, even during the depression, the cars of middle-class
whites were much newer and shinier. Upon reaching town,
Mrs. Branton and I went to the best boarding house, and I
was able to get the only room with a private bath in town.

By now, everyone in Indianola knew that I was an "old

friend" of the Percy family. The white people in town were almost entirely on the lower or middle rungs of the middle class. A few, such as a judge and a banker, were slightly above these levels. No upper class, no aristocracy, and no intelligentsia were in Indianola. Mr. Percy, very aware of his aristocratic background, had no respect for Indianola's white citizens and actively disliked them. They were the enemy to whom his group had lost power. He liked his old car partly because it was so different from their cars. Mr. Percy was fond of Negroes, who he thought had mysterious Pan-like qualities, and he regarded himself as their protector.

He was the most liberal white person I met in Mississippi. Yet as my study progressed, I intuitively realized the quite definite limits for any discussion of Negroes with him. With Mrs. Branton, I never talked about any aspect of my study. However, I could drive to Greenville any time I felt so inclined, to see Mr. Percy or Mrs. Branton, dine with one of them, and occasionally stay overnight with the latter. I never knew exactly why they accepted me. They were each lonely and I was someone to talk with: about literature with Mrs. Branton and about the South, its history, some aspects of its contemporary life (Negro and white), and poetry with Mr. Percy. Although from different backgrounds and classes, Mr. Percy and I had considerable in common. We both respected knowledge that came through our senses. Although I was not a poet,[2] my attitude to poetry was similar to his: "When you feel intensely, you want to write it down—if anguish to stanch the bleeding; if delight, to prolong the moment."[3] As a poet and an aristocrat, he was apart from the main stream of this middle-class "Bible Belt," and, as an anthropologist, I was decidedly outside of it. He was interested in my study and seemed intrigued by what I might find out. He also appeared to be amused at the idea of a person like myself living in a boarding house in Indianola, something I took for granted. Perhaps the most important reason for the good relationships I had with Mr. Percy and Mrs. Branton was that we liked each other.

---

[2] My occasional poetry was private, amateurish, and never shown to anyone.

[3] William Alexander Percy, *Lanterns on the Levee, Recollections of a Planter's Son* (New York: Alfred A. Knopf, 1941), p. 132.

I was profoundly grateful to Mr. Percy. My planned entrée
had been a flop and he had made it possible for me to begin
working in Indianola. As "an old friend" of the Percy family,
I had a high status in this status-conscious society. The white
people in Indianola were not socially accepted by Mr. Percy
or Mrs. Branton. Accepted by them, I could not be really dangerous, even though I was interested in Negro life. The status-
conscious upper-class Negroes also approved of my friendship
with Mr. Percy, although they had no contacts with him.

I was indebted to Will Percy for other reasons. He was my
only informant from the aristocracy. Mrs. Branton was not a
good informant, except indirectly. The fact that none of this
class lived in my community (and that only a very few were
in the whole state) did not mean that the tradition they represented was without contemporary strength. The middle-class
whites carried the burden of complete rejection by them, and
also of straining after a tradition they did not understand.
Talking with Mr. Percy always increased my knowledge and
insight into the complex web of social relations between whites
(aristocrats, middle- and lower-class) and Negroes—a web
which, perhaps, has been oversimplified by the sociological
label of caste structure.

During the first twenty-four hours in Indianola (and nearby
Greenville), and without a single interview or question, I had
been made intensely aware of the complexities of social class
among the whites, of the aristocrat's contempt for the middle
class, and of their respect for him. I had seen the immediate,
hostile, automatic response of the middle class to any possible
threat, no matter how small or unrealistic, to the status quo
with the Negroes.

XV

FIRST MONTH
IN INDIANOLA

*Now began the process of settling in. First, I bought a seven-*year-old Ford (not because I was an aristocrat, but because it was all I could afford!) to take me across the tracks to the Negro section of town and over the gravel roads to plantations.

I phoned Mrs. Wilson, the Jeanes supervisor of Negro education whom I had met in Jackson, and made an appointment to see her. All our visits were in her home since she would have had to use the back door if she had come to my boarding house. Her home was comfortable, white frame, with a porch —one of the nicest on the main street across the tracks. She was a vital, small, bright-eyed, middle-aged woman with brown skin, and long straight black hair which she later mentioned came from an Indian ancestor. More important than her looks was her high level of intelligence, enthusiasm, and dedication to working for the Negroes. She had a college degree, as did her husband, who was a representative of a leading Negro insurance company. Their two daughters were away, attending a Negro state college; a fourteen-year-old son was at the local school. It did not take long to learn that Mrs. Wilson was the leader in the Negro community, and that her leadership was not restricted to educational functions. She was admired and liked by all the Negroes. Her sponsorship of me and her friendship were certainly as important with the Negroes as were Mr. Percy's with the whites.

On this initial visit, Mrs. Wilson and I talked in general terms about the study, and she agreed that for the first month it would be best for me to meet people, acquaint them with my study, and have them get acquainted with me. The visit ended with Mrs. Wilson's inviting me to go to church with her the following Sunday.

When I had visited Fisk University, both Charles S. Johnson and Franklin Frazier had strongly advised me not to reveal my Jewish background to Negroes or whites in a Bible Belt community. For both groups there, they explained, the Jews were still "Christ killers," and the few Jews these people knew were small shopkeepers of low status. So I "became" a Methodist. These and Baptists were the major denominations among the two races; Mrs. Wilson was a Methodist. My sense of Jewish identity was not too strong; yet I was relieved that I could casually mention the Jewish background to Will Percy. Mrs. Wilson was deeply religious, a teacher in Sunday school, and a hard worker in all the activities of her church; her husband was a deacon in it. Considerably later, as our friendship developed, I think she knew, without my saying much, that I was not deeply religious, but that I was much interested in the Negro church and regarded it as a very important institution. She considered me a far better Christian than the religious whites of Indianola, because of what she called my "Christian behavior," i.e. my attitude towards Negroes as fellow human beings. However, I do not think it would have been possible —at least in the beginning of our relationship—for her to have understood and tolerated my being of Jewish background. Nor could Mr. Percy have really comprehended and endured many of my attitudes towards Negroes.

When I went to church with Mrs. Wilson, she introduced me to the minister and he made me welcome from the pulpit and called on me for a "few words." I talked briefly about what I wanted to do: to get to know them and learn about their lives. After the services were over, I participated in the customary sociability in the church yard, meeting and shaking hands with many members of the congregation who invited me to come and see them. I then had dinner with the Wilson family, knowing that I was breaking a taboo by eating with Negroes. Mrs. Wilson had invited me in advance for dinner and I had merely mentioned to my landlady that I would not be home for dinner. I think she assumed that I was having dinner with Mrs. Branton or Mr. Percy.

Every Sunday morning I went to a Negro church, to each denomination in turn. This was a useful way of meeting many people representing all social classes, since everyone went to church. The services were, of course, interesting as a significant part of the social system completely controlled by Negroes. During the week I also attended church socials such as a chitterling supper in a church basement or an entertainment, each to raise money for the church. At a meeting of the Negro Parent-Teachers' Association, I listened to the discussion and talked informally with the members. With Mrs. Wilson I went to the county meeting of Negro teachers and spoke simply and frankly to them about my research project, and ended by asking for their help. After the official part of the meeting was over, I met many of the teachers personally; they were friendly and eager to have me come to their schools, and more important, promised to introduce me to the farmers in their vicinity and give me any other help I needed.

Through Mrs. Wilson, I met socially the members of the small Negro upper class: the dentist and his wife, some of the school teachers, an occasional plantation owner, a woman doctor and her Eurasian husband, and a few others. During this first month I conducted no interviews, except with the Negro agricultural agent in Mrs. Wilson's home. He gave me good background data: percentage of Negroes who were sharecroppers, renters, and land-owners, a list of all the latter, and other useful economic information.

In making these first contacts, the entrée through the state's education department had a limited usefulness in providing some kind of institutional connection. But it would not have been effective without Mr. Percy's and Mrs. Wilson's friendship and helpfulness. I used the state superintendent's letter only once—to Mr. Smith. To him and to all the whites, I said I was studying Negro life; to the Negroes, I said I was studying the community—Negroes and whites. It never occurred to me to waste time pretending to be a "visiting teacher." Besides, I did not know how the role should be played. That I was doing a social study would have been obvious to anyone, regardless of what I would have said.

As I drove around the Negro section of Indianola and met the people, I was struck by the diversity, particularly in contrast to the homogeneity of the white section. Houses ran the

gamut from modest cottages in good condition, such as Mrs.
Wilson's home, to dilapidated one-and-a-half-room shanties.
Two streets were paved. Unpaved streets and narrow alleys
intersected them. Small stores in private homes selling groceries and soft drinks, a shoemaker, a cleaning and pressing
establishment, a barber shop, a couple of beauty parlors (literally, the parlors in two homes), two eating places, an under-
taker, and a pool room represented the commercial aspects of
the Negro section. The dentist, doctor, and insurance agent
had offices in their homes, and the bootleggers worked from
their homes, too. (Mississippi had and still has prohibition,
and corn liquor was the common alcoholic drink.) Churches
ranged from relatively large brick buildings to small deterio-
rated frame structures.

The social heterogeneity across the tracks was even greater
than its physical diversity. Living side by side were the small
upper class of educated people in the professions or in insurance business (not more than 5 per cent of the local Negro
population), a large middle class with three subdivisions, and
a lower class—much larger than the upper one. The income
levels of all the Negro classes were far lower than those of
the equivalent white classes. As field work progressed, I learned
that income was not necessarily the most important criterion
for class membership. Education, occupation, differences in
behavior (primarily marriage and sex life), and the form of
religious worship were part of a complex whole, including
income, by which Negroes assigned class membership. But,
the classes did not live separately. In close proximity were the
pious and the disreputable, known for their drinking, gambling
and fighting; respectable women with Victorian standards and
prostitutes; college graduates and peasants who believed in
voodoo; the dusty blacks, the medium browns, the light creams;
all thrown together because they were all Negroes. The contrasts gave a sense of drama, lacking in the one-class white
section of town.

By the end of the month I knew the general contours. Indianola and the surrounding rural area were economically and
socially fused. The town was the center for business, educational, and social activities. Negroes, even more than whites,
drifted from the country into town for a few hours a day, a
week, or a season. Teachers came to town to attend meetings;

Negroes and "poor whites" came to use the services of the
public health department. On Saturdays, Negro and white tenant farmers came to look about, to shop, and to gossip. The
tall angular poor-whites with their red-burned skins, keeping
to themselves, were easily distinguished from other whites.
During a slack season, a Negro family was likely to move into
town and stay with a relative until it was time for cotton planting or picking. Some former plantation workers had recently
come to town to live. Only a small group—the upper class and
a few of the middle class—were relatively permanent town
dwellers, and many among them had made a crop at some time
in their lives. Sociological problems were becoming more
specific and I saw that the relations between the two races
were even more complex than I had assumed.

I felt secure with the Negroes and accepted by them. A
rumor spread among them that I was really Negro, and passing
for white in order to study the whites. I suppose this was the
only way they could account for me, since I differed so much
from every other white person with whom they had any contact. Probably, the most significant point was that I felt comfortable with Negroes. Black-skinned people did not make me
feel self-conscious. I had also broken a few of the white man's
taboos. I was amused at the rumor and denied it. I had been
accepted and the denial did not alter that fact. Many years
later I happened to tell a social scientist about the rumor, and
his immediate reaction was, "But why didn't you let the rumor
stand as if it were true?" My answer was that no need existed
to play this false role, and that I would have been uncomfortable in it.

During the first month I saw much of Mrs. Wilson as we
drove around the country to various meetings, churches, and
schools. We became friends, and she talked freely about many
things: herself, the social and educational problems of the
Negroes, the white people, and anything else that interested
her. I enjoyed her cynical humor, particularly when she told
me of some incident about acting "proper" before the white
people, in order to get advantages for her people, such as more
and better schools, books, higher wages for the teachers, and
playgrounds. While I was there she managed to get the use
of a piece of land (owned by a white man) for a Negro playground and equipment, or the money to buy it, from whites.

They said, "She is an educated nigger, but she knows her place." Her behavior reduced their guilt and anxieties, and she manipulated them into giving many things white Americans received as their due.

But in spite of her having told me quite cynically of her play-acting before whites, I was not prepared the first time I saw it. This happened unexpectedly when I saw her in Mr. Smith's office, to which she was officially attached. There she looked and acted like a different person from the strong, vibrant personality whom I had seen in her home, at meetings, in church, and alone with me. In Mr. Smith's office, she was the essence of meekness: eyes downcast, accepting with a smile being called "Annie" by white people, although she used the proper social titles for them, waiting patiently to speak with Mr. Smith, who saw all the whites first regardless of the time of their arrival, and who remained seated when, standing, she finally talked with him. She noticed me only with a slight formal nod and "Good Morning." I was startled by the metamorphosis and would not have believed that "Annie" and Mrs. Wilson could be the same person, if I had not known it to be so. Yet, she was no "Uncle Tom," as some would have described her if they had seen her only in Mr. Smith's office and in similar situations. She was a strong self-respecting person, chuckling as she deliberately fooled the whites, and she did it supremely well. In the mid-thirties this kind of accommodation to the white power structure was realistic. The protest movement which became active thirty years later was not yet born.

During the first month I was also getting acquainted with the white people in Indianola. I soon realized that an understanding of them, of their behavior and their attitudes was essential. I knew, too, that they had to trust me as a person if I was to work freely with Negroes and if no harm was to come to them. Will Percy had secured my initial acceptance, but I had to establish my own identity among the whites.

When I was visiting Fisk University, on my way to Mississippi, Charles S. Johnson had told me that a connotation of sociology in the white South was socialism. Fortunately, since I was an anthropologist, I could use that label. Many did not know what anthropology was, and did not want to indicate their ignorance by asking, while for others the term had a vague association of digging for prehistoric remains. In any

case, it was respectable. I was more comfortable, and therefore more effective, in being as candid as circumstances permitted.

Mr. Smith was cordial, gving me the feeling that I had at
least a toe-hold in the community. He made available U.S.
census reports, county education reports, and other official
records. Among other facts I learned that slightly more than
half of Indianola's approximate three thousand inhabitants
were Negroes, in contrast to the 70 per cent Negro population
in Sunflower County. Less than forty white people in Indianola
were foreign-born according to the 1930 census, and these
were mainly Italians, a few others being Russian Jews and
Chinese. My first impression of uniformity in the white section
was strengthened.

Outside of Mr. Smith, the white people whom I knew first
were my fellow boarders: a public health nurse, a secretary,
and two school teachers, all from other parts of the county or
state. They were pleasant, friendly young women in or near
my age group. Mrs. Stewart, the landlady, a widow, and her
eighteen-year-old daughter completed the group. The girls
each had a boy-friend; their necking and petting was done
fairly openly in the parlor. A good-looking young man who
worked at the service station where I bought my gas indicated
that he would like to be my "steady." I mentioned that I was
loyal to an absent boy friend, a foolish reason according to
him, but one that did not hurt his pride. Any kind of friendship
with a white man in Indianola would have been fatal to my
working among Negroes. He would have wanted to accompany
me at night when I went across the tracks. Actually, I could not
have been close friends with any white person in Indianola,
male or female, and been accepted by the Negroes, for they
would then have wondered if I might not be in agreement with,
or influenced by, the whites. No white person was really accepted by these Negroes, because none gave them respect. But
I could be friendly with all the whites and the Negroes knew
I was studying them. The white people did not know it specifically, but they were pleased that I was interested in them
and in their opinions.

I mingled with the whites casually and easily. I went to a
white church some Sunday evenings and was invited to an

afternoon meeting of a missionary society, whose members collected clothes to be sent to the "heathen" Chinese. When called upon, I managed to say something about the importance of their work and restrained the impulse to talk about the needs of people much closer to home. Mr. Smith asked me to talk to the white teachers in the county at their monthly meeting. To them I spoke of education problems; he had told me about some of the specific ones they faced. The Rotary Club invited me to talk at its regular luncheon meeting on any subject I liked. I chose a few aspects of the late Stone Age culture of Lesu. I was something of a novelty to the whites—a Ph.D., an anthropologist, and a friend of the Percy family.

During the first month, two white women invited me to their homes for lunch. One asked me if I (a Yankee) thought they (the Southerners) were "as bad as they were painted." I replied that I wasn't interested in whether people were good or bad, but in trying to understand them. She was relieved. Since this was my real attitude, it got across to her and to others, usually, without much specific verbalization. Buying a tooth brush in a drug store was a sociable incident and provided data. The clerk held forth on his opinions about "niggers"; I listened attentively and he did not seem to notice or to mind that I said nothing. People having their Cokes invited me to join them, which I did. Mid-morning and mid-afternoon many people went to their favorite drug store for a sociable Coke. Even buying stamps at the post office, where I had a box, was not impersonal. The postmistress chatted about the local news and commented that I received many letters from France.

By the end of this first month, all the whites knew who I was and more or less accepted me. But I walked warily among them. I knew that sooner or later white people would know that I was addressing Negroes by their proper titles of Mr., Mrs., or Miss, since I would do it even if whites were present. For Negroes, this would be a crucial test and for the whites, a serious infringement of a basic taboo. They called all Negroes, regardless of education, age, or social status by their first names, or "auntie" and "uncle." State education officials sometimes called a Negro school principal "professor"; an M.D. would be called "doctor"; neither of these conferred social status. Mrs. Wilson was called "Annie" by whites with half her education or half her age, and who knew her only casually. I decided that I would tell Mr. Smith about my breaking the taboo on social titles for Negroes in advance of his finding out about it indirectly, which was sure to happen. During my youth and while still at home, I had always thought that if my parents or anyone else in authority were bound to learn that I was following a disapproved form of behavior, it was better and easier psychologically for them to learn about it directly from me than to hear of it surreptitiously from others.

Operating on the same principle, I dropped in to see Mr. Smith, thinking I would casually mention my according social titles to Negroes. In his office I lost my nerve and left without telling him. A few days later I went on the same mission; again my courage failed. I had the feeling that my telling him would end our friendly relationship and leave me without any institutional foothold in the community. Although the relationship with his office was, to some degree, intangible, yet it was important and I did not want to lose it. Besides, I had come to like and respect him. He was one of the few whites who did not boast about an aristocratic background and who admitted frankly that his ancestors came from the hills—small farmers, who had never owned a slave—and that he was the first person in his family who had finished high school. Such honesty about this kind of family background was unique in white Indianola.

After my second failure, I felt shame. I asked myself, "Are you a mouse, or a woman?" The next day, strongly determined to go through with the "confession," I returned to the office. Mr. Smith was in a good humor and immediately began telling a long, funny story. I hardly heard what he was saying, but laughed at appropriate intervals as I waited for him to finish. As soon as he stopped talking, and before he could begin another story, I said, "I have something to tell you," and proceeded immediately to tell him that I was calling Negroes "Mr.," "Mrs.," or "Miss." His face, which had been smiling, froze. He stood up, as if for emphasis, and said in tones of a Moses laying down the Ten Commandments, "You can't do that." I replied that I had to do it—that the Negroes were not my servants, and that I was accustomed to addressing people whom I did not know well by their proper titles. He again said sternly, "You can not do it; something terrible will happen." I asked what would happen. He could not give me a definite answer, but conveyed the idea of a catastrophe, the collapse of society, of danger to me, to him, and to everyone. While he was talking I thought of Lesu, and that a Melanesian would probably have had a similar reaction if I had asked him what would happen if he did not make a feast to honor his dead maternal uncle. The taboo on titles for Negroes was apparently as basic to the functioning of society in Mississippi as were the *Malanggan* rites in Lesu. But I persisted, and said that I had to go my own stubborn way, even though something terrible would happen.

By this time, I actually thought a calamity might occur. I then made it clear to Mr. Smith that if and when this happened, I would shout from the roof-tops that he had done his best to dissuade me, and that he was in no way responsible for my behavior. I even thought of, and mentioned the possibility of, taking an advertisement to this effect in the local paper in case the assumed disaster occurred. After all, Mr. Smith was an elected official—elected by the votes of white people only; he had given me informal sponsorship, and I was seen not infrequently in his office.

So the situation was left. Mr. Smith looked forbidding as I left his office and returned to the boarding house for the noonday dinner. What would happen, I wondered? Would Mr. Smith withdraw his support? Could I continue to live peaceably in Indianola and do my research without it?

My fear, as well as Mr. Smith's, showed clearly that I was breaking a basic taboo. As my study progressed, I learned that the white man's consistent withholding of respect from Negroes was the foundation of relations between the two races. The symbolism of social titles for Negroes was strong and deep for both groups. For the Negroes, the titles represented their strivings; for the whites, the titles symbolized their fears.

I had read books and papers on the subject of taboos, one of the much-discussed topics in anthropological literature. But for the first time I really knew their strength in a small face-to-face society, and truly comprehended Durkheim's point: breaking a taboo is a crime against the communal solidarity.[1] I had grown up and lived in large cities and was accustomed

---

[1] E. Durkheim, *The Division of Labor*, trans. by George Simpson (Glencoe, Ill.: The Free Press, 1949), p. 68.

to their heterogeneity of people, of opinions, and of forms of behavior, as well as to the relative anonymity for individuals. Lesu and the white section of Indianola were my first experiences in small, homogeneous societies where dissent was practically unknown and anonymity completely absent. I had seen the operation of taboos in Lesu, but I was uninvolved in them. I was not prepared for my fear in Indianola. I, who was not a Mississippian, who was in the state for only a year, who would return to Yale at the end of it, whose life was not bound to the South, had been afraid to tell Mr. Smith that I was breaking the taboo on social titles for Negroes. And I did not think I was a person without courage. The experience added not only to my deeper understanding of taboos, and of the South, but also to my stock of humility.

This tale had an anti-climax. A week or so later I made an excuse to drop in and see Mr. Smith, to find out whether his attitude to me and the study had changed. To my pleased surprise, he invited me to dinner for the first time. The subject of social titles for Negroes was not mentioned again between us. But I assumed that he must have respected my breaking this fundamental taboo. However, I never quite lost my fear that something terrible might happen and I doubt if he did, either.

XVI

INTERVIEWING
THE NEGROES

I was now ready to begin working systematically: interviewing,
participating, and constantly observing both Negroes and
whites. Hardly a day did not combine all three as I drove back
and forth between country and town and between the town's
Negro and white sections. Sunday services in Negro churches
(and, less often, in white ones), interviews and visits with
Negroes in their homes, conversations in my boarding house
and in white homes, a walk down the street, sitting in the
county superintendent's office or any other place I happened
to be, everything I saw and heard was data, with varying degrees of significance. I was thoroughly immersed in the complex pattern of life in Indianola, and always taking mental
notes. However, in writing such a book as this, it is simpler
and perhaps clearer to separate interviewing from participant
observation, and the work with Negroes from that with whites,
although actually they were closely interwoven.

My first interviews were with members of the small upper
and upper-middle class of Negroes in town, because this was
the easiest way to begin. I had already met them and they
were closest to me in background; they were friendly and had
invited me to come and see them. Since I always have a little
stage-fright before the first interviews, I chose the most favorable situation for beginning. Later, I discovered that it was
good technique to have started with the upper class. They
were proud of their success and of their respectability and
eager to offset the common stereotype of the poor, shiftless
Negro with his freer sexual life. By the time I had begun to
interview the lower classes, upper-class people already knew
that my study included all social groups. It was important also

155

to the members of the lower class and to those who did not
follow the canons of respectability that I had been accepted
by the leaders of their community.

Although it was relatively easy to eventually have a sample
representing all classes in interviews, I sensed from the beginning that I would have to work far more with Negro women
than with men. If I interviewed a Negro man, his wife or some
other woman member of his household had to be present. A
Negro man would be in danger if a white person should see
him alone with me. Actually, it was unlikely that any white
person would witness an interview in a Negro home. But the
Negroes were taking no chances. Their careful arrangements
contributed to my understanding the strength of the taboo
between Negro men and white women and to my awareness
of the Negro man's ever-present fear of lynching. This situation circumscribed my activities and limited my data. But the
handicap was not as serious as it might have been elsewhere.

Among these southern rural Negroes, women were far more
dominant than men in family, economic, religious, and social
life. The leader of the community was a woman—Mrs. Wilson.
With the exception of a few upper-class families, a woman was
often the head of a household, which might consist of a grandmother, her daughter, and her grandchildren. The daughter's
temporary mates came and went. Women worked on equal
terms with men as sharecroppers, and enjoyed more job opportunities in town. Many more women than men participated
actively in church life. Underlying the women's dominant position were their actual or potential sex relations with men of
both races; Negro men were restricted to women of their own
group. Aware of the unavoidable limitations imposed by my
sex in getting to know men in this bi-racial situation (much
greater limitations than in Lesu), I did the best I could to learn
something of the male point of view as revealed by the women,
in the men's observable behavior, and through interviews and
conversations with men when a Negro woman was present.

I used no interviewing schedule, but I had well in mind the
problems to be discussed, and the interviews tended to follow
a general pattern. They were always by appointment and usually in the informant's home. The tone was that of a social
visit. After an exchange of polite greetings, my hostess often

made an admiring comment on my dress or suit. I might note a photograph on the mantel over the coal grate fireplace, and the informant would point with pride to the members of the family in it and this often led to talking about them. My questions were open-ended, and directed towards certain areas for both factual information and attitudes. I usually began by eliciting data about the past—the informant's grandparents, parents, and his or her childhood. It was easy to obtain, through direct or indirect questions, basic sociological data such as the composition of the household, the education of the informant and of other members of the family, church membership and activity, work experiences, and other such factual details.

I did not ask questions about attitudes towards white people. These were given spontaneously, as informants talked about working for them and about their other contacts. Nor was it necessary to ask about sex life, the form of mating (licensed marriage, common-law, temporary "friends," prostitution), the legitimacy or illegitimacy of children, and other such normally private details. These women, like most people, thought their personal lives were of interest and were pleased to find a sympathetic listener. Nor were private lives really "private"; they were well known to friends, neighbors, and practically all members of the community. I usually knew something about my informant's status before the interview, and after it I could, if necessary, check some points with discreet questions to a few people whom I knew well and trusted.

An interview lasted at least an hour; many went on for a whole afternoon. Whatever the length, it ended with my having light refreshment, such as a cup of coffee and a hot biscuit, a piece of pie, or cake, and being invited to come again. As time went on and we became better acquainted, the social nature of the interview became more prominent and informants talked with increasing freedom about their personal lives, their feelings, and their attitudes.

During the first couple of weeks I experimented with taking notes during the interview and with not writing, but doing it immediately afterwards, sitting in my car a short distance away. The latter method gave fuller data and more intimate details, even though I ran the risk of forgetting some points. I was aware, of course, that my memory, like all memory, is to some degree selective. But people did not talk so freely if I wrote during the interview. The flow of conversation was not impeded if I occasionally took a small inconspicuous notebook out of my pocketbook and asked for permission to write down an economic fact such as income or amount of money received from making a crop, or the number of acres farmed, explaining quite truthfully that my memory for numbers was weak. I also used the notebook for jotting down a particularly pungent colloquial phrase which I wanted to quote exactly.

The more I left to memory, the better it became. But I did not rely on it for any extended period of time. As soon as the interview was over, I drove a short distance and when out of sight, wrote it up roughly while sitting in the car. I was able then to reproduce the interview with relative completeness. In the beginning some of the data were so vivid and interesting that I thought I could not possibly forget them and, occasionally, I did not stop to write in the car. But when I came to writing in my room that night or several nights later, some of the details were lost. To lose data was my idea of a cardinal sin! So, I was conscientious about the write-up in the car.

Soon I began working on plantations as well as in town, and moving freely between social classes. In the rural area I went first to the school house and saw the principal (always male) whom I had met previously at a meeting of county teachers. Accompanied by his wife, he would drive me around to meet sharecroppers, renters, and an occasional landowner. (Later, I returned to interview them.) The company of the principal's wife was necessary since white people were sure to see us. I left these matters of protocol to Negroes, who knew what could and could not be done far better than I.

Only twice did I have to take the initiative. In one situation, the principal of a rural school, like the other principals, offered to drive me around to meet farm operators in his neighborhood. But unlike the other principals, he did not ask his wife to join us. I noticed the omission, but said nothing, thinking that perhaps his position in the white community was unusually good. We went in his car and I sat on the front seat beside him. As we drove down the main street of the nearby small town to get out into the country, the usual white loafers were sitting in rocking chairs on porches, lolling about on the streets, or standing in the doorways of buildings. I saw them start up from their chairs in amazement or turn to see us better. I did not like the expression on their faces: intense surprise and great hostility. Just before we reached the end of the street, I said quietly to my companion, "I think this is damned foolish." He said nothing for a minute, and then muttered, "Perhaps you're right." He turned around, drove back to the school, got his wife, and shortly the three of us drove down the main street. The white men sat back in their chairs or returned to their own affairs; their faces were expressionless or, at least, indicated no interest in us. I was relieved.

As I later became friends with this principal and his wife, he talked freely and I understood his defiance. A native of Chicago and decidedly better educated than most principals in Sunflower County, he had come south in an idealistic mood to help his people. His large, modern school, one of the best in the county, had been built a couple of years earlier with the help of the Rosenwald Foundation, contributions from the white people, and the volunteer labor of the Negroes. (The Foundation gave relatively small grants which were matched by donations from the community.) The principal had enjoyed creating the school, but now he was disappointed and frustrated. The Negroes had not come up to his high expectations; he had to work more slowly than he liked and the results were not as good as he wanted. He had learned the necessary play-acting with the whites, but he could not accept it with the ironical inward smile or laugh of the southern-born Negro. Instead he was bitter and constantly indignant. He even fantasied shooting white men who humiliated him. Sometimes, he said, he thought it might be better to die killing a white man than just to go on living. But this idea went no further than talk, and that far only occasionally with someone in his family or with me. Driving alone with me down the main street of the white section of town had little to do with me personally, but was an act of bravado to "show" white men who had so often humiliated him. This release of bitterness, however, was obviously too dangerous to go through with completely. I think he was relieved when I suggested turning back. His pride would have made that difficult without my suggestion.

The only other incident of this type was smaller and happened in Indianola. As I came out of the post office one morning, I met one of the upper-class Negro men, who detained me in conversation. It was Saturday and therefore more white men than usual were loafing on the street. They were too interested in this chance meeting, and I did not like the hostile expressions on their faces. I was having dinner the next day with this man and his family, and there was no need for a long conversation on the street in the presence of white loafers. I knew that his motivation was the same as that of the principal—to "show off." But I was concerned for him and as soon as I politely could, I looked at my watch, said I was late for an appointment, and hastened off.

No danger existed for the women in their relations with me. We sat, without fear, before the fire in the small coal grate in the parlor of a comfortable cottage or in the front room of a two-room shanty, or, if the day was warm, on the porch. On a hot summer evening, I sometimes called for a Negro woman and we drove around for a couple of hours to "cool off." Such a drive was one of the best situations for interviewing. Few cars were on the unlighted gravel road; the dark country on each side stretched to unseen horizons. I kept my eyes on the road and said little. Something about the privacy of the car, the darkness of the night, and my passive role almost inevitably produced a flow of conversation from my companion about meaningful experiences of her past and of today. Stories of loving husbands and "mean" ones, of joys and sorrows, unfolded as I drove slowly along the road. After one such drive, I was concerned that my companion might have been upset by the stirring up of painful memories. The next day I dropped by to see how she was. She said she had never felt better, or slept so well as she had on the previous night. It must have been the cool air, she thought. The telling of her troubles had probably served as a catharsis. I assume that other interviews may have had this function.

The small group of Negro landowners liked to tell their success stories—long years of patient hard work, thrift, ability, and initiative. They were not too unlike the stories of white pioneers who had gone west and settled on the land, with one exception: the Negroes had to act "humble." They laughed

cynically, rather than bitterly, as they described their acting
"humble." In none of the interviews was I expected to talk
much. The Negroes whom I saw often and who became my
friends knew something about my family—my parents, sisters,
and brother—and a few details of my life. But all of the Negroes, whether I saw them once or many times, understood
that my function was to learn about their lives.

Most of my time was spent with the sharecroppers, who were
the large majority in the county. In the sharecropping arrange-
ment the family was the economic unit (even children counting
for half a hand) and was supplied by the plantation owner
with a cabin, seeds, implements, animals, land, and an advance
in credit or cash for living expenses. In return the sharecropping family gave the landlord half the cotton they raised; the
other half belonged to them. Almost always the landlord sold
it for them. At the end of the "season," in December, a settlement was made.

The system had a certain function after the Civil War when
the white planters had land but no capital, and the Negroes
had neither land nor money. It might even have had certain
advantages for the Negroes at the time of my study, if it had
operated in a social milieu in which the Negroes had legal
rights. But whether the sharecropper received an honest settlement depended completely on the character of the individual
landlord. Only an exceptional planter gave his tenant a sales
receipt for the cotton sold, an itemized list of supplies purchased at the plantation store or note of the exact amount of
cash advanced, and the difference between the two. Most
planters merely told their tenants that they came out even, or
that a small amount was due them, or that they were in debt.
At the time of my study, the federal government was making
payments for "plowing under," but the tenants received no
part of this money even though they collaborated in planting
a smaller crop and therefore had less cotton in their share.

As I sat in the cabins, many of them not much different from
the cabins of slavery times, and listened to the discouraging
experiences of tenants, I realized that I had never heard of any
economic system functioning in such a completely unstructured manner. If no statement was presented by the owner or
manager, a tenant could not ask for one. No social force, such

as the law or public opinion, existed to back up his demand. Physical force was out of the question since it would probably lead to a tenant's being shot. Even if the request for a statement was made politely by a sharecropper, it could lead to trouble: being "cussed out," getting no settlement, being told he was in debt, or even having his house looted (of bits of old furniture, a painted vase on the mantel, or a picture of his father and mother) and his chickens and corn stolen. The tenant's only recourse (if he was not in debt to the planter) was to move to another plantation, hoping it would be better. Two years on one plantation was considered a good average.

The data from Negro sharecroppers and other farm operators were confirmed through interviews with white planters and other whites. No white person claimed that the majority of planters gave honest settlements. The highest estimate from whites, as well as from Negroes, was that not more than 25 or 30 per cent of sharecroppers received an honest settlement. The whites took for granted the personal and irresponsible character of the economic system. I wondered what would happen if the wages of factory workers in the North (or South) had to depend only on the honesty of their employers, and surmised that the results would be no better.

Some Negro sharecroppers quit farming in discouragement and moved to town. The men tried to get jobs as truck drivers, yard-boys, delivery-boys, or helpers in gasoline stations, or jobs in public work. More jobs were open to women, as cooks, laundresses, nursemaids, and general house servants. In the country, or in town on a small patch of land behind the house, the Negroes raised their "greens" and often kept chickens and a hog. Some who had quit sharecropping became day workers during the few months of the picking season.

In spite of all the discouragements, many of these people had the peasant's feeling of closeness to the soil. I asked a woman who had returned from a visit to her son in Chicago whether she would like to live there. She replied that although she had enjoyed the visit, she wanted to live where she could "put a stick in the ground." A school teacher remarked wistfully that she wished she had time to pick cotton. The fine texture of the Delta cotton and its size were often spoken of in loving tones. Casual small talk had the same earthy quality

as that of peasants everywhere: the muddy road and its hard-
ships for a woman with holes in her shoes when she walked
to church; a leaking roof and having to move the bed during
the night to avoid the rain; a man getting up early to plow
two furrows before breakfast. The spontaneous conversations
were, as always, revealing of the tone of life.

The joys and sorrows of private life were not too different
from those of many other people, except for the ever-present
overt or latent conflict between the races. In the beginning of
an interview I had with a middle-class woman, she asked me
if many marriages occurred between whites and Negroes up
North. My negative answer disappointed her. She said she
supposed that it was only the "worst element" of white men
who would do it, for, she continued, "who would want to marry
a Negro? Not that there aren't some colored folk as good as
whites!" Then out came her story. She had had a relationship
with a white man for twenty years. Regularly twice a week
her lover had come to see her. She was faithful to him, never
looking at another man. She always hoped that he would take
her North and marry her. Then one night, he told her he was
through with this kind of life and was marrying a white woman.
The hurt of being discarded by a lover was compounded by
the blow to her self-esteem as a Negro. This matter of self-
respect was becoming increasingly important with the women,
and some told me that they would not sleep with a man who
did not greet them if they met on the street the next day. This
situation is not unknown in unconventional sex relations among
whites, but for the Negroes it was tied in with their race.

For the Negro men whose women took white lovers, the
situation was painful. One woman told me that when her husband found out about her white lover, "he didn't say a word, he
just cried." She told him she had something to show for the
affair and brought out her bank book, but her husband said
nothing. Later she discovered him with a girl-friend. The wife
was furious; the husband said he only did it because he was
drunk. She forgave him but he drank more and more heavily
and began beating her. After a particularly severe beating, he
left home and never returned.

As I listened to tale after tale, it became clear that the potential or actual relations between Negro women and white

men were a constant threat to the self-esteem of Negro men. I wondered if some of the intra-Negro violence—beatings of women, fighting and shooting between men—might be one way of meeting the threat. But I had no way of checking this hypothesis.

The talk of informants about their intra-Negro mating was revealing about class status as well as sex life. Quite early in the study, I was intrigued by the high degree of class consciousness among the Negroes. Mr. Percy did not outdo them in this characteristic. But what were the symbols of class in a group with a low standard of living and whose traditions went back to slavery? The conventional class symbols of western society were not adequate guides to the Negro social system in Mississippi. Nor would it have been feasible to ask direct questions on this subject except of the upper class, and I could not be content with knowing only their point of view. Much of my knowledge and understanding of the class system came through the conversational type of interview with Negroes of all classes and through my participation in, and observation of, Negro social life.

The kind of sex life and form of marriage or mating were important status symbols. Women boasted if they had a marriage license and proudly showed it to me. Others, who had accepted their common-law marriage or their casual mating with "friends," talked in tones of respect about women with a marriage license. During one interview a middle-class widow proudly showed me her marriage license. Over the date were pasted five small red valentine hearts. Her marriage had been common-law for eight years, before she managed to get her husband to wed her with a license. The ceremony was secret to make people think it had been this way from the beginning. But I knew (and I think she did, too) that the years of common-law marriage were known to all her neighbors, and she talked frankly about it to me. Yet the valentine hearts, concealing the date on the marriage certificate, were a poignant expression of her longing for respectability and status.

I never asked about color preferences, i.e. whether my informants preferred dark, medium-brown, or rather light skins in picking mates. But the preference for light skins—at least by the women—came spontaneously when they described husbands or lovers, or mentioned the complexions of their different children. Looking at photographs, always lighter than the subjects, confirmed this point.

The relative advantages of love and money in mating—not a problem unique to Mississippi Negroes—was mentioned by women when they were talking about men with whom they had lived. Like many women, the Negroes would have liked money and love, but they were realistic about the infrequent achievement of this ideal. I particularly enjoyed one woman's distinction between having a man for love and for money. She told me that to hold the latter, she put a small bottle of voodoo in bed, but relied only on her personal charms to keep the man she loved.

It was rather refreshing to me, as well as good data, to listen to women talking freely and without hypocrisy about their unconventional relations. Even prostitutes talked freely. A particularly good interview was with one of the most notorious. The day was warm and we spent the afternoon, each in a rocking chair, on the porch of her home. She was friendly and at ease as she talked about her life, in which there had been no even relatively long-time mating. Four of her six children (each by a different man) were alive. Two daughters were with her and attending school. She talked of her ambitions for them, stumbling over the word "stenographer," her goal for the oldest. A younger daughter wanted to be a trained nurse. Although expressing no dissatisfaction with her own life, this woman wanted her daughters to live differently.

Among the Negroes in Mississippi, as among all Americans, education was a means of upward social mobility, sometimes the only one. Parents talked freely of ambitions for their children with little prompting from me. It was not unusual for an illiterate woman to stop bending over a wash tub in the yard when I came to see her, and then, when we were sitting in the front room of her shanty, talk about her son, or grandson, whose picture in a college cap and gown was on the mantel. She was proud that her earning from doing laundry for the "white folks" was helping him go to college. She envisaged an upper-class life for her son, without problems. I could not tell her that his problems would only be different from hers, and I speculated on the refinement of problems as one index of progress. From all my interviews and observation, it was obvious that education was an even more significant criterion for class in Negro society than in our society as a whole.

Money was also important as a status symbol, but not by itself. From listening to conversations I knew that a local bootlegger, with more money than most members of the upper class, did not belong to it. His common-law marriage, his way of earning money, and his lack of education prevented that.

It would have been redundant to have asked questions about how the Negroes felt on the denial of social titles. Almost everyone mentioned the constant irritation and anger from this insult. One woman told me that she had christened her baby, "Missjulia," thus insuring a title.

It was not easy to find out how children first became aware of relations between the races, a problem in which I was interested. I did no work with children, partly for lack of time and partly for lack of training. For collecting this kind of data, I thought a psychologist was needed. Yet since the problem was important, I tried to find out something about it. I asked mothers about the type of questions children asked, their approximate age at the time, and the answers given. I learned that many children asked the question of "why": Why don't colored and white children play together? Why is his mother called "Sarah" by a white person and "Mrs." by Negroes? The usual response to the "why" was: "I don't know, that's just the way it is," followed by admonitions about how to behave when with whites and warnings if the advice should not be followed.

I could get little by questioning adults about their early experiences with white people. One woman in answer to a question said, "No'm, I never had any special dealings with white folks when I was young." Later, when she was expressing complete hopelessness about the biracial situation, she spoke in vivid detail of how at the age of ten, she had seen her father shot down by the white overseer of the plantation. The overseer had told her father to work in another part of the field, and he had answered, "No, it is too wet over there."

The longer I was in the field, the more I noted consistent differences between age groups in attitudes towards white people. Negroes sixty years and over (born before the Civil War, during it, or immediately afterwards) tended to accept the alleged superiority of white people. But even among them, I found no one who represented the stereotyped "contented darky." A woman in her seventies believed the whites were superior and talked with affection of her dead white "missus" and of the latter's son, whom she had taken care of as a baby, but she also recalled her youth with bitterness. She remembered her father's being sold away, and that she was not able to go to her mother's funeral because she had to stay at home and work.

The middle-aged did not believe in white superiority, but pretended to this belief when they were with white people. "Acting humble," they called it. I saw the acting and heard the ironical laugh when they talked about it later. Illiterate, little-educated, and well-educated Negroes shared this attitude. It cut across all class divisions. Servants, schoolteachers, sharecroppers, landowners, the few professional people, all said over and over again, "I want to be treated like a human being." They acknowledged no innate inferiority between themselves and other human beings, regardless of how they acted before white people.

Younger Negroes in their teens and twenties also did not believe the whites were superior but they refused to act as if they did. Their "solution" was to avoid contact with whites and to make it as slight as possible when unavoidable. Many parents feared trouble for their daughters and sons and were relieved if they went north. The most resentful young people were often, but not always, among the better educated. However, the strongest correlation was with age. Out of my data came the concept that age groups are an excellent way of studying social change. It had not occurred to me before going to Mississippi.

Unfortunately, however, my data on young people were very limited. I did not interview adolescents, or study them except through what their mothers told me and through observation if they happened to be at home when I visited. But they rarely were, except at a Sunday dinner, and then I was a guest of their parents and young people did not talk much. I do not think it possible to interview adolescents in any society in their parents' presence. Even if they were interviewed separately, I would be skeptical of the results if the field worker had also interviewed parents or was considered their friend. I was aware of this gap in my study while in Mississippi, but I did not know how to remedy the situation.

Some years later I served as a consultant to Charles S. Johnson on his study of Negro children and youth in the deep South.[1] Returning to Mississippi, but to another county, for a summer, I interviewed only adolescent Negro girls. (A male Negro sociologist was interviewing adolescent boys in the same families.) Schools were closed during the summer vacation, and I managed to have one opened in the vicinity of my interviewing. I always called for the young girl, together we drove to the empty schoolhouse, and I drove her home after the interview. My relations with parents were restricted to polite greetings. The young man worked similarly.

In my Sunflower County study I had to accept the gaps in my knowledge of men, children, and adolescents. Actually, even if I could have sampled all groups, there would not have been time to do it in one year. I was aware, too, that I did not have a true random sample of adults, either women or men. It is difficult to have such a sample in any situation where interviews are set up by appointment. But since practically all Negroes I met were pleased to be interviewed, the selection was relatively unbiased. However, the usual unavoidable personal bias occurred in the making of friends, whom I saw more often than acquaintances.

Interviews with two Negroes, each important sociologically, were failures. One was a midwife, president of the Negro midwives association, to which position she had been appointed by a white nurse in the public health department. The nurse lived in my boarding house and had suggested that I come with her to a meeting of the midwives. Against my better judgment I went. The nurse addressed the meeting and then left. I stayed on. The president conducted the meeting like a sergeant giving orders to privates. She yelled commands, ordering people to stand up and sit down. After the meeting, she was all subservience to me. Having been introduced by her boss, she obviously could not feel free, and I knew it was hopeless to

---

[1] Charles S. Johnson, *Growing-up in the Black Belt* (Washington, D.C.: American Council on Education, 1941).

interview or try to get to know her. What she was really like,
I never found out. I knew, however, from some of the midwives whom I later met, that they did not like her.

The other failure was a man of whose reputation I had
heard from Negroes. He boasted that he "wasn't raising his
daughters for any niggers." They would be prostitutes for
white men. He was also known as a tattle-tale, carrying tales
from across the tracks to white people. I went to see him, but
could get nowhere; I did not return. He talked to me only in
the formal clichés which he assumed white people wanted to
hear. I have always felt badly about this failure and wondered
whether it could have been successful, if I had been more
skilled.

Aside from these two, each interview yielded some data and
understanding. At the end of each month, I checked on the
class distribution of interviews and informants. If one class was
over- or under-weight, I tried the next month to correct the
balance. During the year I interviewed 97 Negroes, with a total
of 450 interviews. All classes were represented in approximate
proportion to their numbers. However, the upper class was a
bit more heavily weighted in the sample—but their significance was far greater than their numbers. Class, as it emerged
from the data, appeared more significant than I had assumed.

Patterns emerged from the interviews. Some, such as attitudes towards the denial of social titles, were universal. I
coded and counted only those patterns whose proportionate
significance was not obvious. It did not occur to me to present
data from interviews in quantified form. Perhaps I would today—in an appendix.[2] I am amused by the pretentiously
elaborate quantifications used sometimes for twenty or twenty-
five cases.

I typed and filed notes as I had in Lesu, making two copies
of each interview (and of all other data). One copy was filed
under the name of informant and the other broken into sociological categories such as economics, religion, family, and so

---

[2] In Lesu, my data came from the entire but small village of 232 people,
and I saw, and would still see, no need to quantify it, with the exception
of the vital statistics gained from genealogies and published separately.
However, in my study of a mining community of 30,000 Africans in
Northern Rhodesia, the matter of an adequate sample was important and
I quantified that part of the data which lent itself to this method.

forth. Reading over each section, I was able to note the gaps. I resented having to give so much time to typing. Obviously, I could not trust my material to any white secretary in town. No Negro secretary was in the community and even if there had been, it would probably have been equally unwise for a Negro to have seen all the data while I was collecting it. Doing my own typing had an advantage in that I sometimes saw relationships and got ideas and hypotheses as I typed. Occasionally, I stayed home for a day and did nothing but type. Much of it I did at night, when I would rather have been participating in Negro social life.

XVII

PARTICIPATION
IN NEGRO LIFE

Participation in Negro life added another dimension to the study and had many functions. While interviews enabled me to see patterns in experiences and attitudes, and variations according to class and age, direct observation of people in action enabled me to study the actual functioning of the social structure. This is the heart of the participation-observation method.[1]

Participation had the further advantage of enabling me to see the Negroes enjoy themselves, at Sunday services, at the many weekday church socials and entertainments, at club meetings, at picnics, or at social activity at home. An understanding of the pleasures and recreations in Negro life was as important as knowing about the inequities of the economic system and other Negro problems, and could be gained only through participation. Without this participation, interviewing would probably have been less successful. Finally, I enjoyed the participation. I am the kind of person who likes to participate.

I knew of the importance of the church from my reading before coming south. But an understanding of the broad and deep ramifications of this key institution in both secular and religious life came primarily through continuous participation over an extended period of time. In this Mississippi community the church was the one institution completely controlled by Negroes. (Economic life was regulated by whites and family

---

[1] Cf. W. F. Whyte, *Street Corner Society* (2nd ed.; Chicago: University of Chicago Press, 1953), p. 285 and Bronislaw Malinowski, *Argonauts of the Western Pacific* (New York: E. P. Dutton & Co., Paperback edition, 1961), pp. 1–25.

life was directly affected by sex relations between white men and Negro women.) Almost all Negroes, regardless of class or age, belonged to a church and attended services. Among the exceptions were the prostitutes, for whom the weekend was their busiest time. But they often came to the church entertainments on weekday evenings, and several told me they expected to be church members when they were old.

Methodists, Baptists, and Methodist-Episcopalians were in the majority and drew their membership from all classes. Little feeling of denominational difference existed between them and members of one church attended the services of the other, when their own church was not meeting. Churches had their pastoral Sundays, the first and third, or the second and fourth of each month. The members of these churches, however, looked down on other sects, such as "The Christians" and The Church of God in Christ, known popularly as the Holy Rollers, regarding their noise and "dancing" as "heathenish." On the other hand, the congregations of these two churches, mostly illiterate and among the poorest people, considered themselves more religious than the others. But in all churches, services were highly emotional and beliefs fundamentalist. I went to a Negro church in town or country almost every Sunday. After several months, my presence was taken for granted (an ideal situation for a field worker), and I was no longer called on for "the few words." It was primarily through my regular attendance at church services that most Negroes in the county knew me, or about me—another function of participation.

It is well known that although the Negroes learned Christianity from the whites, they have transformed it and made their church peculiarly their own. Spirituals may have originated in the white man's hymns, but they express with poetry and deep feeling the Negro's anguish and his hope. The Judaic-Christian God has become their personal God; over and over again in sermons and in personal conversations I heard that the Negroes were His chosen people. The drama of the Sunday services, their spontaneity, their strong emotional tone, the beautiful and fervent singing of hymns and spirituals (usually without an organ accompaniment) had me spellbound, but this did not interfere with my taking mental notes. I continued going to church long after the diminishing returns of new data set in.

It was one way of having an important part of Negro life seep into "my bones," similar to my constant attendance at *Malanggan* rites and other feasts in Lesu; also, in Mississippi my presence was expected in church, as it had been at the rites in Lesu.

It is difficult to describe adequately the drama of the Sunday services, and I have never seen a play which did justice to them. The minister usually began his sermon in a low monotonous voice, which gradually became louder as it developed into a chant. He pulled out certain words for emphasis. One Baptist minister chanted the word, "Ev-er-y-bod-y," making the most of each syllable and vowel as his voice rose in pitch. His voice boomed and sometimes broke as he chanted of earthly sins and the glories of heaven and of being saved through repentance and God's mercy. It mattered not that the words became less and less distinguishable. The "A-mens" and shouts of "Sure enough!" and "You're right!" from the audience continued. Some women shouted, waved their arms, and threw themselves about; often one of them had to be carried by several men out of the church. The sermon had then reached its desired climax.

An elder at the Baptist service took the collection of pennies and nickels jocularly. He announced a total of $2.84 and pleaded for just sixteen cents to make it even. Several people walked up the aisle and dropped coins in the plate. The elder announced the sum of $3.07. "Who will make it $3.25?" he asked, and added that he would sing them a song. His body swayed and he tapped his foot as he sang. The total became $3.43. "Who will make it even?" he chanted. At last, when the sum of $3.60 had been raised, he stopped. He and everyone else had thoroughly enjoyed the slow taking of the collection.

I was fascinated by the women who "shouted," particularly because they regained consciousness so quickly after losing it. Men rarely "shouted" in church. I went home with one of the "shouters" after the service, hoping to learn more about her emotional experience. But she told me only what I had already learned from others, that the Lord was in her and speaking through her. She, like many other middle-aged women, had had a "getting religion" experience in her adolescence. The common pattern, as they told me of these experiences, was feeling "heavy with sin," of fasting and praying to God for forgiveness, of the sins falling away, hearing God say they were free, and then feeling "light as a feather."

Although the minister, deacons, elders, and superintendents of Sunday schools were male, women far outnumbered the men at Sunday services and were much more emotional in church. Likewise, many more women than men seemed to have "got religion" in their youth. I kept wondering about the women's greater and more intense participation in the church. In most modern communities women outnumber men at the church services and a familiar psychological explanation is that religion is a means of sexual sublimation for them. The Negro woman's shouts of Jesus being inside her, of her happiness, of losing consciousness, seemed to be symbols of erotic satisfaction. But why would Negro women, able to have both Negro and white lovers, have more need for sexual sublimation than Negro men? Could it be that this very lack of inhibition predisposed them to religious exhibitionism? I wondered. Hard as I tried, I could get no further data on the phenomenon of shouting. Perhaps, detailed case histories of shouters and non-shouters would have given more clues or answers. At any rate, the cultural study with the methods of participation-observation and interviewing was not adequate on this problem, even more so because my data on men's emotional life was unavoidably limited.

But the participant observation method provided good data on differences in age and education groups (as well as in sex) in religious behavior. Young women in their teens or twenties, particularly those with any education, were not among the "shouters." As far as I could ascertain, young girls at school were not "getting religion," as had their uneducated mothers and grandmothers. The school boys and girls were going to church for its social function and to please their parents more than out of conviction. When I was having Sunday dinner with a Negro family, after the services, I sometimes heard the young people make fun of the minister's grammatical mistakes. The ministers in rural Mississippi at this time had little, if any, education or training. While ploughing, a man might have a vision of God telling him to go and preach to his people. These ministers were paid no salaries, but depended on the collection at the services; usually they farmed or did other manual work.

As my presence in the churches became more and more taken for granted, I would sometimes surreptitiously take a few notes on the sermons, noting colloquial expressions. My pocketbook was large and the notebook in it was small. Many of the sermons I heard were similar in some respects to those preached to Negro slaves by white ministers before the Civil War, which I had read. The formal dogma was unchanged and the Bible was accepted literally. The ministers of both periods stressed the sins of their congregation. But now the joys of heaven and God's merciful love were stressed more than the torments of the damned, a major theme of the early missionizing period. The accent had changed from fear to hope, but the emphasis was still largely on the rewards in future life rather than today. A couple of the ministers mentioned worldly affairs, such as President Roosevelt's inauguration in Washington. Only one occasionally made an indirect attack on whites. In one sermon, he mentioned a scene in heaven, in which a white woman lived in a shanty similar to that occupied by her cook in life, while the latter was living in a big house, much like that occupied by her former mistress. This sermon might have been an indirect attack on the *status quo*, at the same time supporting it by limiting social change to heaven. I did not think to check with the minister whether this double meaning was purposeful, or if he was even aware of it; it is decidedly uncertain that he would have been articulate on this problem if I had asked him about it.

All ministers constantly emphasized the need to love—to love one's neighbors, one's friends, and even one's enemies. The same theme was stressed in Sunday schools, which I also attended. In them, informal discussion replaced the minister's monologue. I listened to a poignant discussion in a class for adults, in which the teacher telling the tale of a sharecropper who was cheated out of half his earnings by a white planter, asked the class, "Is it possible for us not to hate him?" One man answered, "Yes, it is possible, but it is hard." This opinion was shared by others in the class, who talked about their fear as well as hate. The discussion ended with an admonition by the teacher to feel sorry for the whites, and to drive out hatred with love.

I cannot think of any method, other than that of participant observation, which could have given an understanding of how the church functioned. By going to church Sunday after Sunday I learned which themes were emphasized and which excluded in the sermons. I saw and felt the fervor and emotional participation of the congregation. I was constantly aware of the paradox within the functioning of the church. On the one hand, it served as a palliative and escape. On the other, it helped the Negro maintain his self-respect in a situation geared to destroy it. The equality of all people before God and their importance to Him was the theme of sermons and Sunday school lessons. Negroes could even regard themselves as superior because they thought they were following Christ's precepts far better than were the white people, whose behavior was called "unchristian."

It was not until a number of years after my Mississippi study that I saw a connection between the Negroes' Christianity and their highly successful role-playing before the whites. When I was in the field, the Negro's skill in "acting humble," when he felt the opposite, fascinated me, and I never quite understood how he was able to do it so well. I generally assumed that satisfaction must underlie playing any role exceptionally well over a long period of time. A more specific clue was given me when I happened to read Reik's book on masochism,[2] which went beyond the usual concept of the masochistic enjoyment of suffering. Reik indicated that the masochist felt assured of his eventual victory over his enemy. The Negro was not a masochist; his sufferings were not neurotically self-induced but were caused by the social milieu, which also provided a "solution": the promise of eventual triumph over the whites, even if in another world, which Christianity gave him. The Negro did not enjoy his suffering but he did enjoy fooling the whites. This enjoyment and the promise of a final victory apparently underlay the sustained and successful play-acting before whites.[3]

---

[2] Theodor Reik, *Masochism in Modern Man* (New York: Farrar & Rinehart, 1941).
[3] Hortense Powdermaker, "Channeling of Negro Aggression through the Cultural Process," *American Journal of Sociology*, XLVIII, No. 6, (1943).

Church activities were by no means confined to Sunday services and Sunday schools. The major social diversions were the occasional church conventions, revival meetings in the summer, weekly entertainments and "socials" in church basements—a nickel admission—to raise money for the church, and meetings of women's clubs whose members arranged the entertainments and socials. These included "candy-pulls," chicken hunts (the head of the chicken was hidden and the finder won the whole chicken), chitterling suppers, popularity contests with the crowning of a "Queen," and many others. I was invited to all of them and went to as many as I could.

As I watched a deacon (a "yard boy" in daily life) play politics at a church convention, a laundress preside as president of the "Willing Workers Club," men and women from all classes put on shows and skits in the church basement, it became apparent to me that one function of the churches' secular activities was the same as their religious role: helping the Negro to maintain his self-respect. In all the church activities, whether secular or religious, he functioned as a whole human being, without the presence of whites to make him feel less than human.

The churches also provided major leisure-time activities, means of enjoyment, and release from the biracial tensions which clouded so much of Negro life. Here, too, the stress on class (in part, a response to the white man's stereotype of lower-class for all Negroes) was forgotten. Everyone came to these social affairs and enjoyed themselves. I did, too. I assume that if I had been totally unable to enter into the fun, my knowledge of the "feel" of Negro life would have been reduced; and I cannot think of anything more boring than watching people having a good time without getting some pleasure, too.[4]

The social affairs in the basements of the churches were hilarious. The games were the simple well-known ones such as "Simon Says" and "Thumbs Up," which centered about the payment of a forfeit by the one who made a mistake. The forfeit usually took the form of burlesque love-making. Many of

---

[4] Occasionally, I wonder what would happen to the dour and grim picture of society conveyed by some social scientists, if they would really enjoy themselves, just once, at some lowbrow and perhaps bawdy party given by the economically depressed people they study.

the games were the same ones I had played at parties with
the factory girls during my organizing days. In the beginning
I was self-conscious at these church socials, but I was soon at
ease and enjoying them. The Negroes took my presence at the
parties for granted, and, as far as I know, it had relatively little
effect on what went on. Participation did not prevent me from
making mental notes, and occasionally a written one in the
ever-present notebook concealed in my pocket.

Short parodies and skits were the usual forms of entertainment in the church basements. In one, "The Brideless Wedding," all the parts were taken by men. The "groom" was the
smallest boy and the "bride" was the tallest one. The hit was
the "matron of honor," a large stout man and a leading member
of the upper class. Costumed in a coverall apron, kimono, and
broad-brimmed hat, he walked down the aisle in his usual
masculine fashion with hands clasped behind his back and
was greeted with shouts of laughter.

Shortly after a national election, a skit was put on in which
Mrs. Roosevelt gave a tea party. After the tea was served,
"Mrs. Roosevelt" said to her guests, "I have invited some of
my Negro friends who will render a few of their songs." At the
words "Negro friends," the audience burst into prolonged
laughter, which stopped the show for at least five minutes. The
spontaneous laughter was more indicative of certain attitudes
towards whites (even a benevolent one like the late Mrs. Franklin Roosevelt) than data from fifty interviews. Among the entertainments also were style shows, in which women wearing
dresses they had made competed for a prize, and Biblical
plays. In one of the latter, a young man portraying Judas,
dressed in a pink kimono, strode across the stage and stam-
mered, "I didn't want to do no harm; I just wanted the money."

The symbolism underlying many of the entertainments,
shows, skits, and "forfeits" was fairly obvious to me while in
the field. But somehow, it did not occur to me then or when
I was writing up my material to make serious use of it—a
paper, or an additional chapter in the book which evolved from
the field work.[5] Although interested in recreational activities,

---

[5] *After Freedom, A Cultural Study in the Deep South* (New York: The
Viking Press, 1939).

I rather belatedly realized their full sociological significance.

The meetings of women's clubs in the homes of members were quite formal, and helped me to understand still another side of Negro life. The members of these clubs were house servants, laundresses, and an occasional housewife who did not have to work out; meetings were always on Thursday afternoon, the time off for house servants. These were the women who ran the entertainments and socials to pay off church debts, to help needy members, and to "beautify" the church.

I remember particularly well one club meeting. It was in a humble home. The bed had been removed for the occasion from the front room, which shone with cleanliness from its recent scrubbing. Chairs were carried in from other rooms and other houses. When the members had crowded into the small room, the president opened the meeting by reading a chapter from the Bible; this was followed by everyone singing a hymn. The hostess then prayed. She began each sentence with "O Holy Father" and asked Him to bless the individual members, the club activities, and the church. During the prayer, I closed my eyes as did the club members. The prayer was so fervent and so personal that I almost expected to see the Lord standing in the doorway when I opened my eyes.

I was struck by the punctiliousness with which the business of the meeting was conducted. The chairman and the members knew their parliamentary rules, and a copy of them was on the table. Minutes of the previous meeting were read and approved. Reports from the finance committee, the sick committee, and the treasurer were formally given; motions were made and passed that these be accepted. As the treasurer called the roll, each member arose and paid her dues of ten cents.

After the business was concluded came the "program." At one meeting, it was a short paper on the subject of "love" written and read by a member, a hymn sung as a solo by another member, and a Bible selection read by a third. The author of the paper was glad to give it to me when the meeting was over. The theme was to love all people, "because they are made in the image of God, because they are interesting, and because they need loving." The climax was, "For the short, the fat, the lean, the tall, I don't give a rap. I love them all."

As a guest, I was called on for "a few words," when the program was over: I praised the club members on their work and wished them well. Then came the refreshments—spaghetti, coffee, and lemon pie, and the hostess was complimented on her pie. The mood of the meeting became informal, with good-humored joking and gaiety.

Now and then my participant observation was accidental. I happened to be sitting in Mr. Smith's office one afternoon shortly before Christmas. A number of people were there, including teachers waiting for their pay checks. Actually, these were not checks, but "certificates," cashable in a bank, at a loss of 8 or 10 per cent. I never understood the fiscal policies of Mississippi's educational system; teachers—white and Negro —often had to wait for their pay. On this afternoon, Mr. Jones, a Negro principal, was among those waiting in the office. I knew him fairly well from my work in the area of his rural school. We exchanged, of course, only a formal greeting in this situation. I watched him, affable and smiling, telling the kind of jokes enjoyed by the white people, who were also waiting. I saw white people who had come in after Mr. Jones receive their "certificates" or transact other business. When Mr. Jones finally received his "certificate," it was long after three o'clock and banks were closed. But his affability was undiminished as he said, "Thank you, sir."

Having lingered a couple of hours to see the end of this incident, I was now late for an appointment with Mrs. Wilson. So I drove quickly to her home. She was waiting for me and with her were three teachers from Mr. Jones' school, to whom he had promised a lift. Their homes in the country were difficult to reach by bus, but on the route to Mr. Jones' destination for Christmas. They were wondering why Mr. Jones was late. I explained that I had just seen him in Mr. Smith's office, and that he would probably be along shortly. As I finished speaking, he strode up the steps of Mrs. Wilson's house, looking, as one of the young women said, "like a thunder cloud." She asked him, "Why don't you smile?" He replied, "Smile, hell!", strode out of the house, and angrily threw their baggage into the car. One of the girls asked him to wait a minute, while she got her suitcase from the house next door where she had spent the night. But Mr. Jones was in no mood to wait. He had done all his waiting for the day. He drove off with two of the teachers, leaving Mrs. Wilson and the third teacher astounded and aghast at his behavior. I tried to explain and described what he had just been through in Mr. Smith's office, but this did not help the teacher who was wondering how she would get home in time for Christmas, or satisfy Mrs. Wilson, who found it difficult to understand the principal's sudden change from his usual courteous behavior. For me, the incident was data contributing to a hypothesis concerning intra-Negro aggression. I had just seen a man repress aggression induced by the biracial situation and let it out on Negroes immediately afterwards. Again, this was the kind of data obtainable only by participation and observation.

I have already alluded to my having dinner with Negro families—usually on a Sunday, after a church service. I even went on a boat picnic with one family at the far end of the county, where I knew no white people. The few who saw me assumed I was Negro. But in Indianola and its vicinity, where all the white people knew me, not one of them, as far as I know, was aware of my breaking their taboo on eating with Negroes eating together being a symbol, of course, of social equality. However, I could not be a participant-observer in certain areas of Negro life, such as the Saturday-night parties in the "flats," the poorest and most disreputable section of the community. Heavy drinking, gambling, and fighting prevailed at these parties. It would have been clearly unwise for me to have attended them. The Negroes would have been extremely embarrassed by my presence and the whites would have known about it since a white policeman appeared on the scene when the violence or noise was greater than usual. My presence would not have been condoned.

But this and the few other unavoidable omissions did not prevent me from having a sense of being within the Negro community, nor did they hinder my increasing understanding of the people and of their institutions. I more or less took it for granted that adult Negroes should speak frankly to me. At the same time, I knew their openness with me—a white person—was unusual. I am not sure that I know all the reasons. I have already mentioned that I lacked self-consciousness with Negroes, and I assume this contributed to putting them at ease.

With other whites they were constantly on their guard. Their play-acting was perfect, but it was apparently a unique and comforting experience to know one white person with whom it was not necessary. One upper-class Negro particularly skilled in playing the role demanded by the whites said it was "a relief to pull up the blind (window shade)" with me. Saying what they really felt and thought to a friendly and trusted symbol of the feared dominant white group was probably a catharsis. They knew (without my making speeches on the subject) that I was trustworthy, that I would reveal nothing to the whites among whom I was living, and that though my study would be published, names would be changed and that my informants would all be protected by anonymity. In no study would I reveal anything that could bring trouble to any individual.

My hunch is that over and above these reasons, the Negroes felt my genuine concern for them, my liking, and my strong desire to find out how things really were. Most people anywhere respond to these attitudes. They are not in themselves enough to make a good field worker, but they make a good base for training and for working as a participant-observer.

Some Negroes thought my study would do them good. Occasionally I argued this point with a friend, saying that I was uncertain that my book would do them good, and mentioning that my basic drive was curiosity to understand their lives. The answer was that if I wrote the truth, this would help them. They were perhaps more right than I, since the famous 1954 Supreme Court decision on school desegregation made use of sociological data.[6]

---

[6] I have been told that my book on Mississippi was one of those providing data, but I have not checked on this point. (I was in Africa when the decision was announced.)

XVIII

WHITE SOCIETY

My life was not segregated, but it was compartmentalized into Negro and white spheres. Living in a white boarding house gave me a base in the white community. My fellow boarders and I ate three meals a day together, and in addition to good food, I absorbed local news and gossip and was continuously aware of the behavior and attitudes of a half-dozen white people. On the other hand, I paid the price of being unable to get away from the research.

The boarders and my landlady seemed to accept me even though they knew I broke the social title taboo. Mrs. Wilson phoned occasionally, usually at meal time, since she knew I was apt to be home then. The phone was in the hall and conversations could be heard anywhere on the first floor. Whoever answered the phone would call out to me, "Annie's on the phone." I knew Mrs. Wilson had heard the "Annie" and I began, "Good morning, Mrs. Wilson." I could feel the strained silence at the table in the next room. Our phone conversations were brief, making an appointment or changing the time for one. My fellow boarders had all told me that "Annie knew her place" and this belief probably kept them from being more disturbed by my calling her "Mrs."

Knowledge of the white people I obtained in different ways: systematic interviewing, considerable informal participation, and an attitude questionnaire administered toward the end of the study. My original plan had called for studying only the behavior and attitudes of white people in their relations with Negroes. But I soon realized that it was not possible to understand these relations without knowing more about the class system and the traditions and history of white society. It never occurred to me not to expand the study, within the limits of the available time.

Planters were systematically interviewed. The sample included those with "mean" and "good" reputations, solvent and
insolvent; many were owners of the plantations on which I had
interviewed sharecroppers and renters. Interviews with the
planters were almost always by appointment; I did not write
during them, but always immediately afterwards, as was my
custom with Negroes. The frankness of the "mean" planters
surprised me. One opened his books and, boastingly, showed
how he cheated his sharecroppers. He admired his own cleverness, and was apparently so much a part of his social milieu
that he was unaware of, or unconcerned about, other values.
However, other planters rationalized their behavior with the
commonly-held belief that a "nigger" had to be kept in debt or
on a subsistence level in order to get him to work. Whatever
the planter said, I maintained the "poker face" of an interviewer, and expressed only interest which was real, and an
assumed naïveté.

Before coming south I had known that Negroes had no
political or legal rights. But the total absence of economic
rights was a minor shock. I had not before known of such a
society. Tribal societies had their well-defined rules and customs of reciprocity. The Middle Ages, of which the South
reminded me in some ways, had an established system of duties
and responsibilities between lords and serfs. But the rules on
which the sharecropping system was based were broken more
often than followed.

Much of my data and understanding of the white people
came from a seemingly casual social participation with the
middle-aged and older people in Indianola. I did not participate in the parties of young unmarried people, because I could
not take the heavy consumption of corn liquor, and going to
them would also have necessitated a boy-friend, which, as already indicated, would have been disastrous to working with
Negroes.

I was invited to white people's homes, and used the occasions to direct the conversation along the lines of my sociological interests. Sometimes useful information came up spontaneously. Each social visit or any encounter giving data was
written up as soon as I was back in my room. Women invited
me to afternoon bridge parties; since I did not know how to

play bridge, I dropped in on a party now and then for sociability in the late afternoon when refreshments were being served. More rewarding for data were an afternoon visit or lunch with a woman alone, and dinner or supper with a family. When I dined at a white person's home, I usually knew the servant who waited on the table. We exchanged only a quick knowing look. I may have interviewed her, had refreshments in her home, or been with her on some other social occasion. I could trust her and she could trust me not to reveal our relationship. I was often amazed at the freedom with which my white host and hostess talked in front of their Negro servant. It was as if she did not really exist. The Negroes' awareness of the realities of white society was no accident.

White people talked freely about themselves, including their feelings and attitudes towards Negroes. Revealing also were their frank opinions about white neighbors and friends. Planters were described as "mean" or "good" to their sharecroppers; these evaluations usually agreed with those given by Negroes. The "mean," as well as the "good," planter might be an elder in the church, and this situation was regarded as normal. My host and hostess did not seem to notice, or did not care, that I said little and never expressed an opinion. They were pleased—and, perhaps, flattered—that I was genuinely interested in what they had to say.

Conversation about family background was always a source of data. Almost everyone boasted about having an ancestor who had been a Colonel in the Confederate Army, and tried to give an impression of being descended from men who had big plantations with a large number of slaves. Common sense told me that the Confederate Army must have had more privates than Colonels; reading had informed me that in the whole pre-Civil War South, not more than 25 per cent of the people had owned any slaves and the majority of these had owned but one or two. Only about 6 per cent had as many as twenty slaves. Since Mississippi was settled late, the percentages were probably even smaller in that state.

The pretenses to an aristocratic background, which could also be called fantasies or lies, were significant data on cultural values in the community. Lies frequently reveal much about the values of a society, even when the field worker can not check on them. The situation in Mississippi, in which it happened to be possible to distinguish between the equally important lie and fact disclosed two related points: the absence of a middle-class tradition, and the white peoples' burden in carrying a tradition that did not belong to them.

Having perceived these points in listening to fantasies about family background, I gained evidence of them in other places. For instance, the whites talked condescendingly about a planter from Ohio who was openly a middle-class farmer and without pretense to a higher social background. His late father, he said, had been a dirt farmer in Ohio. When I interviewed this midwestern immigrant to Mississippi, he was in overalls, doing manual work. This was completely atypical for a white planter. The man from Ohio owned one of the few solvent plantations in the county; he had a good reputation among the Negroes and his sharecroppers were busy all year long, rather than only during the short planting and picking seasons. He planted other crops besides cotton, and had an extensive and profitable peach orchard. As I had a cup of coffee with him and his wife at the end of the interview, he mentioned that he had little in common with his fellow planters and his wife said she had almost no contact with their wives.

White women as well as men thought all manual work beneath them. Some who were hard up during the depression and were even on Federal relief employed a Negro laundress. The traditional American middle-class tradition of the virtue of hard work and its function in "getting ahead" was absent from this Mississippi community in the mid-thirties. However, it was not beneath a white woman's dignity to run her household and be a skilled cook. Women of the pre-Civil War aristocracy had run large plantations and taught house slaves their skills. The Negroes' term "strainers," for most middle-class whites, was sociologically apt. While it is not difficult to understand why people want to pretend to a background to which culture gives a higher prestige than their own, it is almost axiomatic that this situation produces anxieties, as in cases of Jews denying their backgrounds, Negroes passing for whites, and so forth.

Conversation and behavior revealed that the white people in this middle-class community also had a heavy burden of anxiety or guilt, or both, in reference to the Negroes. No household was without its gun. The whites seemed to live in fear of the tables being turned. I was advised to carry a gun in my car as I drove alone at night "across the tracks." When I laughingly mentioned my total ignorance of firearms and said that I was more afraid of them than of people, I was considered courageous. Some women, particularly those who took their religion seriously, expressed in hesitant manner the contradictions they felt between their Christian beliefs and the accepted code of behavior towards Negroes. Their obvious guilt was, I think, somewhat allayed by my not being interested in assessing blame. I can think of no worse technique for getting data than making an informant feel guilty.

This was a Bible Belt community for white people as well as for Negroes. All the whites went to Church. As among the Negroes, the majority were Methodists and Baptists (with a small minority Episcopalians and Catholics), and again like the Negroes, the young white people went more to please their elders than out of conviction. Many Sunday evenings I attended the services of a Methodist white church, and occasionally visited a Baptist one, because it contributed to my being accepted. The services seemed dull in comparison with those in the Negro churches. In sermons the white ministers stressed hell more than heaven; the biracial situation was never mentioned. After the services, I chatted sociably with members of the congregation. Occasionally, I accepted an invitation to attend an afternoon meeting of one of the women's missionary societies.

The Bible Belt atmosphere contributed to my feeling of being in the Middle Ages. A white woman better educated than the average stopped me one day, when I was in a bank to cash a check, to ask my opinion about a Biblical saying on the stars and moon. Did I think it was true, she asked. I replied that I was completely ignorant of astronomy and got away as quickly as possible. During the slack season I had come across two uneducated Negro men sitting on the porch of a shanty, arguing with much seriousness a literal Biblical point. I have forgotten the point, and its details are not in my notes, but I remember it was similar to, "How many angels can dance on the point of a needle?" The feeling of the past was always with me, even if it did not go back to the Middle Ages. When middle-aged white people talked about "the war," they meant the Civil War. I had first mistakenly thought they meant World War I. The talk of ancestors—usually mythical—and of the glories of a past epoch strengthened this impression of not being in the twentieth century.

As I mingled with the white people, with values so different from my own, I was surprised at my tolerance and, even more, at my liking some individuals. I remembered that when I was working in the labor movement, I thought that anyone who did not believe in trade unions as the hope of society was beyond the pale of my liking or even socially recognizing. In Mississippi, I wondered if I would have been different from the other whites, if I had been born in this community and had never left it. I had learned through breaking the taboo on social titles for Negroes how difficult it was to go beyond the group uniformity and consensus. As I tried to understand the historical and social situation which had produced these white people, I occasionally wondered about my new self; anthropology had become part of my personality. But my values remained as strong as ever and the effort to understand people with an opposing code did not mean that I condoned it.

Instead, I felt compassionate. The whites seemed to be worse off psychologically in many ways than the Negroes, and I sometimes felt that if, Heaven forbid, I had to live in Mississippi, I would prefer to be a Negro. The oppressed group were sure God was on their side and sure of their eventual victory, and had a sense of satisfaction in successfully disguising their real attitudes and fooling the whites. Many of the dominant group felt either guilt or hypocrisy, or both, and fear. The initial resistance of the leading white citizens in Indianola to my study clearly indicated fear of what I might find out, and was in sharp contrast to the attitudes of Negroes who wanted me to learn the truth. Then, too, the area for reality thinking was larger among the Negroes than for the whites. The former knew well their own group and the whites, both of whom they regarded as ordinary human beings—good and bad. The white man's knowledge of Negroes was limited to opposing stereotypes: a child-like person always enjoying life or a potentially dangerous sub-human type.

However, my compassionate attitude towards whites was severely jolted late one afternoon when I ran into a crowd of about twenty-five rough-looking white men with dogs on a country road. They separated to let me drive by. I stopped for a couple of minutes and found out what I had immediately suspected. They were out to "get a nigger" who, they said, had raped a white woman in a neighboring county. He was supposed to have fled into Sunflower County. Shaken, I drove on. I knew the Negro would be lynched if caught. The would-be lynchers belonged to the poor-white group so easily distinguishable by their clothes and their red-tanned necks. Their faces, now transformed with brutality and hate, were frightening.

I could make only a pretense at eating supper when I returned to the boarding house. My fellow boarders had heard of the alleged crime, and were unconcerned about the possibility of lynching. It was too bad, they said, but after all, it was in the next county, and Negroes had to be taught a lesson once in a while, otherwise no white woman would be safe. That night I could not sleep. I felt I had to do something to prevent a possible lynching. I saw myself as a kind of Joan of Arc on a white horse. But what could I do? I knew that an appeal to police or other authorities was useless. The Negro and the white men hunting him lived in a county where I knew no one. By morning I had not thought of anything I could do to help the Negro. At breakfast I saw the local paper with a headlined story about the "sex crime."

But at least I could function as an anthropologist. The Negroes in Indianola stayed indoors and there was no need to study their attitudes. But I could study the middle-class whites who would not have participated in a lynching, although they condoned it. During the next couple of days I walked around the white section of town, sat in drug stores drinking Cokes with men and women, visited people I knew, listening all the time to what they had to say about the impending lynching. The story was almost always the same: no one believed in lynching, but what could one do with these "sex-crazed niggers." Only one person—a woman—wondered if the Negro was really guilty. She was a deeply religious middle-aged housewife whose family background was a bit higher in terms of education and wealth than the norm in Indianola.

The Negro man escaped to another state, and was not caught.

The excitement died down. Whispers and rumors circulated that he had committed no crime, but had attempted to get back some money owed him by a white man, who happened at the time to be accompanied by a girl friend. The story of the Negro's attempted rape of her had been spread by this man.

I felt I had won my spurs as a field worker. I had interviewed, observed, and gotten data in a situation which had deeply disturbed me.

I was curious to find out about the "poor-whites," when they were not in a mood of violence. They lived in a small community not far from Indianola, but I could not study them for two reasons: lack of time, and the open hatred between them and the Negroes. It would not have been possible to have associated simultaneously with each group without incurring the suspicion of both. But out of curiosity, and using an interest in religion as an excuse, I went to a revival meeting of "Holy Rollers," all poor-whites, and then went back one afternoon for casual visiting. They did not talk like the Faulkner characters I had expected. I learned little from this brief contact, but enough to make me think that a study of them would have been possible and rewarding. I regret that I never made it.

At the other end of the social spectrum was the aristocracy. Although their number was infinitesimally small in Mississippi, yet the traditions they represented were historically and sociologically significant. Limitations in their knowledge, awareness, and behavior have been as important as their positive contributions in setting the contours of the white social structure. I knew only two Mississippi aristocrats: Will Percy and Mrs. Branton; and of these Mr. Percy was much the better representative and the most articulate. As already indicated, they lived in Greenville, about forty miles from Indianola.

I learned much about Will Percy's attitudes and personality through long conversations, but frequently did not have adequate documentation. After my field work and the publication of the results, Will Percy wrote an enlightening autobiography.[1] A more detailed analysis of his aristocratic point of view is now possible and is sociologically significant. It is difficult

---

[1] William Alexander Percy, *Lanterns on the Levee, Recollections of a Planter's Son* (New York: Alfred A. Knopf, 1941).

to say how far he was typical of his class since he was the only aristocrat I knew even moderately well, and the only one to my knowledge who wrote such a frank autobiography. He thought he represented the aristocracy, and both whites and Negroes thought so, too. As a poet and a sensitive human being, he was probably more aware of himself and of his society than others of his class. He had been to Harvard, lived in Paris, and traveled in many parts of the world. But he remained a provincial aristocrat of Mississippi.

Will Percy was born in 1885. His background of French *bon bourgeois* and southern aristocracy provided him with complete certainty about his place in society: "the certainty I was as good as anyone else, which because of the depth of the conviction was unconscious, never talked of, never thought of. Besides Southerners, the only people I have ever met graced with the same informal assurance were Russian aristocrats." [2] "As good as anyone else," an understatement, contrasts sharply with the social anxieties of the middle-class whites.

Will Percy knew and loved many Negroes in his childhood. First was Nain, his nurse, "sixteen, divinely cafe-au-lait," whom he loved "for her merry goodness, her child's heart that understood mine, and her laughter that was like a celesta playing triplets. Chiefly, I remember her bosom: it was soft and warm, an ideal place to cuddle one's head against. . . ." [3] Then came childhood playmates, and his most constant companion was Skillet, the son of his grandmother's cook, "the best crawfisher in the world," who "as a conversationalist outdistanced any white child in inventiveness, absurdity and geniality." [4] He had other Negro playmates on his aunt's farm in Virginia, where he spent many childhood summers. These experiences convinced him that Negroes were happy Pan-like beings living only in the present, fundamentally and mysteriously different from white people. (This point of view came out over and over again in conversations with me.) Actually, the spontaneous gay play he happened to experience with Negroes could have been duplicated by many white children who simply enjoyed the freedom to explore the world of nature.

---

[2] *Ibid.*, p. 41.
[3] *Ibid.*, pp. 26–7.
[4] *Ibid.*, p. 48

Yet in spite of the love for his nurse and Negro playmates, none of them seem to have been real people to him. Of Nain, his nurse, he said, "She comes back to me more an emanation or aura than as a person." [5] He wrote that before he went to college, "I had liked children whose pleasures were my pleasures, *but they had not been persons to me and left no mark*" [6] (author's italics). Of his boyhood friend, he wrote, "I like to imagine Skillet is not in jail or dead, but that he lords it in a Pullman car or pulpit, or perhaps he has a family of his own and many little crawfishers. . . ." [7] This was the best he could conceive for his imaginative boyhood playmate. That Skillet could have become a poet, a teacher, a business man, or left his humble status in some other way, never seemed to have entered Percy's mind. In Greenville were Negro teachers, doctors, business men, members of an educated middle- and upper-middle class. In Percy's book they are mentioned only once, when, as head of the Red Cross during a crisis caused by the Mississippi River overflowing its embankments, he appointed some of them to a commitee. The ever-present Negroes in his life and in his book were all uneducated servants or children of servants.

Percy delighted in their charm. He wrote, "Just now we are happy that the brother in black is still the tiller of our soil, the hewers of our wood, our servants, troubadours, and criminals. His manners offset his inefficiency, his vices have the charm of amiable weaknesses, he is a pain and a grief to live with, a solace and a delight." [8] The same attitude is expressed more specifically towards Ford, his chauffeur, houseboy, and general factotum, who duns and exploits him continually. Percy writes, "I must [support him] because Ford is my fate, my Old Man of the Sea, who tells me of Martin and admonishing cooters and angels that do the loop-the-loop, my only tie with Pan and the Satyrs and all earth creatures who smile sunshine and ask no questions and understand." [9] However, Ford left Percy's employment, and came back drunk to see him

---

[5] *Ibid.,* p. 27.
[6] *Ibid.,* p. 94.
[7] *Ibid.,* p. 49.
[8] *Ibid.,* p. 21.
[9] *Ibid.,* p. 296.

after he had lost another job. He is quoted as saying, "You can't do no good, Mr. Will. It don't make no difference how hard I try or how good I been, I ain't never gonner be nuthin' but jes Fode." According to Percy, Ford was facing ". . . the tragedy of himself and of his race in an alien world." In South Africa, Morocco, Harlem, or Detroit, ". . . his pitiful cry would have been equally true, equally hopeless and unanswerable." [10] Percy, the poet, could understand at least a part of the Negro's tragedy. But Percy, the aristocrat, could not imagine a social system in which the Negro's fate would be no more or less tragic than that of all people.

As Negroes were innately different from whites, so also were white groups different from each other. Percy's analysis of the white population in the Delta was: [11]

> Old slave holders, the landed gentry who were the governing class in the past, and their descendants. These were the aristocracy.
> Poor whites, whose manual labor had lost its dignity from having been in competition with slave labor. The descendants of these whites control local government in many countries; mutual hatred exists between them and Negroes.
> Managers and slave drivers, mostly illiterate but with ability, who had become plantation owners. Their educated descendants are the "professional southerners" and future aristocrats.
> Jews and other foreigners—Italians, Irish, Chinese, Syrians

Percy thought the poor whites intellectually and spiritually inferior to the Negroes. The "crime" of the southern white masses was the same as that of the Russian communists, the German Nazi, organized labor, and capital in the United States: "the insolence of the parvenu." [12] No wonder these southern white masses felt socially insecure: the duty of the aristocrat was to protect Negroes from them. Both Percy and his father had courageously played this role. At considerable personal risk they had spoken against violence and demagoguery to hostile groups such as the Ku Klux Klan.

For Percy, Jews were "different," although not inferior to other white people. According to him, they arrived as peddlers with packs on their back. "Today they are plantation-owners

---

[10] *Ibid.*, p. 296–97.
[11] *Ibid.*, pp. 16–24.
[12] *Ibid.*, p. 153.

and professional people and merchants; their children attend
the great American universities, win prizes, become connois-
seurs in the arts and radicals in politics. . . . Why shouldn't such
a people inherit the earth, not, surely, because of their meekness, but because of a steadier fire, a tension and tenacity that
makes all other whites seem stodgy and unintellectual." [13] Percy
did not "see" the stodgy unintellectual Jews in his community
any more than he knew, in a real sense, middle-class Negroes.

He had the charming manners of a southern aristocrat with
women but considered them inferior to men in their ability
to exercise the privilege of voting. He writes, "Some of us still
remember what we were told of these times (the Reconstruction period), and what we were told inclines us to guard the
ballot as something precious, something to be withheld unless
the fitness of the recipient be patent. We are the ones I suppose
who doubt despairingly the fitness of Negroes (and under our
breath be it said) of women." [14]

Percy the poet and the aristocrat, the educated man who
knew the world's literature and art, who had traveled and lived
abroad, and Percy the provincial Mississippian, a man who
loved Negroes but regarded them as inherently alien and
unknowable, together made up a complex individual indeed.
I was truly grateful to him for having made it possible for me
to work in Indianola, and I enjoyed his company. Naturally,
I sent him a copy of the book which resulted from the Mississippi study as soon as it was off the press. I was eager to know
his reaction to it. After a few weeks passed and I had received
no acknowledgment, I wrote asking if he had received the
book. He answered immediately, thanking me and writing that
he had not yet had time to read it. I am almost certain this
was a polite evasion of the truth. I knew him well enough to
know he was not that busy and that his curiosity to learn the
results of my study would have probably made him read the
book as soon as it arrived. I did not hear from him again. He
was probably unable to "take" my description of Negroes as
people not innately different from whites, and my discussion
of Negro class differences and middle- and upper-class Negro
values and behavior. But I assume he could not depart from his

[13] *Ibid.*, p. 17.
[14] *Ibid.*, p. 274.

code of charming politeness to tell me how he really felt about the book.

While still in the field, I felt the need of a systematic check on my observations and impressions of middle-class white attitudes towards Negroes. Towards the end of the study my position was good enough to use a questionnaire. Nothing indicated that it had originated at Fisk, a Negro University: Charles S. Johnson had prepared it for a large study of public opinion.

Six hundred questionnaires were given out and two hundred and fifty-six were returned answered. The groups covered were the Chamber of Commerce, Rotary Club, students at a nearby junior college, women's missionary societies of the Methodist, Baptist, and Presbyterian churches, and the sisterhood of a synagogue in Greenville. I explained the purpose of the questionnaires to each group; they were returned anonymously by mail. Both sexes were about equally represented, and for the first time I had data on attitudes of a group of young people in their teens. The results showed no consistent differences from those of adults, although minor differences existed.

Only a half-dozen or so Jews lived in Indianola, but a sizeable group (most of them belonging to a Reform congregation) were in Greenville. The rabbi was from Philadelphia and I traded on my maternal grandfather's reputation there. The Greenville rabbi knew of him, invited me to dinner, arranged for my coming to a meeting of the sisterhood, and cooperated in my giving questionnaires to its members. The data from the questionnaires confirmed my impression of no difference between the attitudes of Jews and Protestants towards Negroes. Conversations with a few Jews who had moved from the North to Greenville indicated that some had become more southern than the southerners in these attitudes in order to be accepted by the community.

In Indianola the questionnaires provoked considerable discussion, and some people made a point of asking me to come to see them so that they could explain their attitudes more fully. In general, the questionnaire provided a useful confirmation of what I had already learned by participating in the community. It could not have been used without this previous participation.

The constant participation and observation among Negroes and whites had its costs, too. Occasionally I wondered who I was, as I passed back and forth between the two groups. When I inadvertently "passed" for Negro, I would return to the boarding house and look in the mirror, wondering if the color of my skin had changed. There was always some tension in the situation for me. I never was sure that something terrible, or at least disastrous for my field work, might not happen as Mr. Smith had predicted. But I evidently managed fairly well; I do not remember having any even minor illness when I was in Mississippi.

As in Lesu, there was no escape from the inevitable note taking. Since most of the data in Mississippi had to be remembered until after the interview, social visit, or other incident was over, the note-taking there was harder. But the weariness from never being free of taking mental notes was similar in both field situations. It was difficult to escape into a novel or book of poems as I had occasionally done in Lesu. The room in my boarding house, with its large double bed, was cluttered with personal things, typewriter, and notes. I could not lie in bed for the day and relax sufficiently in the midst of the disorder to lose myself in a novel. Letter writing was one escape. But I did not write the long full letters as I had from Lesu. My enjoyment of the Negro "socials" in the church basement and of the church services was real, but accompanied by the inevitable note-taking.

Going to movies was my best relaxation. The storefront theater showed grade "B" and "C" films. But I have always loved movies, good and bad. Most everyone (Negro and white) went to the movies—twenty-five cents downstairs for whites and fifteen cents upstairs for Negroes. After I had seen a movie, I listened to my fellow boarders discuss it as we ate, and later I heard Negroes talk about it. Slowly I began to realize that whites and Negroes were seeing the movie differently from how I saw it. For them, the movies represented life—true life —different from their own. Fantasies were being received as real culture patterns. I began to listen to the discussion of movies with sociological interest and a new problem, thus emerged quite by accident out of experience. I did no work on the problem in Mississippi, but later it became part of another research project.

Nashville was four hundred miles away and by driving hard, I could reach it in one day. I spent two holidays there—Christmas and one other time when I was just fed-up with Sunflower County. Part of the vacations were spent on the Fisk campus, where I mingled with Negroes socially. But in this ebony tower I did not have to take notes and it was likewise a relief not to be concerned with possible reactions of white people to breaking some of their taboos. I knew one white family, Northerners, the man on the faculty of Vanderbilt University. Staying with them was relaxing; I don't remember what we talked about, but it was not Mississippi. I returned to Indianola, refreshed, after a Nashville visit.

Occasionally in Indianola, I was tired and depressed and wondered why I had come there. I remember one hot August night when the damp heat seemed to close in on me. It was more oppressive than the nights in Lesu, where cool sea breezes filtered through the thatched roof. I lay bathed in perspiration, although hardly making any movement. I asked myself, "Why do I have to suffer this heat?" The next day as I was getting some interesting data, I had the answer: I enjoyed field work more than any other. It was a form of experiencing life, of stepping beyond the boundaries of my background and society and of making the latter more intelligible.

In the discussion of the Mississippi field work, I have occasionally touched on some of the differences and similarities with the Lesu experience, in terms of method and techniques. Here, I would like to emphasize a few major points. The culture of Lesu was sufficiently strange and esoteric for me to be really outside of my society. Although the standards of living in Lesu were decidedly lower than in Mississippi, neither Melanesians nor I regarded this or any other aspect of their social organization as social problems—in the colloquial sense of presenting situations for which change was desirable. (Today, after the long contact with Japanese and Americans, as well as Australians, the situation might be quite different.) In Mississippi, it was impossible to escape the inherent social problems. Inevitably, I viewed the mores, behavior, and attitudes of Negroes and whites from the background of the larger American culture in which I had been reared and in terms of my personal values. Yet, I did manage to acquire a considerable social distance from the Mississippi community. Seeing it in historical perspective and as a kind of anachronism was helpful. The previous experience of being involved and detached in Lesu was invaluable. Finally, my identification with both racial groups and with the different classes in each gave me a measure of objectivity.

Of necessity, my roles in the biracial situation and power structure of the deep South were more complex than in Lesu. In the latter place, I occasionally was naïve; in Mississippi, I had sometimes to pretend to a naïveté. In Lesu, I had no anxiety about unknown dangers (once I got over my initial panic). As far as was necessary, I followed the Melanesian taboos, and when I broke them, such as going to a men's ritual feast, it was done at their invitation, with their help and with the approval of the community. In Mississippi, I had to break some taboos of the white power structure openly, and some secretly, never knowing what might happen in either case. "Carrying" two groups mutually hostile and fearful was far more difficult than the clear-cut role in Lesu. My involvement in the two situations was quite different. No matter how high the level of my empathy with the people of Lesu, I never wondered if I was a Melanesian or a Caucasian, a member of the stone-age society or of my own. As already mentioned, in Mississippi, there were times, when passing back and forth between the two groups, being identified with each and occasionally mistaken for a Negro, that I wondered what group I really belonged to. Psychologically, I did belong to both, which in some cultures other than Mississippi would create no problems.

For all the differences between Lesu and Mississippi, many similarities existed. I was not only accepted in each place, but my presence and the study eventually taken for granted. In both the culture seeped into my bones, as I went over and over again to Melanesian feasts and to Mississippi churches, participated in the daily lives of Melanesians and Negroes, interviewed many people, and became close friends with a few.

XIX

LOOKING BACKWARDS:
MISSISSIPPI 1934—
SEEDS OF THE
NEGRO REVOLUTION

Writing in 1965, it is difficult to end the section on Mississippi without, at least, a postscript on the seeds of the contemporary Negro revolution, although I have done no further field work in the South.

In 1932–34, I did not foresee the revolutionary demand of the Negroes for full civil rights "now." Then the young Negroes whom I studied had rejected their parents' role of placating the whites through pretending to believe in the latter's alleged superiority, but were uncertain about what new role they should adopt. "Nevertheless," I wrote, "beneath this present confusion and discouragement he (the young Negro, particularly the educated one) does have a new belief in his race, his own potentialities, the possibility of eventual amelioration . . . Above all, he has, in the sense of a cause which must be served, a potential integrating force, capable of being mobilized by some new formulation of values and aims and some new leadership in which he could have confidence. Given this sense of urgent need, it seems likely that some new faith will supersede education for those who have been disillusioned concerning its promise." [1]

Today, "Freedom Now" is the cause which must be served, the integrating force for those in their forties (the youth who had not found themselves at the time of my study), for their

[1] Hortense Powdermaker, *After Freedom, A Cultural Study in the Deep South* (New York: The Viking Press, 1939), p. 363.

children not born then, and for their parents who had played a role of compromise. All are now social pioneers.

Yet this radical movement in the South has its roots structurally and ideologically in the past. In the mid-thirties and earlier, the church was the one institution completely controlled by the Negroes. In it, I had noted, they were trained in administration, in handling finances, in exercising leadership, and in working together. Today the church is still the heart of the civil rights movement in the South. The people meet in it to hear their leaders urge them on in the struggle for equality and to pray for its success. Dr. Martin Luther King, Jr., a dominant leader and a symbol of the revolution, is a minister in a Baptist church in Atlanta and chairman of the Southern Christian Leadership Conference, an alliance of a hundred or so church-oriented groups. Although well educated, he still has the charisma or mystique of southern Negro preachers of the past, rather than the sophistication and brilliance of secular leaders in the North such as Roy Wilkins, Whitney Young, James Farmer, and John Lewis. Descended from a militant maternal grandfather and father who fought for civil rights in their days in Atlanta, the Reverend Dr. King continues to be guided by the Christian doctrine of love, as he preaches nonviolence in an often violent situation. The faith in God's and man's love which enabled the Negroes in Indianola to maintain their self-respect and to channel their aggression in acting the meek role demanded by the whites now sparks the forthright demands for full equality. In the face of much provocation, Southern Negroes have the courage to act on their faith. Their remarkable ability for self-discipline is not a new achievement. Thirty years ago I saw it demonstrated over and over again by Mississippi Negroes in their relations with whites. The respectability and legitimacy of the Negro revolution is likewise assured by placing its roots in the traditional ethos. The Reverend Dr. King says, "We will win our freedom because the sacred heritage of our nation and the eternal will of God are embodied in our echoing demands." [2]

The leadership of women in family and community life,

---

[2] *The New York Times,* July 14, 1963.

their greater buoyancy and hopefulness for the future, as compared to men, was revealed in the Mississippi study. It is therefore not surprising to find women in the forefront of the contemporary struggle. To mention only a few: Mrs. Rosa Park, a seamstress, who refused to give her seat up to a white passenger when commanded to do so by a bus driver, triggered a successful boycott of the bus line by Montgomery's Negroes in 1955. A year later the first effort of a Negro to enter the University of Alabama was made by Miss Autherine Lucy. It was a woman chairman of the N.A.A.C.P. in Little Rock who organized the Negroes in 1957 to protect nine children trying to go to a formerly all-white school from the hatred of white mobs. Many other women, following a traditional pattern along a new path, have been in the forefront of the movement.

More significant in terms of social change is the fact that Negro men have taken their rightful place in the leadership of the revolution. The political and economic power of the white men had been intricately meshed with sexual power, and with the willingness to use violence if necessary to maintain it. In the thirties, Negro men in Sunflower County were far more deeply frustrated and anxious than were their wives. White men maintained their traditional prerogative of access to Negro women at the same time that they reserved the right to lynch a Negro man if it was rumored that he looked with desire at a white woman. Considerable evidence existed then that sexual relations between white men and Negro women were decreasing and that extramarital and premarital relations among whites were increasing. Negro women, out of self-respect, were saying "No" to white men, who were also probably making fewer demands because of the opportunities within their own group. Both trends seem to be stronger today. The open defiance of Negro men to white men who refuse to grant them civil rights may not be unconnected with the changing sexual mores.

The protests of the Negro men in Mississippi are not confined to civil rights. Economic rights have also come to the fore. In the 1930's an effort of some Mississippi sharecroppers to organize was repressed with violence. But in 1965, the sharecroppers in Panola County were sufficiently well organized to present written demands for improvements in wages and conditions of work to plantation owners. Their organization is tied to the civil rights drive, as are other labor unions.[3]

Both the leadership and membership of the civil rights drive increasingly broadens. The Negroes' resentment, formerly concealed through cynical and clever play-acting, is now channeled into open hostility to the entire social system which has kept them in an underprivileged position. At this writing the civil rights movement in the South is still non-violent and still rooted in the church. Men, women, and children pray on the streets as well as in churches and go to jail singing hymns, revised spirituals, and freedom songs.

The anxieties of the whites are out in the open, too, and they fight to maintain the traditional mores with any means they can command—the courts, the police, and violence. In 1963, a prosecutor in an Alabama court addressed Negroes arrested in a racial demonstration at Gadsden (and only Negroes) by their first name. Miss Mary Hamilton, age twenty-eight, refused to respond. "My name is Miss Hamilton. I will not answer a question until I am addressed correctly," she said. The Court held her on contempt; the sentence was five days in jail and a fifty-dollar fine without a hearing, later upheld by the Alabama Supreme Court. The N.A.A.C.P. took the case to the Supreme Court, noting that Miss Hamilton had responded to one of the most distinct indicia of the racial caste system—the refusal of whites to address Negroes with titles of respect. The Supreme Court ruled in favor of Miss Hamilton.[4] But Southern whites continue to affirm their belief in the social inferiority of the Negro, symbolized in the taboo on titles of courtesy. The violation of this taboo is still regarded, as it was in the mid-thirties, by whites and by Negroes as a threat to the traditional social system.

It is unusual to find young people as eager as their elders to uphold traditions. In western countries and in developing African nations, youth are usually more liberal or radical than their elders. This was not, and still is not true among the whites in Mississippi. The students at a junior college who took the

---

[3] *The New York Times,* March 7, 1963, p. 78.
[4] *The New York Times,* March 31, 1964.

attitude test administered during my study shared the opinions of the adults. Both age groups regarded as true such statements as: [5]

"Negroes are all right as long as they stay in their places".
As equals, the races cannot and will not exist together.
Race prejudice has an acceptable utility in preserving the purity of the racial stock.
Negroes are inferior to white people in innate capacity.
The Negro should remain a separate and distinct race.
Racial intermarriage should be prohibited by law.
The Negroes' place is in a manual work.

There was also unanimity on the falseness of statements, such as:

Negroes and white children should be educated in the same schools.
Colored people should fight for social equality.
All races of men have the same faculties, and general ability to learn; they differ in no important degree.
Negroes should be accepted now to complete social equality with white persons.

The leaven of youthful idealism, of awareness of the forces of change, of the desire and courage to change, is still absent among young white Mississippians. A survey of student attitudes at the University of Mississippi made two years before the riots against the admission of a Negro student, James H. Meredith, to their campus, indicated that they were isolated from American culture and traditional in outlook.[6] The survey and the opinions of the faculty at the time of the riots over the admission of Mr. Meredith drew attention to the absence of any tradition of dissent and any rallying point of liberal thought on the campus. The students had no active debating society, no even faintly liberal organizations, no humor magazine, and no beatniks. The campus bookstore was limited to required texts. A small selection of paperbacks could be found in a shop in an out-of-the-way corner of the Student Union

---

[5] Hortense Powdermaker, *op. cit.*, Appendix A, pp. 381–91.
[6] Survey made by Dr. C. Robert Pace, professor of education at the University of California, Los Angeles, was designed to draw a picture of a college or university as seen by its students and is a form of opinion poll. Quoted in an article by Thomas Buckley, *The New York Times,* Sunday, October 21, 1962.

Building. "No magazine of even middling quality is available on the campus and few are sold in Oxford." [7] All signs of more or less normal post-adolescent rebellion were lacking. The profile of these young people, emerging from the survey, is similar in many ways to that of their parents who were young at the time of my study and to their grandparents who were then middle-aged.

As late as 1963, Mississippi whites were intensely committed to maintaining the traditional status quo. Hodding Carter, editor of the *Delta Democrat Times* in Greenville, and an outspoken liberal editor, described Jackson, the capital: [8]

> ". . . it is a town obsessed with a determination to maintain existing relationship between the races. Its politics and social order are monolithic. One can count on two hands those Jacksonians who are willing to speak against any status quo. . . . Almost the sole source of the city's newspaper information comes from a morning and afternoon combination owned by a family whose animation can only be described as an admixture of fundamentalism, furious racism and greed. (This paper is widely read throughout the state.)
>
> Rare is the Jacksonian citizen of any prominence, or even of no consequence, who does not belong to the Citizen's Council. . . . Hardly a week has gone by for many months in which some agency—political, journalistic and even clerical—has not issued an inflamatory statement of defiance or contempt for government, the United Nations, or any other idea of world government."

Two years later the situation changed. The editor of a newspaper in McComb, Mississippi (a center of strife and violence over civil rights), published an editorial urging compliance with the Civil Rights Law, and quoted Tom Paine to support his stand. Even more important, the Mississippi Economic Council (equivalent to a state chamber of commerce) urged respect for the Civil Rights Law and compliance with it.[9] The change of attitude is due, at least in part, to the power of Federal dollars, which can be withheld from industrial contracts and schools and from the establishment of government bases, if the Civil Rights Law is not enforced. Private business

---

[7] *Ibid.*
[8] Hodding Carter, "Mississippi Now—Hate and Fear," *The New York Times Magazine,* June 23, 1963.
[9] *The New York Times,* March 3, 1965.

is also the loser if a community is known for racial strife; northern companies may fear to establish subsidiary companies and
large cities will lose the patronage of conventions. Slowly,
leadership seems to be shifting from the die-harders of the
Ku Klux Klan and the White Citizens Council to leading business men and less reactionary whites. Leroy Percy, a member
of the late Will Percy's aristocratic family, testified before the
Civil Rights Commission in Jackson that Mississippi is "tired
of being led by the dead hand of the past," a quite different
attitude from Will Percy's nostalgia for the past. Mr. Leroy
Percy continued: "The people of Mississippi want a change and
I believe they are going to get it . . . (they) want to be in the
main stream of American life and not in the backwater." [10]
The contemporary aristocrat is no longer the provincial aristocrat. When the issue is joined, it is not beyond the traditions
of southern aristocracy to side with the Negroes against their
middle- and lower-class oppressors.

But the aristocracy has some responsibility for the bitterness
and violence of these whites today, as well as for having kept
the Negroes in their so-called place in the past. Scorned by the
aristocrats, and without a respected middle-class tradition, the
individual and group identities of the middle- and lower-class
whites are apparently tied to their feelings of alleged superiority over Negroes. The identity of these white men is meshed
with their status in a caste-like social system. The civil rights
struggle threatens the system and the traditional status positions. Members of the White Citizens Council and of the Ku
Klux Klan fight with passion to maintain their personal and
group identities. They fight the more desperately, because they
know they wage a losing fight. They prefer to go down fighting than to become an integrated part of a modern nation.

---

[10] *The New York Times,* Feb. 20, 1965.

PART IV

HOLLYWOOD

INTRODUCTION:
Why Hollywood?

The study of Hollywood grew out of my sociological interest in movies, which had begun in Mississippi. After I returned, I could not forget the comments I had heard there about movies. Both whites and Negroes had seemed to look at them as "a slice of life," or in anthropological terms, as culture patterns.

I wondered about the reactions of other audiences and, accordingly, my students in a class on field work methods did an exploratory study in a low-income housing project in Long Island City. We gave tickets to a number of its adult residents to see selected movies in a neighborhood theater, and then interviewed them. The results indicated that the audience tended to be critical of the "truth" of those parts of a film which touched their experience, but to accept as "true" what was outside of it, such as a tale of a successful girl artist and her two rich boy-friends. This study and another smaller one strengthened my original impression from the comments on movies I had heard in Indianola, namely, that unsophisticated and relatively uneducated people viewed the movies more or less as representations of real life.

What were the culture patterns in movies to which these people were being exposed and which they were taking seriously? Always a movie fan, I now became an anthropologist in the theater, taking notes on certain films which I later translated into terms of culture patterns. Occasionally, I was lucky enough to see an American and a foreign movie with the same or similar themes and to compare them.

For some time this interest was only an avocation. Eventually it became more serious. In 1939 the Mississippi book had been published and in 1944 another on prejudice was published. World War II was just over, and I no longer was under the pressure of two jobs: one at Queens College and the other (two days a week) at Yale University in its Army Specialized Training Program for the southwest Pacific. A publisher asked me to do a new book on the race problem. I was not interested. "What am I interested in?" I asked myself. "Movies," was the answer.

I planned a content analysis of them. Since time for research was limited by a rather heavy teaching schedule, I needed a small grant to buy a tape recorder and to employ a typist. Although not sure that the new interest fell within the discipline of anthropology, I wrote to Paul Fejos, director of The Viking Fund (later The Wenner-Gren Foundation for Anthropological Research), describing the project briefly. He answered immediately and asked me to come and see him.

I did not know until that first visit that his many-sided career in medicine, archaeology, and anthropology had also included his being a theater director in Europe and a motion-picture director in Hollywood. In 1928 he had made a distinguished film, "The Last Moment." One of the most creative and imaginative people I have ever met, he immediately saw possibilities in the movie project that had not occurred to me. He told me that I could not possibly understand movies as part of our culture unless I knew the social-psychological milieu in which they were made. As I later learned, his thesis was correct. He suggested that I go to Hollywood for six months. Accordingly, I submitted such a project to the Fund and was fortunate in receiving a grant. The original plan was to write a book on movies, in which Hollywood would be either one section or a theme running throughout.

I arrived in Hollywood in the beginning of July, 1946, and stayed one year. During the first month the department of anthropology at the University of California in Los Angeles invited me to teach during the coming academic year. (A new appointment had not materialized. I accepted the position on a half-time basis, teaching only familiar courses, because this permitted an extension of the original plan for a six-month study to a year. Being a visiting professor at U.C.L.A. was likewise a useful sanction for the role of anthropologist, a new one in Hollywood.

Much of the Hollywood of 1946–47 has gone. Then it was still controlled by powerful and passionate personalities in the

front offices of major studios. But there were new trends pointing to changes; these I studied, too. During the year a book
on Hollywood took shape and the original plan of a book on
movies, of which Hollywood would be only a part, was
shelved.

Today I am critical of the Hollywood field work, more so
than of any of my other field experiences. Hindsight tells me
that the problems were formidable because of inherent difficulties in the situation, and because of certain patterns in my
personality. A discussion of both may be as useful, if not more
so, as that of more or less successful field research. Although
the sociological and psychological aspects are, of course, interwoven, they are discussed separately.

This section of the book has been the most difficult to write.
It is not easy to unravel the tangled threads of an exceptionally
complex personal and social situation which occurred almost
twenty years ago. Even more important is the fact that Hollywood was the only field experience in which I made no notes of
my personal reactions. This, in itself, is significant. I was not
the functioning feeling, as well as thinking, human being that
I was in other field research. Feelings were muted. I saw myself
as an objective scientist.

XX

THE SOCIOLOGICAL SIDE

The first difficulty I encountered in Hollywood was situational.
When I left my apartment, on foot or in a car, I could not perceive a community. Hollywood was not a structured geographical locale; studios and homes were spread for many miles in the sprawling city of Los Angeles, which I thought ugly. In both Lesu and Indianola, the communities were definite, and it had been relatively easy to observe constantly and participate in their life. Experiencing the culture in each had been continuous and escape had been difficult. This kind of constant and seemingly casual observation was not possible in Hollywood.

Another difficulty was that, as far as I knew, no comparable research existed to serve as a model for the study of Hollywood. The hypothesis underlying the research was that the social structure of Hollywood was an important determinant in the content and form of the film. The problem narrowed to an examination of the continuing process which underlay the making of a film and the study of the human roles necessary to that process at any one point. This approach was quite different from that of the study in Lesu, in Mississippi, and later in Northern Rhodesia (and in most anthropological research), in which the focus was on a network of multiple roles. In the Hollywood study, the roles were segmented, and research was limited to their interplay at specific points in the making of a movie.

Without definitive research models, my methods were frequently trial and error. The basic technique was the interview. I had arrived with a few letters of introduction, some of which were helpful, and in the beginning I met anyone and everyone who was available. Several were influential people,

213

who, fortunately, became interested in the project. News of their helpfulness—too informal to be called sponsorship— spread rapidly via the Hollywood grapevine and opened doors for interviews. The grapevine was as effective, or more so, in Hollywood as in smaller and more homogeneous groups. If at any time I had thought of it, and had been able to trace the paths in the maze through which gossip and rumors circulated, the results might have been illuminating. Gossip is, of course, a universal in all societies. But the attention given to the gossip columnists in the two daily papers (*The Hollywood Reporter* and *Variety*) and to the tales they peddled was far greater than in other industries and in most modern communities. The columnists were only one part of the grapevine. Another was a constant social interaction between members of different groups of elites, in the studios and out of them. Several times I saw the effectiveness of gossip in relation to my work, and I glimpsed its function in the lives of the movie makers. But I did not understand its full significance, or, unfortunately, view it as a problem for study. Instead, my attitude was a combination of amusement and of gratefulness when the grapevine functioned to my advantage, as it did in securing interviews and on a few other occasions.

I attempted to have a stratified functional sample of interviewees, i.e. representatives of the front office, producers, directors, actors, writers, agents, and of the very successful, the medium successful, and the unsuccessful. Among the actors, writers, and directors, I found further subdivisions ranging from the creative to the mediocre which did not necessarily correspond to degrees of financial success. The subdivisions within the sample of approximately three hundred were not in proportion to their numbers in the movie colony, but assured representation of practically all groups and types. At that time people were openly "left" and "right" and, as I was curious to find out if any correlation existed between political position and attitudes to movie-making and movie content, I deliberately chose to interview people of opposing political groups. This part of the study was admittedly not extensive, but no correlation apparently existed. In general, men of many different ideologies worked within the same social system, more or less accepting it because of the large financial rewards.

The sample was secured through a broad range of contacts, one leading to another. If a producer talked about relations with the writers in his current production, I tried to meet one or two of them. The Screen Writers' Guild was helpful in making contact with members who were in different categories such as writers of originals, westerns, comedies, and so forth. A director often helped me meet actors. Two friendly and intelligent agents arranged interviews with some of their clients. An actor would introduce me to some of his friends, and later I would interview them. It was a partly accidental, partly planned chain of contacts—decidedly not the random sample of a statistician. But picking names for a random sample out of a directory would have produced no interviews. Each one had to be carefully set up, through a contact. The interview took place in a studio office, in the home of the interviewee, or over lunch in a restaurant, but never on a set. Newspaper columnists and magazine writers often interviewed on the sets, and I had to differentiate myself from them.

Conversation was directed in a seemingly casual manner, and never completely directed. I began by getting the respondent to talk about the picture on which he was working and usually he was only too eager to do that. If he was currently not employed, we began on his most recent picture. I tried to get data on his specific role in its production, his relations with others working on it, his attitudes toward them and to his own role. From there we went on to his other occupational experiences in Hollywood, to his work background before going there, and to his general goals. His values came out directly or indirectly, as did also his feelings about their realization or lack of it. Often the "leads" came spontaneously. Among the best interviews, in both quality and quantity of data, were those with a gifted and well-known director, who definitely directed the interviews, which he gave me once a week for a month. He had the time because he had just finished a picture and had not yet started another. I had waited three months for this free period.

Usually I took no notes during an interview and followed the Mississippi pattern of driving around the corner and, sitting in the car, writing it up roughly. Within twenty-four hours, the interview was part of a dictaphone record, later transcribed by a secretary. This was the first field experience in which I did not have to spend many hours at the typewriter.

Most people talked freely about themselves and their roles in moviemaking for a number of reasons. The gifted individuals had a high level of frustration, and frustrated people generally love to talk. Some, who came from Europe or from the Broadway stage, were helpful because they saw Hollywood in the perspective of other societies. Others were good respondents for exactly the opposite reason, their naïveté—they knew not what they said. A few others had long been disturbed by the chaotic complexity of Hollywood and enjoyed discussing it. There are, in addition, two basic reasons underlying success in all field work: most people love to talk about themselves and rarely have enough opportunities to do so; and they are flattered at having their opinions taken seriously.

Respondents talked about each other as well as about themselves. It was therefore possible to see a subject not only through his own eyes, but through those of his friends, acquaintances, co-workers, and bosses, and to catch glimpses of him in roles outside the making of a movie. In this way I learned the current status of anyone in the movie colony. The sketches of individuals in my book on Hollywood are portraits of real people (with fictitious symbolic names) based on an integration of the data they gave me with what I learned from other sources, and on any intuitive insight I had of their personalities.

A significant omission from the sample of interviewees was representatives of the front office. With the exception of one atypical front-office executive (who has long since left Hollywood), the few interviews with the powerful men at the top in major studios resulted in only superficial data and impressions. Many would not consent to be interviewed at all and others agreed only if their public relations aide was present—not an interview in my estimation. Accordingly, I never knew the top level of the Hollywood hierarchy, as I had known its equivalent in all other field work. I was well aware of the lack of direct contact with the most powerful segment of the social structure, but all efforts to include it were rebuffed.

On the other hand, there was an abundance of gossip, folklore, stories, and jokes—probably some true, many clever, all hostile—which circulated about the top executives, and these tales far exceeded those about any other groups, including stars. Almost no one in Hollywood had a good word to say for the front office. The fulsome flattery to their faces had its opposite side in hostile jokes behind their backs. The folklore and jokes revealed the attitudes of those who told them, and the shared hatred of the front office seemed to be a bond between the tellers of the tales. But anecdotes could hardly substitute for direct contact with the subjects.

The picture of the front-office executives given by everyone else was of men without gifts or talents, driven by a lust for domination over people and films, and by a desire for enormous profits. I can now only guess at the reasons they did not want to be interviewed. Perhaps they thought they were too important. Then, too, accustomed to the protective care of public relations aides, the front-office executives may have feared the prospect of facing directly a prying social scientist. They did not suffer the frustrations of the artists, neither did they have the naïveté of some of their employees, nor were they interested in unraveling the sociological complexities of Hollywood. What could they gain from talking to me?

However, the realities of the power struggle all along the assembly line of creation—between producer and writer, director and actor, everybody and the front office—and the relationship of this struggle to the final product, the movie, became increasingly apparent during the study. It became equally clear that the personalities and values of the individuals, as well as their positions in the hierarchy, were significant for the form and content of the movie. There were those who accepted the social structure and their place in the power hierarchy, and did as they were told, while others—a minority—struggled, with varying degrees of success, to manipulate the structure and to leave their own mark on the picture. I was much interested in the exceptions, who often highlighted the norm. These two unequal groups illustrated well the paradox in movie-making: a creative process which was also a big business with an assembly line for production.

Among the exceptions was a successful movie writer who became disgusted with the quality of the movies made from the scripts he wrote to the orders of the producer and the front office. He quit, even though it meant giving up a large salary without anything to take its place. This action was unusual. For many people, even a threat of suspension sufficed to bring them to heel, not only because of the loss of salary, but also because the studio was their whole life and apart from it they were lost. But this writer took a vacation to think and to plan what he would do. The front office of the studio where he had been working wired him an offer to be a producer-writer which carried the power to produce his own scripts. He accepted the offer and was able to work on pictures which he could respect, and which, incidentally, were also profitable. Sometimes the front office permitted a dissatisfied talented writer or director to do one picture as he wanted, in order to keep him. The premise of the front office was that such a film would be a flop and then the artist would have learned a lesson. However, such a picture was not infrequently a box office, as well as an aesthetic, success, and thereafter the writer or director had a broader choice of material and of working conditions.

I found that the sociological problem of the content of movies, with which I had started, was fused with the aesthetic problem of all drama and story telling—the inner truth of character and plot. The latter was more apt to be achieved when a talented man (director, writer, or, occasionally, actor) gained sufficient control to use the medium as a form of self-statement. The trend towards becoming producer-writer, director-actor, producer-director-actor, producer-director-writer, and towards independent production (apart from the major studios) had begun when I was in Hollywood and I viewed it as promising.

Interviews with many writers, directors, and actors in the minority group of artists (those who did not accept the social structure) revealed certain personality traits in common which must have been formed long before they ever saw Hollywood. First of all, they wanted to do something more than make a lot of money. They were not uninterested in financial rewards, but they had a deep drive to project their own fantasies (rather than those of a producer or a front-office executive) on to the films they made and to illuminate a segment of life as they saw it. Their values were deeply rooted, they had courage, they

were willing at times to oppose the powerful men at the top
and to take chances.

The run-of-the-mill writer, director, or actor, however, was
quite different. So many people worked on a picture that it
emerged as a hodgepodge without the stamp of any personal
idea or fantasy, unless it was that of a top executive who had
the final say. The people who worked, seemingly without protest, on the assembly line varied: artists, satisfied not to function as such or according to their ability, mediocre people who
had neither ability nor point of view, and pretentious frauds.
The primary concern of all was a large salary. Data on them
and on the detailed functioning of the assembly line came not
only from interviews, but also from filing cabinets.

An important one was the file of the Screen Writers' Guild
on the arbitration of screen credits, to which the Guild gave
me access. When many writers worked on one script (as often
happened), the awarding of credit might be difficult, and any
writer who had worked on the film had the privilege of object-
ing to the studios' award. The case then went for arbitration to
a rotating panel of three members of the Screen Writers' Guild.
Hearings were not oral, but consisted of communications from
the writers involved and from other relevant studio people. The
relations of writers with each other, with the producer, sometimes with the director, and, occasionally, with a star, were
recorded from as many points of view as the number of people
concerned. The recorded hearings provided excellent detailed
case histories of script writing, with a minimum of time and
energy expenditure on my part. The file also enabled me to
check on data from interviews.

In one case from the files, the executive head of a studio
purchased a novel, two story treatments, and a script from
another studio. He then employed Writer One to do a new
screen play which would conform to his and to the producer's
ideas. A director sat in on story conferences and contributed
his suggestions. But when the script was finished, the producer
and front-office executive did not like it and employed Writer
Two to do a new script. Later, two other writers were added,
one to polish the dialogue. At the end the executive, with no
experience in writing, rewrote much of the script. I saw the
result, a mediocre film from every point of view, although a

greater than usual amount of money was spent for its exploita-
tion. All the writers on this film earned large salaries, and those
I interviewed appeared to accept their roles as part of the
game.

In the office of the Production Code Administration of the
Producers' Association (MPPAA—Motion Picture Producers'
Association of America) was another filing record which I
thought would be relevant to this study. The staff members
charged with implementing the self-imposed code of morality
read all scripts and worked with producers from the beginning
of a film to the end, advising on those points they considered
unacceptable and often suggesting changes which would enable the film to receive the Association's seal of approval. In
the file for each movie was not only the correspondence about
the implementation of the code, but also a detailed record of
all conversations about it. In interviews I received only tidbits
about the implementation of the code on this or that picture,
but never the whole story, which often covered many months
of conferences and exchange of letters. I therefore had an eye
on the file, but was told it was completely secret, and that absolutely no one outside of the Production Code office had access
to it. There did not seem to be anything I could do about
seeing this file.

Then one day the Producers' Association unexpectedly offered me a job. I had met a few of their staff to whom I happened to mention my analysis of movies in terms of culture
patterns. The Association, threatened by pressures from the
Legion of Decency and other would-be censors of movies,
thought it would be helpful to have an objective content analysis of them, and asked me to do the job. I immediately declined. Startled, the vice-presidents asked me if I was not even
going to consider it. Realizing I had made a *faux pas*, I hastily
said that I would give it serious consideration and let them
know my final decision in a week's time.

When we met again I played my role better, telling the vice-
presidents how much I regretted that I could not accept the
position. Shocked, they upped the salary and held out many
other inducements of what my future might be with the Producers' Association. I still refused. The reasons were: I was too
interested in my research project to stop working on it or to
give it part time, as was then suggested; it would not have been

good to be aligned with any one group, such as the Producers'
Association or a guild; working for the Producers' Association
was not my idea of a desirable professional future. At first I
said nothing to anyone about the offer, but then I told a half-
dozen people—in great confidence! By the end of a week many
knew of the Association's offer, and that I had said "No." In
the retelling, the tale was much exaggerated in regard to the
offered salary. A frequent interpretation was that the producers
had tried to "buy" me off. This, I think, was incorrect. They
really wanted and needed a content analysis of the movies
they were making. But regardless of the motive for the offer,
saying "no" was unusual in Hollywood and my prestige
went up.

More important was my manipulation of the situation. One
of the men working for the Association considered himself a
sort of sociologist (although with little formal training); when
he heard that I had refused the offer, he phoned to congratu-
late me on my good sense in turning it down. He seemed
almost too delighted and I wondered if he had feared me as a
possible rival. A few days later I dropped in to see him. Again
he congratulated me, and again his satisfaction was apparent.
As I arose to leave, he asked if there was anything he could do
for me. I casually replied that it would be helpful to have
access to the files which recorded the implementation of the
Production Code. I was indeed pleased when my acquaintance
smiled and said he thought he could get the necessary permission.

A few days later he phoned and told me everything was okay
and to come over. Taking me down to the filing room, he introduced me to the head clerk, and told her to give me the file on
any movie I wanted. Leaving the room he said, "It's all yours,"
and winked. He was a small, serious, prim man, and the wink
was decidedly out of character. For a while I sat at the table
with a file in front of me, wondering about the wink and his
remark. Could it mean that he was using me to get back at
the Producers' Association? Previously I had vaguely sensed
some hostility in him to it. Whatever his motivation, the files he
had opened to me were rich in data. I spent a half-day each
week in the filing room until I had the needed material. (In
both the Screen Writers' and the Production Code files, I was
under obligation not to mention the name of the movie, studio,

or people.) From the file of the Producers' Association came the chapter, "Taboos," in my book.

Data from interviews and filing cabinets were supplemented by a limited and rather superficial observation and participation. Occasionally, I went on a set and watched the director, actors, camera man, script-girl, and the many technicians involved in the shooting of a small scene. But repetition of this kind of observation neither gave new data nor deepened my understanding. The few hours on a set did not enable me to feel even vicariously the genuine excitement which at times pervades the making of a movie. I knew about it intellectually, primarily through interviews with creative directors. The transferring of an image, originating in a novel or script and taking form in a director's mind, to the screen where it will be seen by millions of people *is* exciting. But I did not feel it, in the way I felt the emotional impact of religious services in a Negro church in rural Mississippi.

The observer's role, as well as the participant's, was lacking in my Hollywood study. I did not *see* and *hear* people in actual work and life situations. Instead, I learned through interviews: people told me what happened when they worked on a movie and of their reactions. I had similar useful data through the files. In all field work I have relied on interviews and, when available, on written sources of information. But except in Hollywood, these were always combined with, and related to, participant observation of spontaneous life situations. What people told me and what I read was constantly checked with what I saw, heard, and experienced, just as the latter was checked through interviews. Equally important, I lacked in Hollywood the deep feeling tone of the society which a field worker acquires through constant observation and participation. I never felt its culture in my bones, as in Lesu with my continuous participant observation in daily secular and ritual life.

In order to be more on the inside, I considered accepting a job as script writer which was offered me. But I declined because I knew of the strong possibility that I would spend my days isolated in a studio office, only to leave the studio with little more data than could be gained from chit-chat and gossip with other writers in the lunch room. I could get that without taking a job.

Nor was participation in social life as rewarding for research as it was in other field work. In Hollywood, there was no more or less permanent group. Relatively few people were indigenous; they came and they left; personal and professional relations were constantly shifting. It is difficult for an anthropologist to get a toe-hold in this kind of "community." However, it was easy to observe casual inter-personal relations dominated by pseudo-friendliness; the "darling" and "sweetheart" terms of address and demonstrations of affection and love in situations of hostility, hatred, and lack of respect; the crude domination and the sycophantic dependency. I knew about, but did not participate in, the continuous cycle in which people were together in work, in weekending, in love and sex relations, horse racing, card-playing, drinking, and so on.

Some social life was different, and I participated in it a bit. Dinner and long evenings of discussion with a gifted English writer whom I had known slightly in my student Bloomsbury days were always pleasant and rewarding. He had a hard brilliance which illuminated all discussions of Hollywood with him. Others writers I knew gave elaborate dinner parties in upper-class style. But conversation was usually dull and the gossip repetitious. Only occasionally was a little data gleaned, such as the time I heard two talented writers go into a long serious huddle over a problem in a script for which neither had any respect.

A few parties were personally enjoyable. Among the latter were those given by a European woman, a writer, to whom I had an introduction from an old friend of hers in New York. She was not in the high salary-prestige group, and food at her parties was always simple. But the occasions approached the European salon in style, and the guests were all creative, regardless of their salary bracket. The high light for me at one of her supper parties was meeting Charlie Chaplin, a hero of mine since the days of the silent film. He seemed to be genius incarnate, and I could not keep my eyes from his face and hands, the most expressive I have ever seen. He pantomimed his formal butler and a process server from the sheriff's office who was trying to reach him in a paternity suit; he sang Cockney songs and was the center of the stage for the whole evening. One of the other guests—a playwright—told me later that Chaplin was playing to me, the only stranger at the party and, obviously, an admiring one. I did not ask for an interview because I was almost certain that it would not have contributed to my knowledge of the social structure of Hollywood. But meeting him and having a sense of his great vitality (he had just passed his sixtieth birthday) and of his genius in a face-to-face contact was exciting and gave me a feeling of euphoria.

I had friends in a small circle of actors whose parties were enjoyable for their gaiety. From them I had a sense of the actor's personality and of his deep need to act. At one party, a well-known comedian said, "Why can't we be intellectual tonight, when we have an anthropologist to talk to?" The others booed! We played charades, as usual. I liked them for their spontaneity and lack of pretension.

Although friendly with a number of people, I had no intimates as I have had in all other field work. No sense of mutual identification, so productive in understanding both an individual and his society, existed with even one person. Close friendships were rare in Hollywood, I was told. I had friends in the anthropology department of U.C.L.A., where I was teaching part-time, and a small number of other acquaintances and friends outside the movie industry. I enjoyed these contacts and thought they were of value as an antidote to Hollywood. Now I question this value. I had one foot in my own world and was functioning in it. I was never totally immersed in Hollywood as I have been in other field situations.

However, from interviews, files, a limited number of friendly contacts, and a minor degree of participation certain problems and issues emerged quite clearly: the assembly-line method of creation, the struggle for power and domination, the star system, the self-imposed code of morality for films and the amorality of most human relations, the 100 per cent guild organization in a company town, the diversity in values between artists and business executives, the phoniness of would-be artists. I knew the exceptions as well as the norms. I had some answers to my original problem of the relationship of the social structure of Hollywood to its movies. A book on Hollywood had taken form in my mind and I even had its title before I left there.

XXI

THE PSYCHOLOGICAL SIDE

As I wandered through the Hollywood maze, I saw myself as an objective scientist, and took pride in a Jovian detachment. Now, with hindsight, I know the situation was quite different.

As I left Hollywood after a year and drove past a sign marking the boundaries of Los Angeles, I burst into song, as is my habit when feeling joy. But even that reaction did not make me realize how deeply I had hated the place. When leaving other field sites, I have usually been both glad and sorry—glad to depart because I have been tired and fed-up; sorry to leave my friends and life in the field. Except for the Hollywood situation, I have never been joyous on leaving, nor have I hated a society I studied. Although it might be difficult, there is no reason why an anthropologist could not study a society he hated, so long as he was aware of his feelings at the time, and was able to cope with them. But my rage was bottled up, and never fully conscious.

I happen to be a person of strong feelings, and it might have been predicted from the previous conditioning of my personality that I would feel rage in Hollywood. The plunge into the labor movement had been a rebellion from authority in the family and against the subjugation of unorganized workers by employers. Nor was it irrelevant that World War II, in which we fought a totalitarian concept of man, had just ended before I went to Hollywood, or that I had always been (and still am) concerned with the moral problem of freedom. I had, also, always been hostile to a way of life in which the accumulation of wealth was the primary motive. My identifications had long been with scientists and artists, and I have never seen any real ideological or temperamental incompatibility between them.

But I played it cool, as today's jargon would express it. I pretended a role of amused detachment. I knew, of course, that the fraudulence of the human relations, the treatment of people as property, the debasement of taste, and the whole dehumanization which occurred in the making of most movies were foreign to my values. But instead of letting my deep feelings spill over into rage, I felt superior. I now wonder what would have happened if the men at the top of the power hierarchy had been accessible to me. It is possible that I might have acquired a feeling of compassion that would have allowed me to get inside their roles and then detach myself, as I had done with white planters in Mississippi. Or I might have seen that the behavior of the front office did not necessarily spring wholly from malice, but could be the all-too-frequent denegation of the talented by the untalented.

My role as a field worker was also affected by the fact that the Hollywood study attracted more attention than anything I had ever done. Colleagues and people outside the academic world were intrigued by the idea of an anthropologist studying Hollywood. Unfortunately, I, too, became intrigued with playing a role and doing something unusual. In no other field work had this happened. I had merely followed my interests and my profession: any other role-playing was secondary and incidental.

Given my personality, it was inevitable that I should be on the side of the artists in their struggle against the power of the front office, and this attitude was not detrimental to the study of the artists. Through my identification with them, I was able to get inside their roles, then detach myself and see them with considerable objectivity. The best parts of the book on Hollywood are the chapters on directors and actors, precisely because I was openly and consciously identified with them.

It had not taken me long to learn that the director was the key person and belonged to movie-making in an organic sense. Even without actually seeing directors at work, I was able to understand their creative excitement in interviews and to be sympathetic with their frustrations. The chapter on directors gives far more data on the creative ones than their number warranted. But they were the key to understanding the translation of a fantasy into a film. Furthermore, the relationship between director and actors is natural, i.e. indispensable for the making of the film, and not imposed by the financial power structure.

I quickly understood a basic fact about actors: that acting is a way of life for them. I saw them as human beings with the kind of personality whose needs were best met by acting. Whether the script and directors were good or bad, the actor usually did the best he could and thus maintained his integrity as an artist. Acting was essential to his being fully alive. This I could understand. Field work, writing, teaching are among the ways in which I feel alive.

Then, too, I saw actors, regardless of their success or wealth, as an underprivileged group; many of them knew they were looked down upon by other members of the Hollywood hierarchy. In the chapter, "Actors are People,"[1] I discussed their resentments to the seven-year contract, by which they were legally owned by the studio for that period, and to being treated as synthetic products of publicity and make-up departments, camera man, producer, director, and front office. The talented artists were deeply sincere about their work, and I related to them easily. Naturally, I met and interviewed many actors without much ability, who were of interest only as they represented certain types. But they intrigued me, too. The actor's personality was new to me and I was constantly trying to understand him.

I think, too, that I was not immune to the charm and "glamor" of some of the actors. I remember interviewing a handsome well-known actor, as we lunched beside a pool. I wondered if any observer would call that work! However, the interview did produce good data, as did similar ones.

My relationship with writers, however, was quite different from that with directors and actors. Although closer by temperament and profession to the writers than to any other group in Hollywood, I failed to identify with them or to get inside their roles. The producer-writer relationship was not functional in the social structure as was that of director-actor. As I interviewed producers and writers and read the files on the arbitration of screen credits, the cliché of the writer being the producer's lead pencil seemed, and was, only too true. I was

---

[1] Hortense Powdermaker, *Hollywood, the Dream Factory* (Boston: Little, Brown & Co., 1950).

indignant at the writers for getting into this position and *horrified* when I found gifted writers (whose work before coming to Hollywood had been literature) working on admittedly mediocre scripts and taking them *seriously*. But was this any different from the actor taking his role in a mediocre film with seriousness? Obviously not. For both it was a way of preserving some measure of self-respect. But at the time I did not see this. I wrote that the writers had become "soft," that they sacrificed their integrity as artists for monetary rewards. To a large extent, this may have been a true value judgment, i.e. for those who were artists and who possessed integrity. But indignation limited my understanding.

I duly listened as the writers told me of the compensations they enjoyed: for the first time they were free of debt, able to buy pretty clothes for their wives, save money for the education of their children, and, in general, live in upper-class comfort. All this left me "cold"; I wrote, "the creative person who functions as such has to make some sacrifices." [2]

Many of the writers not only experienced a prosperity unknown before coming to Hollywood, but also enjoyed, for the first time, participation in an occupational group. Writing is generally a lonely condition. But in Hollywood writers were with each other in the studio dining room and at conferences and, away from the studio, they had a lively social life among themselves; some were also active in the Screen Writers' Guild. Although "a producer's lead pencil," they enjoyed having an essential role in a multi-million-dollar industry and knowing that the film on which they worked reached a world-wide audience. Writers, gifted or not, talked quite honestly about the advantages of Hollywood for them. But I scornfully thought of the gifted ones as moral prostitutes and labeled many of their ideas about the advantages of Hollywood as rationalizations. The fact that most writers, left, center, and right politically, accepted the system, received satisfaction from it, and even defended it, primarily because of financial rewards, or for the glamor of being part of Hollywood (though they also lampooned it), put them beyond the pale for me—not a favorable situation for understanding. I could not step outside their

---

[2] *Ibid.*, p. 136.

roles for objective analysis because I had never been inside them.

I was (and am) a writer. Writing is a way of life for me. The writers had let me down, because they had not come up to my expectations of professional integrity. Yet, I had understood and objectively studied white Mississippians whose standards of behavior towards Negroes certainly lacked integrity and were far different from mine. Why were my reactions to the Hollywood writers and to the white Mississippians (both members of my own race and culture) so different? The behavior of each cut clearly across my strongly held values. But in Mississippi, I knew quite consciously that I might have behaved like the white people if I had lived there all my life. I was glad that this had not been the case, and felt compassion for the whites. This was in sharp contrast to my "holier-than-thou" attitude towards the Hollywood writers.

In looking back upon the Hollywood field work, I think I was unconsciously threatened by the writers. Perhaps I had wanted to become one of them but would not admit it. Unconscious envy usually underlies a "holier-than-thou" attitude. It was inevitable that I should be involved with the writers, since I regarded myself as one. The problem, however, was not in my involvement, but that I was unaware of its real nature. If I had been more aware, I might have been able to objectify the situation and to have studied it with more detachment.

In other field experiences I knew when I was involved. When I met a would-be lynching gang on a road in Mississippi, my involvement and wanting to save the Negro were so open that I had an anxious and sleepless night. But the next day I was able to get outside the situation and take notes. In Lesu I was quite aware of my personal involvement when my friend, Pulong, was critically ill; I took notes on my feelings, as well as on the ill woman, her husband and her relatives. Conscious involvements are not a handicap for the social scientist. Unconscious ones are always dangerous.

After the manuscript of the book was completed and accepted by the publisher, he suggested that I insert more comparisons with primitive societies. I had used only a few which were pertinent. I resisted the suggestion, arguing that I did not think more such comparisons were relevant. Then, against my better judgment, I accepted and implemented the publisher's suggestion, inserting many analogies with primitive societies which now seem out of place and weakening to the book. The profuse use of analogies was a gimmick, designed to make the book more popular rather than meaningful, and not too different from the gimmicks used in movie scripts. The possibility of popularity was not unpleasant. I had submitted to the Front Office!

My "holier-than-thou" attitude in Hollywood should have put me on guard, but, unfortunately, did not. I thought that objectivity was obtained by having as good a stratified sample as the situation permitted, allowing respondents to speak freely about their behavior and attitudes without any expression of my values, and recording as exactly as possible what they said. All these are necessary techniques, but do not insure a field worker's psychological mobility to step in and out of the roles of peoples with different value systems.

Is it possible for anyone—artist, social scientist, or reporter —to write both meaningfully and with objective detachment about Hollywood? Lillian Ross's superb reporting of the making of *The Red Badge of Courage* is the most objective writing I know on Hollywood.[2] In a sense she was doing for one picture what I had tried to do earlier for the social structure as a whole. Her success as a participant observer in following the making of an atypical film over a period of two years could be the envy of any field worker. She observed the interplay between John Huston, a fascinating and gifted director-writer, Gottfried Reinhardt, an intelligent, cyncial producer, and Dore Schary, intelligent and optimistic, in charge of the studio's production. She caught and portrayed well their creative excitement, frustrations, and compromises. The description of their relations with the front-office executives is much less detailed and more second-hand, although penetrating. Powerful Louis B. Mayer did not want to make the picture, but the still more powerful Nicholas M. Schenk in the New York office of Loew's, Inc., supported Dore Schary so that the latter would learn by making a mistake, i.e. making a picture that would be a financial

---

[2] Lillian Ross, "Picture" in her *Reporting* (New York: Simon & Schuster, 1964). First published as, "Onward and Upward with The Arts" in *The New Yorker,* May 24th, 31st, June 7th, 14th, 21st, 1952.

flop. But objective as her report was, reviewers referred to its subjects as "victims" and wrote that she would not be welcome in Hollywood again.

Viewing my Hollywood field work in retrospect, I think it succeeded to a considerable degree in describing the social structure in which movies were made and the manner in which this structure influenced their quality, form, and content. My point of view as a humanist and my concern with the human and social costs of movie making gave meaning and strength to the book. Identification with artists enabled me to understand and present their roles, their frustrations, and their occasional victories in a factory producing fantasies. Many readers praised the book for its portrayal of the artists' position in the United States. But I think of what the book might have been if some of my involvements had not been hidden, if I had possessed the psychological mobility and the sociological opportunity to enter and understand all the contending groups, if my value system had not so aggressively dominated the whole study, if I had known more humility and compassion.

PART V

NORTHERN RHODESIA, NOW ZAMBIA

INTRODUCTION:
Why Africa and the Mass Media?

Hollywood was "water under the bridge," but my sociological interest in the mass media remained. Giving a course on mass communications at Queens College increased my knowledge of the literature; a class in field methods studied the attitudes of fellow students towards the mass media and produced a few hypotheses; chairing an interdisciplinary conference on mass communications under the auspices of the Wenner-Gren Foundation for Anthropological Research and editing the Proceedings added to my perspective. And through the work of David Reisman and others I became increasingly aware of a related problem: the significance of leisure in contemporary society.

A sabbatical was due in 1953–54 and it occurred to me to combine my interests in the mass media and in social change with a dormant one in sub-Saharan Africa, where I had long wanted to do field work. Certainly, Africa was an excellent area for studying change, and the choice of leisure activities— traditional or modern—could be used as an index to it. Because of the voluntary nature of leisure activities, it could be assumed that choice was based on values and need; in the case of movies and radio, choice would not necessarily be determined by the level of education, as in reading. The problem— basically one of changing values and needs—was well within my cultural-psychological interests, and I was intrigued by its exploratory nature.

Next came the selection of an area in which mass media were readily available. They were functioning in many African areas and I decided on Uganda, for a number of reasons: I knew more about it than any other part of Africa; it was possible to study Swahili, the *lingua franca,* in advance, which I did through records; my old friend and former classmate at the L.S.E., Audrey Richards, was head of the East African Insti-

tute of Social Research in Kampala and assured me when I
wrote her of help in getting started. A fellowship from the
Guggenheim Foundation and my sabbatical half-pay provided
the necessary support.

But now, as in my first field work, conditions beyond my
control interfered with the choice of locale. Just before I left
New York, a letter from Audrey Richards informed me that
conditions in and around Kampala were not as good for my
study as when we corresponded earlier, and that she was unexpectedly coming to "the States" as a visiting professor. She
added that the Institute would be more or less closed during
her absence and that no one would be around to give me any
help. She suggested that I go to Northern Rhodesia where the
Information Department had a significant program in radio
broadcasts for Africans, and she mentioned that Mr. Brelsford,
its director, would be interested in my study and helpful. His
avocation was anthropology, with several papers to his credit;
she was writing him about my project.

My knowledge of contemporary Northern Rhodesia was decidedly not extensive. I had read the standard old monographs
on the Bemba, Lozi, Ila, and other tribes, but I was not *au
courant* with the recent literature or with the contemporary
situation, although I knew vaguely about the dominant copper
mines. More important was my total ignorance of any of the
vernacular languages, and the lack of time to learn one. In less
than a month I was sailing for England en route to Africa,
and was engulfed in the innumerable chores which accompany
leaving home and college for a year. I vaguely hoped that while
in London I would find that it was still feasible to go to Uganda.

But Mrs. E. M. Chilvers, research secretary at the Colonial
Office, and a few other knowledgeable people whom I met in
England, thought Northern Rhodesia far better for my problem. At Mrs. Chilvers' suggestion, I attended a Cambridge
conference of administrators from British Africa, listened to
their discussions, and talked over the research problem with
a few of them, among whom was Mr. G. S. Jones, Commissioner
of Native Affairs in Rhodesia (later Sir Glyn Jones, Governor
of Nyasaland). Naturally, I also talked to British anthropologists who had worked in Northern Rhodesia, although none had
been there recently. I bought the newer anthropological books

on that area to read on the voyage to Cape Town. Although knowledgeable about the research problem, I was decidedly less prepared on the exact area than on any previous expedition.

But I was more interested in the problem than in a particular location in Africa, and decided to pick the best site for that. Anthropology had moved (and I with it) a long way from the time when the major emphasis was on the selection of an area, and finding the problem after one arrived. Besides, the intensive reading on neighboring Uganda and a more or less general knowledge of Africa made Northern Rhodesia not completely unknown. I counted, too, on my many years of field experience to be of help in a new area and situation. The biggest handicap was that I did not know the vernacular language in the newly selected area. But the fact that the research problem was relatively well planned, plus a natural optimism and the chance to fulfill a very old desire to go to Africa, helped reduce anxieties.

Exhausted from running around to see anthropologists, colonial administrators, and a few old friends, I boarded the ship at Southhampton with relief. Mr. and Mrs. G. S. Jones, whom I had met at the Cambridge conference, were friendly fellow passengers, returning to Lusaka from their leave. I learned that they had been in Northern Rhodesia for more than twenty years, and that he had started his civil service career there as a district officer in the "bush." Naturally, I was interested in everything they told me about the country. Before we debarked at Cape Town, they invited me to stay with them in Lusaka, after they were back in their home.

XXII

FIRST MONTH IN
NORTHERN RHODESIA

Upon arrival in Cape Town, I flew directly to Lusaka. The flat town looked a bit like my imaginary picture of our pioneer midwestern towns, but with many differences. The government buildings (some temporary wooden shacks, others permanent stone), the neat bungalows, the paved streets ending in dirt roads, an elegant first-class hotel on the outskirts of town were all in sharp contrast to the compound with its huts and houses for Africans. It was the dry season and vegetation was a dusty brown. Lusaka being a capital, the large majority of Europeans were civil servants.

I stayed first as a guest at the Rhodes-Livingstone Institute, several miles from town, as Mrs. Chilvers had arranged before I left London. Its library was excellent for my purpose as were some of its director's published and unpublished surveys. But arriving in a new field area, I could not spend all my time reading in a library and I found the Institute's remoteness from both African and European life depressing. I moved to the more cheerful government hostel in town for a few days, and after that to the home of Mr. and Mrs. Jones.

To my great disappointment, Mr. Brelsford, who, according to the last letter from Audrey Richards, was eagerly awaiting my arrival, had been transferred to Salisbury. However, he had left a memo about my contemplated project with the new Acting Director of Information, who kindly made contacts for me with the heads of the radio, cinema, and publications bureaus for Africans. Most interesting was Broadcasting House with its highly intelligent and dedicated European and African staff. I interviewed them, read their reports, and watched the tape-recording of a play. The director and his assistant were friendly and conversations and interviews with them always rewarding. The director's home was the only one in Northern Rhodesia where I met an African socially—a member of his staff.

The able, intelligent staff (European and African) at the Publications Bureau provided useful data, through interviews, conversations, and written reports about their work. I was particularly interested in one of the senior African assistants who wrote many of their small booklets for distribution among literate Africans. He was cordial and I arranged to see him for an hour a day to learn something of his background and his reasons for choosing certain themes for the booklets. He agreed to summarize (in English) their contents and he set his own price for this work, to be done after I left Lusaka. All went well for four days, but on the fifth he refused to speak to me. The preceding day our relationship had been pleasant and without incident, and I could not account for the change. The member of the European staff who had introduced me could only explain that Africans were mysterious and unknowable. I could not accept this "explanation." But I wondered whether I would encounter more of this kind of behavior; fortunately, it remained an isolated incident. If I had stayed in Lusaka, perhaps the mood of this African would have changed again and I could have had an explanation.

The staff in charge of cinema for Africans had no interest in the possible sociological impact of movies on the audience, but were concerned almost exclusively with the purchase of films in a "package" from South Africa and in arranging for them to be shown. Rural cinema tours were part of their activities and when I learned that one would be leaving shortly, I asked for, and received, permission to accompany it.

During these first few weeks I was busy, but restless and a bit discouraged by the difficulties in finding a suitable locale for work. Lusaka, the capital, was too atypical to even consider. I went hither and thither by local plane to various urban centers, such as Livingstone and Ndola. The last town seemed better than the others I visited, and while I was looking it over, a young British anthropologist, Bill Epstein, working in the nearby mining town of Luanshya, came over to see me. I asked him about the feasibility of my working on the Copperbelt,

which seemed to be the best locale for my research. The mine
townships were apparently setting standards for change. Radio
listeners were many, movies popular, and a not-insignificant
proportion of Africans were literate and reading newspapers.
Moreover, I had never been to a mining community and liked
the idea of a new experience. Bill Epstein's description of
Luanshya—the site of the Roan Antelope Mine Township—and
his kind offer to share the large nine-room house which he
occupied were the final reasons for the choice of Luanshya.
I had been told by everyone that it was practically impossible
to find a house in any of the mine townships. The Rhodes-
Livingstone Institute rented the large Luanshya house for its
workers and I agreed to pay half its rent to the Institute.

By this time I knew that formal permission would have to
be secured to work on the Copperbelt. By coincidence and
good luck, I had a letter to Sir Ronald Prain, who turned out
to be the Chairman of the Board of Directors for the Rhodesian Selection Trust, which included the Roan Antelope mine
in Luanshya. The husband of an old English friend from my
L.S.E. days had given me the letter of introduction, just as I
was boarding the ship at Southhampton, and there was no
time to even ask who was Sir Ronald Prain. In Lusaka, when
I asked the question of a government official, the answer was,
"Only the most important man in Northern Rhodesia!" The
situation had similarities to my letter of introduction to Will
Percy in Mississippi. After the conversation with Bill Epstein,
I returned to Lusaka and looked up Sir Ronald immediately.
He was away; his secretary expected him shortly but did not
know the exact date.

In the meantime, the cinema van was about to go on its tour.
I left the itinerary with Sir Ronald's secretary so she could
wire me when he returned. (He might not stay long in Lusaka
and I had to be certain about meeting him.) The tour through
the Western and Northern Provinces was planned to show,
very belatedly, a film of Queen Elizabeth's coronation. An old
Chaplin film, "The Skating Rink," and a news commentary
were included in the program.

The cinema van was a lorry, and the party consisted of Mr.
Rogers, a European technician, Kasabo, an African driver, and
deBeer, a "colored man" (i.e. mixed racial background) who

ran the projection machine. It was soon apparent that Mr.
Rogers was not comfortable with either Europeans, Africans,
or "colored." He appeared to resent the higher social status of
District Officers and District Commissioners and to be afraid
of Africans; he insisted on always calling me "Professor" and
I could not put him at ease. He parroted the "firm but just"
line without understanding, and talked of the danger of "cod-
dling" the Africans. My giving a couple of aspirins to the
African driver when he complained of having a fever disturbed
Mr. Rogers. Under these circumstances I resigned myself to
making almost no contact with the driver or the operator of
the projection machine. The latter looked bored most of the
time, but came to life at night when he operated the machine.

The tour lasted only about a week but was decidedly rewarding: my first impressions of the country, of rural Africans
and of their reactions to movies, and of European district officers and commissioners. I took extensive notes on everything,
much as I had done upon arriving in Lesu.

The monotonous flat bush country on each side of the dusty
road became intensely interesting because Livingstone had
walked through part of it. I read his *Journal* (which I had with
me), trying to "see" the missionary-scientist walking through
the bush, being greeted by chiefs in a village, becoming ill and
suffering many other trials, but always taking notes, on fauna,
flora, and people. I had a pleasant sense of almost knowing him.

The D.O.'s and the D.C.'s were a new part of the social environment since Livingstone's time, and I found them diverse
and interesting. I already knew that Europeans would have to
be part of my study of social change, in much the same way
that white people were part of the Mississippi study. The first
government officials on the tour were at Fort Roseberry, where
we arrived about 4:30 in the afternoon. The government offices
closed at 4:00 P.M. and Mr. Rogers and I found the officials on
the golf links. They had not received the telegram about our
arrival, and now that we were there they could not have been
less interested. Resenting anyone who kept them from their
golf, they said they would see us in the morning. We then
went to a government rest house, the dirtiest place I had ever
seen. I looked at the bath tub and debated whether to exchange
the dust from the road for the dirt of the tub. No cleanser or

disinfectant was in sight. I decided not to bathe. The commissary run by the D.O.'s wife was not open. So we went to her home and borrowed some cans of food: dried milk, herring in tomato sauce, and pears—and a half-loaf of bread, a little butter, and tea. We boiled water over a kerosene burner, and as we were having our supper I felt envious of Kasabo and deBeer, each of whom were staying with friends in the village. I turned in at 8:30. The bedroom was dirty and very hot. Each of its two windows opened only to about four inches. Again I debated whether to sleep under the extremely dirty mosquito net canopy, or suffer the mosquitoes. I decided on the net with all its dirt. The night seemed endless, and I was glad to get up at six in the morning. On the way from the w.c. I met another guest who asked me if he could borrow my comb, since he had forgotten his. I obliged. He returned the comb and then asked for an aspirin, and again I obliged. He told me he was in public works and had only recently come to the country.

The cinema show supposed to have taken place the night of our arrival had been postponed until the following evening. Mr. Rogers was so mad about the dirty accommodations of the rest house that he threatened to leave immediately unless we had a better place to stay that night. The D.C. arranged for us to sleep the one night at the homes of government officials, and because his wife was away, I stayed at the home of the D.O. The latter was a young, rather good-looking Englishman, who expressed nothing but contempt for Africans, saying that they were "useless," "lazy," and had no "culture."

The rest house at Ft. Roseberry was the only uncomfortable experience of the tour. Other places, we stayed at clean, adequate rest houses or at the homes of government officers. These men varied. At Kasama a young D.O. was very different from the one at Ft. Roseberry. He had arrived from England two years previously, and was an unusually objective observer. He mentioned the highly stratified social life and class feeling among the small group of Europeans at Kasama and he talked about the tragedy of those Africans who had taken over European values and were then ignored and insulted by the givers of the values. He talked also at considerable length of the conflicts suffered by the government officials (and I thought he

was talking about himself) who do not believe in many of the
Federation's policies, which they nevertheless have to imple-
ment. A strong sense of justice, a sensitivity to the Africans'
position, and a desire to help them were sometimes in conflict
with official duties. He thought that Africans sensed the doubts
and anxieties of these Europeans and that this, obviously, did
not make the situation better. Then, he compared the situation
of the government officials to that of one of the characters in
Orwell's *1984*, who insisted for a long time that two plus two
makes four, but finally accepted that the answer is five, or
anything else "Big Brother" said. This young D.O. thought he
was "tough" and that he would not succumb. "But," he added,
"the people who do succumb are happier!"

At Luwingu, a small post with only three European families, the D.C. was still another type. A tall, blonde, intensely
serious man, in his late thirties or early forties, born in India
where his father was in the Civil Service, he seemed to have
stepped out of the pages of Kipling. When he was showing me
around the station, I was startled to see an African throw himself on the ground, lie on his back and softly clap his hands
together, the traditional greeting of a Bemba man to his chief.
It was the most servile, obsequious gesture I had ever seen.
The D.C. took it as his due. He thought he was born to command. Fearless, sure of his racial "superiority" and of the right-
ness of his role in carrying "the white man's burden," he knew
no doubts. He loved his way of life and his major problem was
how to avoid being promoted to an administrative post in the
capital. The worst thing he could imagine would be to spend
his time on paper-work. His wife also enjoyed the bush life;
her last child had been born without medical attendance.

While the different types of D.O.'s and D.C.'s intrigued me,
my major interest was in the reactions of the African audiences
to the movies. At the first showing, I noted that the audience
talked all the time to each other (in the vernacular, of course),
so that the sound track could hardly be heard. At the second
place we stopped, I succeeded in having the District Officer
secure a few African clerks to move around in the audience
and take notes (later translated in English) on what the audience was saying. Since we stayed only one night in a place, it
was not possible to interview any African. The notes on the

conversations among the audience provided the first intimation
of their confusion over the reality and unreality of the film, a
confusion which involved an ignorance of the nature of acting.
This became one of the problems for further study. I noted
that the English spoken commentary was usually misunderstood, even by those who knew English, on those rare occasions
when it could be heard. The Chaplin film was the most popular, the "British News" the least popular and least understood.
The Africans were interested in the coronation film, but understood very little of it. Later, I was to find some differences
in urban audience reactions. For instance, in Luanshya, a
Chaplin film was regarded as appropriate only for children.
But further research on the reality or unreality of films, between documentary and fiction movies, indicated that the confusion existed also among urban audiences.

Towards the end of the week, I had a telegram from Sir
Ronald Prain's secretary that he was briefly in Lusaka and
would be glad to see me. Mr. Rogers, the cinema technician,
was suffering from an intestinal infection and had decided to
end the tour, anyway. He took me to the nearest airport and
I flew back to Lusaka.

The next day I lunched with Sir Ronald and Lady Prain.
He was interested in my research project, but mentioned the
difficulty of finding a place to live in any of the mine townships. When I mentioned that I could share a house with an
anthropologist in Luanshya, he immediately offered to write
an introduction to the general manager of the Roan Antelope
Mine, suggesting that I be given all possible cooperation.

I left for Luanshya in a few days. The nine-room house
which Bill Epstein had invited me to share was large enough
for each of us to go our own way. It was an advantage for
me to come into a functioning household, with a cook (even
though his culinary ability left much to be desired) and a "yard-
boy" who cut wood, did the laundry, and other odd jobs. I took
over the planning of meals and most of the marketing. During
the first month when I was feeling my way, I absorbed considerable background from Bill as I plied him with questions.
But as soon as I was actually started on the research, I worked
completely on my own, as did he. Part of the time he was away
in the rural areas. The menage ran smoothly without personal

problems. The differences in our ages was great enough to avoid the lifting of eyebrows. But the shortage of houses was such that the situation would probably have been accepted, even if the age difference had not existed.

Luanshya had two townships—municipal and mine, and the house was in the former. It was the more diverse, having government offices, churches, shops, banks, and other businesses, and provided more freedom. The mine township was a company town, limited to the mining operations and the homes of their employees, and subject to certain restrictions. The European employees, for instance, were not allowed to entertain Africans in their homes. On both townships the residences of Europeans and Africans were segregated, and, at that time, no anthropologist or any other white person would have been permitted to live in the African section of either.

After about a month in the Protectorate, I was settled in Luanshya. The month had seemed much longer, as I had the feeling of marking time or wasting it until I found a locale where I could settle. Looking back, my impatience seems unrealistic. Given the situation, I had done reasonably well and been lucky, and had learned a bit about the social contours.

XXIII

ENTRÉE
TO THE COPPERBELT

It was a relief to be away from Lusaka, and in a locale where I could settle and begin to work. From the beginning I liked Luanshya. It was on a plateau, with an elevation of five thousand feet, and I am at my best in a relatively high altitude. The sky with its continuously changing cloud formations seemed vast, yet close. Sunsets were beautiful and dramatic, with the mine smelters, shafts, and derricks silhouetted against the sky.

I had the sense of a complex social drama, with roles played by ten thousand African workers and their families, fifteen hundred European employees with their families, and management. Supporting roles were those of civil servants, missionaries, teachers, shopkeepers, and so forth, and a small group of Asiatic Indians. The latter, living in isolation from both Europeans and Africans, owned second-class shops which catered to the needs of Africans. The Indians appeared relatively insignificant in the social system, and, besides, there was no time to study them.

The segregated residential areas were strikingly different. Only the enormous ant hills were the same. The pleasant bungalow homes of Europeans were set in gardens, dry and brown when I arrived, but later, with the coming of the rains, colorful with tropical flowers. On the African "compound," as it was called colloquially, few flowers broke the monotony of the orderly rows of rectangular houses of white plastered sun-dried brick. The average house had two rooms and a lean-to kitchen. Communal bath and latrine facilities were in each section of the compound. A few African clerks and others of relatively high status occupied European-like bungalows. My first impression of the African compound was of its hard, stark, unaesthetic quality, compared to the small rural villages with their round thatch-roofed huts which seemed to be an intrinsic part of the physical environment. But the Africans, I later learned, much preferred their homes on the township. Houses on both mine townships were owned by the company and rented to employees. (Rents were on a substandard level.) The company provided all the utilities and amenities. For Africans, these included welfare centers—the main one having a movie theater, radio loud-speakers, library, tea-room, and dance hall —hospital, swimming pool, carpentry shop, beer hall, sports stadium, open-air market, stores, and others. For the Europeans, there was a club with its swimming pool, tennis courts, dining room, library, and large auditorium used for amateur theatricals and dances.

The only unsegregated area was the mine itself. Twenty-five hundred feet underground, reached by a "cage" (elevator), was the buried copper for which all the above existed. I was pleased to accept an invitation from management for an escorted tour underground. Wearing the protective male clothes and helmet, I followed my escort through the wet slippery mud, saw the Africans working with axe, shovel, and drill and drive the underground train. I was impressed by both the machinery and the human physical labor, and glad to have had the experience of being underground. It enabled me to understand better an African when he described his first reactions to being underground: "It looked like a rat's hole, and when you get down you are like a rat . . . You cannot see the blue sky but only rocks . . . I hope to get a job on the surface." On the surface were the smelter, concentrator, and power house. Underground and on the surface, Europeans and Africans worked together, with Europeans in the higher supervisory positions.

At the entrance to the African mining township was a sign, "Private Property, No Trespassing," confirming my impression of a company town. But the power structure was far from unitary. Organized power on the mine was wielded primarily by mine management and two unions—one of African miners and the other of European miners. The District Commissioner and his staff residing in the municipal township represented the power of the British Colonial Government. I needed approval and, if possible, the cooperation of all sides in the power hierarchy.

Sir Ronald Prain had made my contact with management easy. On the second day in Luanshya, I called on the general manager and described the research project. A study of the impact of the mass media was too innocuous to arouse much anxiety in anyone. However, he mentioned that he would like to see data collected on the mine property. Naturally, I had private reservations about showing raw data. But I later showed him and others who were interested the results of an initial survey concerning the mass media. After that he asked for no more data and I showed him none. At the end of my first week in Luanshya, his wife and he gave a dinner party for me at which I met many of the top personnel, most of whom were continuously helpful during the study. The situation and attitudes were quite different from Mississippi, where the white people had been afraid of what I might find out. Mine management was rather proud of the social system they had initiated, and of the new way of life they provided for their African employees. My impression is that the general manager trusted me not to cause "trouble," which to him meant influencing Africans against Europeans. If high-level Europeans in the mine hierarchy had distrusted me, work would have been far more difficult.

I called on the District Commissioner the same day that I saw the general manager. The D.C. turned out to be highly intelligent, knowledgeable, liked and respected by the Africans, and I was lucky to be in his province. He and his family were among my close European friends in the community. No real cordiality existed between them and the general manager and his family, but it was not difficult for me to maintain excellent relations with each. Missionaries were another group of Europeans with whom I later made contact, although their power had become minimal. But they were useful informants and had been important as the first carriers of modern values to Africans.

While in Luanshya, I worked within the European power structure of the mine and more or less "played it safe." Mine management on the Copperbelt had the power (and occasionally exercised it) to request a field worker to leave. Local mine officials were always worried about the possibility of a field worker upsetting the complex status quo between African miners and management, and, therefore, were sometimes unduly suspicious. It seemed obvious to me that suspicions could be eliminated or, at least, reduced if the anthropologist had friends among management and was open and frank with them about what he was doing. The same policy was equally important in relations with the African power structure. But some anthropologists said that they felt they had to "take sides" and that their side was that of the Africans. Actually, the situation was open, and it was quite possible to work with both groups and have friends in each. My impression was that some of the anthropologists took sides for the same reasons (personality factors) that I did in Hollywood, where it was also bad field technique. An exclusive identification with the under-dog (or with the top ranks) may prevent the necessary social, intellectual, and psychological mobility necessary for field work in a complex power structure.

In addition, I did not see how Europeans could be omitted from the study of contemporary urban African life, but at that time I was apparently the only anthropologist in Northern Rhodesia with that view. Western civilization was not completely unimportant in rural society either. One anthropologist, working in the latter, boasted about getting into a physical fight in a bar with a European because of the man's remarks about Africans. My answer was, "But you should have been taking notes."

In some ways the African power structure was more difficult to approach than was the European. I had been told over and over again of the suspicions of urban Africans towards the latter. I knew that the political Federation of Northern and Southern Rhodesia and Nyasaland had been forced on the Africans by white settlers and that the consequent hostile suspicions could be vented on any white person, including myself. Advice on how to make initial contact with the Africans differed. In England, an anthropologist had told me that the only way was through the African Mine Workers' Union. But in Lusaka I had heard enough gossip to make it clear that management was suspicious of anthropologists working closely with the union and I knew that management rather than the union had the final authority to decide who could do research on their private property. I tried, therefore, to think of a broader entreé into the African community.

Remembering the Mississippi field experience, I wondered about the possibility of entering through the African education department, and had talked this over with its head officer in Lusaka. He (a European) and his senior African assistant had thought it a good idea, and passed me on to the African education department in Ndola, the capital of the province in which Luanshya was situated. The Ndola European and African staff, also friendly and helpful, had given me an introduction to the African education officer in Luanshya. He called on me shortly after I arrived and turned out to be intelligent and poised, with a year's background of study in England. He suggested calling a meeting of African leaders for Saturday afternoon. I left the choice of personnel to him, since I did not know enough to make concrete suggestions. Among the fifteen at the meeting were teachers, trade-union officials, social workers, clerks, medical orderlies. All were considered members of the intelligentsia because of their education and occupational status. Most officials of the African Mine Workers' Union were former teachers and clerks; only rarely had one been a miner. The group were all under forty, and three were women. It was a better cross-section of African leadership and of the intelligentsia than the executive board of the mine workers' union, and far less apt to arouse the anxieties of mine management. (I more or less assumed that the latter would know everything I did.)

The meeting was held in a school house on the mine township, probably the most neutral setting in it. The African education officer, acting as chairman, introduced me as "Professor," a high status term among the literate Africans (and also among the Europeans). I explained what I planned to do and stressed that I was an American, and that I had no connection with the mines or with government. They seemed to understand and a few, particularly one school teacher, asked highly intelligent questions about the project. But then one man began asking questions indicating much suspicion: Where did my money come from? Would anyone control what I wrote? and so forth. I answered simply and truthfully that my funds came from the college sabbatical half-pay and from an American foundation, and that neither they nor anyone else had any control over what I wrote. The questioner was not satisfied and continued to raise points indicating mistrust. I did my best to remove his fears but was obviously unsuccessful. Finally one man, a trade-union official, interrupted and said he had not come to listen to Mr. X. orate and that he was tired of his suspicious questions; he added, "You have to trust some one— give the Professor a chance." [1] Mr. X. was silent and the others nodded their approval. I was relieved. The chairman was about to close the meeting when a man who had been silent rose and earnestly asked, "But *what* does your name, Powdermaker, mean?" I was pleased to give its derivation.

After the meeting I chatted informally with the people and talked at greater length with the man who had rescued me from the overly suspicious questioner and with the school teacher who had asked relevant questions about the research, inviting each to come and see me. Both became good friends and were helpful as informal, unpaid consultants. Later, the school teacher did some paid work, part-time, on the project.

I also met with the tribal elders who supposedly represented the leadership in the municipal African township. (Originally, I though of working on both mine and municipal townships, but most of the work was done on the latter because of lack of time.) When I mentioned my interest in the effect of the mass media, such as movies and radio, the elders became very articulate on the theme that movies were the cause of all their troubles with the young people. I thought back to the time when movies were considered by many as the cause of delinquency among young people in the United States. It was obvious that the tribal elders did not understand, and were disturbed by, their children and grandchildren, and that the movies were a convenient scapegoat as they had been in the United States. This was the only point that interested them. As a field worker, I listened and did not argue. But I privately contrasted the tribal elders with the young intelligentsia I had

---

[1] Later I learned that many African trade-union officers had been trained by English trade-union and labor party officials, either in England or Northern Rhodesia. Earlier, their first contact with Europeans had usually been in the mission schools which had given them their start in education. Whether for these or other reasons, officers of the mine workers' union, whom I met, were not unfriendly to Europeans.

met a few days before at the meeting on the mine township, to the disparagement of the former.

The problem of finding full-time assistants and an interpreter was far more difficult than getting the approval of the European and African leaders. I needed first an interpreter-assistant. Bemba was the *lingua franca* on the Copperbelt; English was a prestige language, spoken by a minority—those who had attained at least a Standard V (corresponding to our sixth grade) education. Bill Epstein and others had told me that it took a year to achieve a moderate fluency in Bemba, if one lived in a rural village where no other language was spoken. This obviously was not possible for me since I only had a year to spend in Africa. I discovered also that Bill, who knew Bemba well, and others like him who worked in this area, used paid African assistants to collect much of their data. Each anthropologist usually had several.

My need for assistants in Luanshya would have been urgent, even if I had known Bemba. How otherwise could an initial survey be made among thirty thousand Africans to discover the general patterns for the use of the mass media and the attitudes towards them? Handicapped by my ignorance of the Bemba language, I naturally wanted an interpreter, too. I mentioned my needs to everyone who I thought might be helpful. The intelligentsia had jobs, and what I had to offer was only temporary. Finally, a youth seventeen or eighteen years old appeared as an applicant. His major recommendation was the importance of his father, a judge in the local African court. The youth belonged to the Lozi tribe, but was proficient in Bemba; he had gone through Standard VI (our seventh grade) and his current job was as "pump boy" at a gas station. I was not impressed with him; he seemed too young, without sufficient education, and my intuitive reaction was that he would not be able to handle the job. Nevertheless, I decided to employ him because he was the only applicant, and I was beginning to feel desperate. I made it very clear that the employment was for a probationary period of one month to see how it worked for both of us.

At the end of the first week, I knew he was impossible, both as an interpreter and as an assistant. In the former function he was too slow, and in the latter, he did not appear sufficiently

able. He was unsuccessful in getting quite simple data by himself. His youthfulness and relatively low level of education were
probably the major reasons; his father's high status did not
make the Africans take him seriously. The same factors of age
and education were most likely responsible for his not understanding the training I tried to give him. Before the probationary month was half over, I told him that he could not continue
in employment at the end of it and gave his youthfulness as
the reason. During the remainder of the month I asked him to
collect popular songs to give him something easy to do. But
those he collected were, for one reason or another, unuseable
as data.

I regretted having gone against my intuition in employing
him, but I was not prepared for the trouble which followed.
Rumors began to circulate through the African township: he
was being fired because the household was Bemba and there
was a Bemba plot to get rid of him, a Lozi. (The cook was
Bemba, as were one or two of Bill Epstein's several assistants.)
Much more worrying was the next rumor: I had asked him to
peer into people's houses at midnight. This was associated with
a preliminary technique for kidnaping. A charge of kidnaping against an African or a European was disastrous. Much
disturbed, I went immediately to see the District Commissioner. He, too, thought the matter very serious. We knew
that if the rumor gained strength I could not remain on the
Copperbelt and that it might even follow me elsewhere. I saw
failure ahead, as I had on my first day in Indianola.

Fortunately, the District Commissioner knew how to handle
the matter. He asked the youth and his father, the court judge
(and an employee of the government) to come to see him that
afternoon. I was present, too. The District Commissioner described the rumors. There was no denial. Sternly he told father
and son that the rumors *had to stop.* He said that he would
do his best to have the youth get back his former job. The
rumors ceased. A week later the youth returned to being a
"pump boy" at the gas station and when I stopped for gas
(tipping him was customary) he smiled and was apparently
friendly. He and his father had seemed to think that the job
with me would lead quickly to high prestige. They were reluctant to accept the fact that the young man's low level of
education and his youthfulness made it impossible for him to

function adequately as a research assistant. I was grateful to the District Commissioner for getting me out of a dangerous situation, but annoyed with myself for not having followed my initial intuition of the youth's inadequacy.

I was still without an interpreter or assistant, and very discouraged. I also needed, temporarily, a large number of assistants for a survey to establish the basic patterns in the use of the mass media. In some situations a survey can best come in the latter part of the field work, to check on qualitative data. My survey of attitudes of white people in Mississippi had been of that nature. But in Indianola I knew far more when I started than I did at the same period in Luanshya. Almost no work had been done on the mass media in this part of Africa, and I felt the need first to establish certain basic patterns, such as how many people, and who, used each of the media, the preferred movies, radio programs, and newspapers, the reasons for not going to movies or listening to radio, and many other details about these forms of communicating modern culture. After the survey, I hoped for one or two good assistants to work with the non-English-speaking Africans while I worked with the English-speaking ones. The plan was fine, but where were the necessary assistants?

In desperation, I phoned the headmaster of the Munali boys' secondary boarding school in Lusaka, whom I had met there, and asked if he knew of any unemployed graduates in Luanshya or nearby. He said that students had just gone on vacation and gave me the name of one who could round up others in the town. I got in touch with him and told him of my needs, which he understood. The next day he appeared with six other Munali students, all in advanced standards of the secondary school. One had just left school, because of his father's recent death and his consequent lack of money to continue his education. The others had about five free weeks.

While impatiently waiting for assistants, I had, among other things, devised a tentative schedule for the survey, so I was prepared for the first meeting with the Munali students. They were bright and quick in understanding. I explained the purpose of the survey, and the different kinds of questions. The direct type was to elicit relatively simple factual data: (1) face information such as sex, tribe, approximate age, degree of education, rural or urban born, occupation, religion, and so forth, for possible correlations; (2) the use or non-use of the different mass media (radio, movies, newspapers), frequency among users, favorites in each of the media, and so on. Direct and indirect types of questions were used to get reasons for preferences, for not going to movies or listening to radio, attitudes toward being illiterate, and so on.

Informants were asked for concrete details about what they had last heard on the radio, seen in the cinema, or read in the newspapers. The next question was, "How do you feel about that?" I stressed the need for the interviewers to encourage the expression of opinions and attitudes, and to record verbatim everything that was said, and, also, any question not on the schedule asked by the interviewer. (This practice was discouraged.) Open-ended questions were designed to catch a wide range of attitudes about which neither the assistants nor I knew much in advance. The interviewing was to be done in Bemba, and then translated into English.

When we had finished discussing the schedule and the methods of interviewing, the sample, the pay, the daily quota of interviews, and the hours of working, the assistants elected a foreman whom I could contact quickly to relay a message to the group if necessary. These modern young men followed a traditional African custom, and selected the oldest one out of an age range from early to mid-twenties. His few years of seniority gave him automatically a position of minor leadership.

Before leaving this first meeting, the young men asked where I stood on the political issue of Federation. I answered the question truthfully, saying that I thought Federation was not in the interests of Africans. They were satisfied. I doubt if they would have worked for me if I had been pro-Federation. But I also made it clear that the study was apolitical, and that as a foreigner I could not participate in Northern Rhodesian politics. Many social scientists urge research workers to avoid all comments on political issues.[2] But, obviously, no rule can cover all situations in which such issues are involved.

The assistants came to my house at 8:00 A.M. daily (except Sunday) and handed in interviews done the previous afternoon

---

[2] For example, see: Arthur J. Vidich, "Participant Observation and the Collection and Interpretation of Data," *American Journal of Sociology*, LX, 4 (1955), p. 357.

and early evening (the best times for interviewing). I had read them by the time they returned the next morning, and made the necessary criticisms and suggestions, which grew fewer during the course of the survey. The first couple of days were spent in pretesting, after which the form of some questions was changed. We attempted to have a random sample, which would include municipal and mine African townships, since I was interested in possible differences between them. Roughly calculating the population of each section into which the townships were divided, I instructed the assistants to interview at each nth house. The sample was relatively random and turned out to be similar to those used in other surveys made by the mine and by the Rhodes-Livingstone Institute in such categories as tribe, age, occupation, rural and urban born, education, and so forth.

My previous experience in training college students to do field work was decidedly helpful. The African assistants varied in their interviewing ability as did the students at Queens College, but all of the Africans were good interviewers and the best of them were better than any of the college students had been. It must be remembered that the Africans were older and more sociologically mature because of their life experiences than the American college students.

Several of the assistants had an initial difficulty in getting some people to consent to an interview, even though the innocuous nature of the survey was carefully explained. They said they would cooperate if they heard the study announced over the loudspeaker of the main welfare hall on the mine township by either a trade-union official or an African welfare worker (who was, of course, an employee of management). The assistants said the sponsorship of either was equally good. It was decidedly quicker and simpler to have an announcement made by the senior African worker than to wait for a meeting of the mine workers' executive board. I checked first with the always helpful European head of the African welfare department who gave his okay immediately. The senior African welfare worker then announced the study several times when the large amphitheater was filled to capacity with a movie audience. (The African Mine Workers' Union used the same hall for their meetings.) Interviewing then proceeded without opposition.

This was one of the many revealing accidental incidents. It drew my attention to the possible composite symbolism of the welfare department and the union. Both seemed to represent benevolent authority, at least in some situations. The Western point of view of the union versus management was not always applicable. It was more true during a strike which occurred later during my stay, but even then many of the Africans separated European management from European supervisors who allegedly fired African workers unjustly. The supervisors were considered more hostile than management, and many were.

The survey with its sample of five hundred fifty-one was finished within a month and yielded rich data not only connected with the mass media but also on African life and attitudes. Since movies, radio programs, and newspapers were concerned with many aspects of life—family, love, sex, politics, Europeans, work, and so forth—the comments of the interviewees on what they heard, saw, or read provided far more than the statistical tables, valuable as these were. For instance I learned of the Africans' misunderstanding of European mores and of their concept of European immorality from the comments on news reels which showed Europeans dancing, lying on beaches, and in other such social situations. A father kissing his child was considered a prelude to incest. Reactions to modern popular songs on the radio indicated attitudes to romantic and physical aspects of love. The Africans took their mass media seriously, as if they represented real life. In the case of movies, the lack of understanding of the difference between news and fictional films, which I had noted on the rural tour, was demonstrated over and over again.

The universal hostility to Federation was obvious, although neither the assistants nor I asked a single question about it. When Sir Roy Welensky was in the movie or radio news, reactions were always spontaneously against him. Fears of losing the land, of Africans having to wander from place to place like wild pigs, of more Boers coming to the country, and many other anxieties related to Federation were expressed, spontaneously—sometimes as non-sequiturs—by practically all informants, whether or not they were using the mass media. The study had been planned as apolitical but it was certainly not feasible to omit a situation (political or not) which dominated the thinking and the lives of these Africans.

From the beginning, responses from men and women differed sharply, and I was curious about the response of many women that they were "too lazy" to go to the cinema or listen to the radio. It was clear that I would have to find out more about the lives of the women. Another negative response to movies and radio by both men and women was that they thought it foolish to think that going to the cinema or listening to radio would make them Europeans; this and similar expressions provided hypotheses for further investigation on the meaning to these Africans of becoming modern. Attitudes of the illiterates towards their lack of education revealed basic differences in philosophy, such as that inequality was divinely ordained and was right, or that it was a matter of circumstances. Some adults were going to night school, while others thought that time was better spent in drinking beer.

It was important to establish patterns and possible correlations with age, sex, tribe, education, and the many other categories before proceeding further with the research. Fortunately, this could be done quickly because the head of the Hollorith machines department of the mine offered their use and the help of a man to run them. I did the coding. (I was amused that my first use of these machines was in Central Africa.)

The survey produced not only the basic patterns in regard to the mass media, but also gave richer data on values and attitudes than I had anticipated. I wrote it all up roughly and sent copies to several people in Lusaka connected with the mass media bureaus for Africans, and received helpful comments in reply. The general manager and the European editor of a newspaper published by the mine for their African employees also received copies. The newspaper turned out to be popular, but a frequent criticism by the interviewees had been its omission of English social titles (Mr., Mrs., Miss), before African names although their Bemba equivalents were used in the vernacular section. The editor argued the point with me, but it was not long before English social titles became the practice. I was amused—and pleased—at this small practical result of the survey.

XXIV

THE AFRICANS

The survey was over and six of the seven African assistants had to return to school. Nor could I have afforded to keep all of them for a longer period. The best one, twenty-year-old Phiri, also the youngest, lacked the money to continue his education, and, fortunately for me, remained as my assistant. During the course of the study two African schoolteachers were occasional and part-time assistants, and one African woman worked for me part-time; I also employed an African typist. I gave up the idea of a regular interpreter for a number of reasons: I could train assistants to get excellent data from non-English-speaking Africans; there was plenty of work for me to do with those who spoke English; accustomed to making rather direct contact with people, I was uncomfortable in the interpreter situation. But I continued to regret that I did not know the Bemba language, even though I managed to reduce some of the disadvantages.

Of great importance in this context was my assistant, Phiri. He became a kind of alter ego, and I can not imagine how the study would have been made without his help. He understood what kind of data I needed and he interviewed, recorded, and observed continuously. Born on the Copperbelt, he knew its life and people well. His parents were uneducated and his father had been an unskilled laborer on the mine. Phiri had the advantage of having been away from the mine township: in the village of his mother's family for vacations, and in Lusaka attending school since he was fourteen. An excellent student from the beginning of his school career, he was best in mathematics. The high level of his intelligence was obvious, as was the clarity and logic of his thinking. He had made an empirical test of a widely held witchcraft concept, found it false, and was one of the few Africans I met who seemed to have really rejected witchcraft thinking. Even more remarkable was his memory, the best I have ever encountered and superior to mine, which happens to be good. Pre-literate peoples often have a better memory than literate ones; it is assumed that without writing people are conditioned to remember more. But Phiri, of course, was literate and none of the other assistants could match him in memory. Another anthropologist working in the area told me of one of his assistants—pre-literate—who likewise had a prodigious memory.

Shortly after the survey was finished, I arranged that Phiri and I attend a meeting together as a kind of test; he took no notes, and his write-up of it was like that of a recording machine. At my suggestion, he wrote his biography (forty-five typed pages) and the details of small and big events were rich: family background, play life with gangs before elementary school, reactions to the latter, a description of his first teacher and of subsequent ones, the bus trip to Lusaka (including the clouds in the sky, the weather, the condition of the road, and minor happenings) when he was fourteen, his life at boarding school, girls and falling in love, the death of his father, and so on and on. During the survey I knew he was the best interviewer, but his many other abilities became apparent when he began working more intensively with me. Equally important, he became truly *engaged*, identified with the project and with me.

I had worked out a general format for his interviewing, but he varied it when necessary, and followed up "leads" that we had not foreseen. He wrote down everything—what he, as well as the informant, said. Night and day, seven days a week he worked. Sometimes I suggested he take a day off, but he rarely did. (Neither did I.) Between us there developed a mutual liking, deep affection, and respect. His new young wife was still in her rural village, and a couple of months after he started working for me I contributed a part of the travel expenses to bring her to Luanshya. Their first child, a boy born shortly after I left Luanshya, was named "Powdermaker."

In all my field work, except in Hollywood, there has been one person—Ongus in Lesu, Mrs. Wilson in Mississippi, Phiri in Luanshya—with whom I have had an exceptionally close

friendship, who has helped me, more than I can say, to understand the people and their society.[1] Each was dedicated to the
project and to me. The friendships lasted whether or not we
ever saw each other again. They became a permanent part of
my life and, apparently, I of theirs.[2] Other friends and informants in these three societies were also helpful in sensitizing me
to the people and to the culture. But there was always one or
two who provided the deepest communication. Of the three
people mentioned, who had alter ego relationships with me,
none was paid except Phiri, and he earned his living by working for me. However, his zeal and devotion went far beyond
earning a salary.

Phiri could not work with women, since any young man going to see a woman if her husband was not home would be
suspect. An African woman, better educated than the average,
who had formerly done a little work in the welfare department,
assisted me with non-English-speaking women. She was a
mother and wife and could give only half time. Although intelligent, she did not reach Phiri's high level, nor was she as well
educated. She followed instructions literally, but lacked the
initiative or ability to handle those unexpected situations for
which no advance instructions can be given: nor could she
pursue an unforeseen "lead" in an interview as Phiri did. However, the data she collected from the women were reliable and
useable, although incomplete. A source of strain between us

---

[1] This situation is not unique and a number of anthropologists have described their most helpful informants in *In the Company of Man,* ed.
Joseph B. Casagrande (New York: Harper & Bros., 1960).
[2] Phiri and I corresponded occasionally after I left Luanshya. At this writing he is in England on a government bursary studying in the field of
community relations, which he entered after my project was over. As soon
as he left Africa to study abroad, he began writing long and frequent
letters filled with detailed observations about his new experiences. He was
a stranger in a foreign culture, as I had been in Africa, and it seems that
he had a need to write to one who had also been a stranger.
Mrs. Wilson and I corresponded after I left Mississippi and she visited
me when she was in New York many years after I left Indianola.
There could, naturally, be no contact through letters with Ongus and
my other preliterate Melanesian friends in Lesu. But a man who went
there in the mid-fifties told me that he made his successful entreé by
saying he was my friend, and that everyone, including children not yet
born when I was there, knew of me. I had, he said, become part of the
mythology. Unfortunately, he did not collect the myths.

was her lack of responsibility. We had agreed on the number of hours per week for work and often she did not live up to the agreement, giving both legitimate and non-legitimate excuses, such as her menstrual period, a minor illness of one of the children, going somewhere with a missionary friend, or another engagement. She never offered to make up the lost hours for which she was paid. (Her salary was weekly.) I tried unsuccessfully to give her a sense of responsibility, mentioning that if women took jobs they had to meet the same standards as men did. Uninterested in this point, she seemed motivated only by the salary. She lacked Phiri's interest in the study and had little feeling of closeness to me. Perhaps no anthropologist could expect more than one Phiri in any one field experience! All the work with the women in the mine community sharply revealed their backward position in the social system, particularly as compared to the advanced one of the Negro women in Mississippi.

During the first month or so I was under close observation. In this part of Africa, a plot atmosphere existed among both Africans and whites. Was I part of the conspiracy which had brought Federation to the Africans? was their question. The Europeans' question about any anthropologist was, would he collaborate with Africans to change the status quo? My answer to each was genuinely "No," conveyed not only verbally, but through my behavior.

I was sometimes surprised by the trifling nature of the incidents to which significance was attached in the establishment of my reputation. One afternoon, I was driving on the compound and, as usual, very slowly because of the absence of sidewalks for pedestrians. The hat of an African riding a bicycle in the opposite direction blew off and fell directly in front of my car. I stopped immediately. He retrieved his worn and shabby hat, saying, "You are a proper European." "Proper" meant some one who treated others with respect and had a sense of etiquette, i.e. politeness and good taste; it was a valued trait in tribal society. Africans did not expect any European to become an African or to follow tribal customs. But they wanted to be treated "properly," with respect. The absence of this attitude in many Europeans caused bitterness and hostility. In the hat situation I was not playing a self-conscious role as a

field worker. It was my normal role in life but it differentiated me from a large number of other "Europeans." Two Africans riding with me in the car said that most of them would
have driven over the hat. My reaction had been merely, "a hat
is a hat," and I was rather surprised at the favorable comment
it caused.

I went at least once a week to the large movie amphitheater
on the mine township and occasionally to the smaller hall on
the municipal township. At my first appearance in the mine
theater, the European operator of the projection machine asked
me to sit with him in his elevated cubicle. I replied that I preferred to sit among the audience and added, not to hurt his
feelings, that I was studying their reactions. I later discovered
that sitting among the Africans created an immediate and
favorable impression on them and was much talked about. No
other "European" had ever done it.

The African cinema was an enjoyable as well as learning
experience for me. Fortunately, I am a movie fan and like
"Westerns," and the invariant program (a "Western," "British
News," "Northern Spotlight"—Northern Rhodesia News—an
animal cartoon, The African Mirror—incidents of African life
—and sometimes a very old American farce) did not bore me
unduly. But my real interest was in the audience. Their emotional reaction was as intense and overt as was that of Negro
congregations in Mississippi rural churches. More than a thousand Africans were gathered in the unroofed amphitheater,
sitting in the aisles, often standing against the walls, as well as
filling all the seats. They shouted their pleasure and booed their
displeasure. The climax was when the cowboys wrestled or
boxed. The whole audience rose, flexed their muscles in unison
with the blows, shouting "Come on, Wa! Wa! Wa! Give blow!"
Identification with the cowboy was obvious.

When the audience was not shouting, they talked all the
time to each other about the movie, and to catch the conversations I had a couple of assistants sitting and moving about in
different parts of the hall, recording the comments. Data from
these, literally reams of spontaneous comments, could not have
been secured as well through interviews. Spontaneous comments may often reflect attitudes more truly than do answers
to formal questions. Besides, in some situations a field worker

may not even know the significant questions before he has heard the people talking spontaneously. At the movies, the assistants were invaluable, because even if I had known the Bemba language I could not have moved about the hall as inconspicuously as they did. (Other Africans also moved about.)

The confusion between reality and acting was confirmed over and over again. If something in the cowboy film disturbed the African's sense of reality, he was annoyed and called it "cheating." For instance, this term was used when a new cowboy was being taught how to shoot, because many members of the audience recalled that the same cowboy in a film several weeks earlier had been experienced with a gun.

Comments also revealed attitudes towards Europeans, to Federation, and to other aspects of contemporary life. Large well-fed cattle were shown at one point in "The African Mirror." A typical remark was: "These cows are Southern Rhodesian. When they are brought here for slaughtering, meat is sold to Europeans only, and we are sold only the thin meat (without fat)." Boos followed shots of Welensky and other Federation officials in the "Northern News."

By the end of the first month or so, I felt more or less accepted by the Africans. They knew not only that I had nothing to do with Federation, but they had set me off from other white people. However, it still took courage for me to begin interviewing. I always suffer a kind of stage fright, even after many field trips. It was easy to busy myself doing other things, and I had to force myself to the first interview. I picked a man whom I had met and who had seemed cordial. The interview was moderately successful and, at least, got me started. From then on I interviewed more or less regularly among the men and women who spoke English. The interviews were focused on problems which had emerged from the survey and from the recorded conversations which I wanted to explore more extensively. Some of the interviews had the appearance of a social visit, ending with a cup of tea. A friendship developed with some of the respondents. This happened more often with members of the intelligentsia, and I could discuss problems of the research with a few of them. Sometimes they came to my house for tea, occasionally for dinner.

Unlike Mississippi, the situation presented no problems with the males. No African had to fear being lynched if seen talking to a white woman. The fact that I was considerably older than when I had gone to Indianola was an asset in several ways. Middle age gave me a kind of freedom a young woman might not have had. Moreover, among Africans age is a status symbol. When friends among the uneducated felt close to me, they called me "Grandma." My professorial rank carried prestige among the educated, who usually called me "Professor."

Interviewing by assistants and by me was entirely with adults, but I knew that young people should be included in a study of social change. (Comparison of the attitudes in different age groups in Mississippi had been one of the significant clues to understanding change there.) With the help of a couple of African schoolteachers, I worked out a quick and relatively easy way of getting data from teen-age (male and female) Africans: essays on selected topics given by teachers as part of the regular classroom work. I was interested in the young peoples' values, their self-imagery and imagery of Europeans, their specific ambitions and their fantasies of what they would like to be. The essay topics in the order in which they were written were:

1. If you went to London and met an English person who had never before seen an African and he asked you about them, how would you describe them? Include how they live, how they look, and how they behave.

2. If you went back to your village or your mother's village and you met a friend who had never seen a European, how would you describe them? Include how they live, how they look, and how they behave.

3. What would you like to do when you finish school? Include the kind of job, where you want to live, the kind of person you want to marry, when you want to marry, the number of children desired.

4. If it pleased God to make you anyone or anything you please, who or what would you like to be? Give your reasons.

The essays were written in Bemba or English, whichever was customary in each class. None of the students knew the essays were being written for me, thus guaranteeing more spontaneity than if they knew I was in the picture. (African, as well as any other students, would be inclined to write what they thought the investigator would consider "good.")

The essay-writing technique could not have been successful without the interest and help of the teachers. They not only gave the assignments to their students, but also helped me formulate the topics so that they would be clear and meaningful. A considerable number of the teachers were my friends. They were interested in my project, and I in their problems. Attending a monthly teachers' meeting, I listened to their discussions, and offered any comments I thought might be helpful. I accepted invitations to give an occasional talk to the students about the United States. (Some of the questions asked by the students after the talk gave useful clues to their attitudes.) A social relationship developed between a considerable number of the teachers and myself, and we visited in each other's homes. They chafed at the narrowness of life on the mine township and, it seems, the friendship with me added breadth. Only two of the teachers received any payment from me: one for translating the essays written in Bemba, and the other for working part-time recording audience reactions at the movies.

Data rich in traditional and modern elements came out of the essay project.[3] The girls were more traditionally oriented than the boys and more hostile to Europeans, and a considerable number of the girls wanted to be men in order to enjoy the greater privileges of the latter. The concrete ambitions were realistic: skilled or white-collar workers and shop keepers for the boys; teachers and nurses for the girls. Their fantasies were in vivid contrast; two thirds of the boys and more than half the girls wanted to be nonhuman. Traditional hospitality and helpfulness to kindred and friends and respect were the most important values in interpersonal relations; the absence of these qualities among the Europeans and in their relations with Africans made them seem immoral.

The essay technique did not work well in the evening classes for adults learning to be literate, because they were not yet accustomed to expressing themselves in writing. But I was able to pursue some of the points raised in the essays through interviews with adults. Those going to night school and those uninterested in becoming literate were an interesting contrast in ambitions for themselves and their children.

---

[3] See Hortense Powdermaker, "Social Change through Imagery and Values of Teen-Age Africans in Northern Rhodesia," *American Anthropologist*, LVIII (1956), 5.

I had a sense of poignancy about the adults who came to school at night after a hard day's work on the mine. A teacher asked me to talk to his class to encourage them and strengthen their resolve to become literate. So, one evening I talked informally to a class, and, as usual, left considerable time for questions. A man asked about the proportion of illiteracy in the United States, and I was able to give him an approximate answer. The African rate was, of course, many many times higher. Everyone in the class slumped in discouragement. Naturally, I was troubled by this reaction, and the whole purpose of my talk seemed to be negated. But, luckily, I quickly thought of a way to counteract the discouragement: I compared the men going to night school with those Africans in the past who had cut the first paths through the dense bush. The men in the class immediately saw that they, too, were pioneers; they sat up straight and smiled.

I was well aware that my original problem was being much expanded. The theme of traditionals versus modernists which emerged from the survey continued through subsequent interviews and other data. Although correlations with age, sex, level of education, and so forth, were significant, many questions were unanswered. To understand the differences between the attitudes of men and women to the mass media it was necessary to learn more about women's traditional and changing position in the social structure, the new economic roles of men, and the resulting changes in family life. Nor could the role of the mass media in social change be understood apart from that of other significant agents of change such as the Europeans, the trade union, the welfare department.

Not only did the original problem lead to other problems which I then pursued, but training and personal preference slanted my work in a holistic direction, even though it was necessarily limited by lack of time. I did very little on religion, pagan or Christian. (Only a very few people were Moslems.) I went occasionally to church services and learned that they differed little from their European counterparts. The Africans had not made the Christian church their own, as had the American Negroes. Magic and witchcraft interested me and I was alert to its use through incidents which happened to come to my attention through the recorded conversations or in some other way. It did not seem wise to interview directly on this subject since many of the urban Africans were reluctant to admit a belief in magic and witchcraft. Nor did I consistently pursue the persistence of tribal customs except in particular areas primarily related to the family (such as the bride-price, courtship, divorce, and extra-marital relations) and to relations between old and young, men and women; none of these could be done exhaustively. I knew only by hearsay about the modifications of such rituals as were customary on the appearance of the first menses and at other stages in a life history. There were other traditional practices whose persistence, change, or disappearance I did not study at all. The mine township of 30,000 was no Lesu with its population of 223! A longer study of the mining community and one done by a team could, naturally, have given far more data.

Today, a problem approach is more common than a holistic one. I know well the dangers of the latter; its inevitable incompleteness and a diffused quality. Yet I find this approach rewarding because it contributes greatly to my understanding. Is it not possible for a field worker to focus on a problem and, at the same time, spend a portion of his time noting most anything that comes to his attention? Curiosity also impels me to study whatever seems significant, even though I do not see its immediate relation to the problem. When a strike of the African miners occurred, it would have been almost impossible for me to exclude it from my interest and study, although it had no apparent relationship to the research problems. Yet data from the week-long strike turned out to be both revealing and important. Before the strike I had been wondering about a significant minority in the same age, sex, tribal, and education groups who differed considerably from each other in their place on the traditionalist-modern continuum. In the discussions during the strike a sharp disagreement occurred between the traditionalists and modernists on one of the issues. The difference clearly hinged on the range of identifications—kindred versus a broader non-kin group. The traditionalists were unconcerned if Africans who were not kindred suffered when the strike leaders called out hospital orderlies and nurse assistants from African hospitals; the modernists were appalled at the order which caused suffering to many Africans whether or not they were kindred. Other data became more meaningful in terms of the range of identifications, and it was, indeed, a most fruitful hypothesis. If I were doing the study over again and had the necessary assistance, I would devise a test to check more definitively the range of identifications for a well chosen sample.

Another seemingly tangential but useful approach was my attempt to learn as much as possible about the past through interviewing old people (African and European) and through reading. In the latter context, the published *Proceedings of the African Representative Council* was rich in providing data on the Africans' imagery of missionaries and colonial officials, who were among the first Europeans to communicate Western values to Africans. The imagery was in sharp contrast to that of Federation officials. One could not leave out either the past or the contemporary "Who" in Harold Lasswell's well-known formula of "*Who* communicates *what*, to *whom*," in a study of communication and change.

Problems were developing, data were interesting and substantiated at least some significant points, new clues kept appearing, and hypotheses were being formed. Certainly I was kept busy. Yet I was dissatisfied. Driving around the compound, visiting and interviewing, having a limited participation in African social activities, even my close relationship with Phiri and friendship with a few others did not give me a sense of intimacy with African life in its casual, everyday context, such as I had had in Lesu and in Indianola. I was frustrated that I had to live in the European township and by my ignorance of the Bemba language. The Africans were so verbal, talking literally all the time. If only I could hear them talking to each other, as I had listened to the Melanesians in Lesu and to Negroes in Mississippi. The recorded comments of the audience at the movies gave me some spontaneous conversation, but were limited to that situation.

In this mood of dissatisfaction, it occurred to me that the technique in the movie hall might be extended. I asked Phiri to stay home for a week and write down everything that was said in his immediate family and among the neighbors from the time they arose in the morning until they went to bed. He and his young wife lived with his sister and brother-in-law, both uneducated and more or less typical of their group. Communication with two neighbor miners and their families was close and constant; relatives and friends also came visiting often. At the end of a week, I eagerly read the voluminous notes Phiri handed me. They were the stuff of life: the price of food, the purchase of a new coat, where the native beer was being brewed, rumors of witchcraft, gossip about an adulterous husband, talk about work, the union, a football game, and children, news of rural relatives, the theft of a bicycle, small irritations and larger quarrels. Anxieties, fears, pleasures were open; language was earthy. The conversations gave me what I had been missing—the inside view of life on the compound, without which field work cannot be effective. I was able to see and hear people talk and act spontaneously. My understanding increased many times, and new clues appeared continuously. The conversations revealed individual variations both within a closed group, such as the family, and the more open one of friends and neighbors. I could "hear" traditional values being upheld by some and questioned by others. The experiment had worked far better than I anticipated and this kind of reporting was therefore continued not only among Phiri's family and neighbors, but at a beer hall, a welfare center, a trade union meeting. The strike was reported solely through conversations about it.

The recorded conversations added another dimension of reality to the study, i.e. the reality of life through African eyes and ears, and reduced somewhat the disadvantage of not knowing the language. Even if I had spoken and understood Bemba, it would not have been possible for me to have been present in some of the situations where the talk was recorded unless I had lived on the compound, which was then impossible. Nor could I have mingled too freely with the men at the beer hall or gone to a trade union meeting of African miners. (The latter action would have immediately made management suspicious and endangered the continuance of my field work.) Yet, not knowing the vernacular language continued to be a handicap, although I reduced it as much as possible, and even managed to get part of the inside view without the language.

XXV
━━◄►━━

THE EUROPEANS

The Europeans were also within the spectrum of my interests.
As in Mississippi, it was not possible to understand one racial
group without comprehending the behavior and attitudes of
the other. In a study of social change, such as I was doing on
the Copperbelt, the Europeans had a particularly significant
role. But again, as in Mississippi, there was no time for a systematic study of the whites and I followed much the same
techniques of continuous observation and considerable social
participation.

I made friends with the Europeans, as well as with the Africans, and was pleased to be accepted as I stepped in and out
of white society. The situation differed from Mississippi where
a real friendship with the whites would have made me suspect
among the Negroes. The Africans took it for granted that I
should have some friends among the Europeans, and thought
it appropriate. (Some of the African leaders and members of
the intelligentsia also had friendships with a few Europeans.)
The local women's club invited me to give a lecture, and I
accepted because I thought it necessary for them to have a
chance to look me over. I do not remember the topic of the
talk, but I recall the women's pleased surprise that they could
understand me, an anthropologist and a professor!

Social life among the Europeans had a pleasant warmth and
coziness, and was quite different from white society in Misssis-
sippi. The high level of education and the generally liberal
attitude of mine management, of government officials, and of
missionaries had no counterpart in Indianola. The openness of
the issues in the African biracial situation and the rational
recognition of them was, again, a relief from what I had known
in Mississippi, where a seemingly peaceful situation had cov-

ered a hidden morass of fears, anxieties, and guilt. Most of the
Europeans in the mining community accepted social change
as inevitable. The topic which dominated the conversation of
top-level management was, how to advance the Africans, and
at the same time, not arouse undue anxiety among the European miners. The simple formula of workers versus management and owners (which had served in the days of my labor
organizing) had to give way to a more complex concept which
took into account the interests of African miners, European
miners, white-collar workers of both races, and management.
The enlightened self-interest of the latter happened also to
be to the advantage of the Africans. The Copperbelt was
setting the standards for their advancement in the Protectorate.
Many African leaders thought the advancement should be
greater and quicker, but knew they were forging ahead and
were relatively optimistic about the future.

Most of my European friends were among middle and upper
levels of management, government officials, missionaries, professional people, and relatively few were in the lower class.
Sometimes I interviewed; other times I merely directed the
conversations to problems that interested me. Since African
advancement and related problems were so much a part of the
Europeans' spontaneous conversation, often I only had to listen.

A few of the Europeans probably knew I was observing
them as well as the Africans. My host at a dinner party, where
the guests were top-level mine management and their wives,
said to me, "You ought to be studying us; we are as interesting
as the Africans." I smiled and answered, "How do you know
that I'm not studying you?" He nodded his head and grinned.
Dinners, parties, casually dropping in for a cup of tea, were
pleasant and often provided data, which I recorded as soon
as I returned to my house. The ethics of doing this (recording
what happened on social occasions unknown to the participants
in them) had long ceased to bother me. How could it, when all
of life, whether among family, friends, colleagues, students,
strangers, was, and is, in varying degrees, a kind of field work?

Close friendships developed with a few of the Europeans,
because we genuinely liked each other. One was a young
Canadian in the middle range of management. Knowledgeable
about African life, speaking Bemba fluently, singularly free

from racial prejudice, interested in Africans, liked and respected by them, he was atypical in the European group. A couple—both doctors—were also congenial. The man was descended from a famous medical missionary family, and he and his wife were among the few Europeans I met who seemed to really belong to Northern Rhodesia. The D. C. and his family were among my close friends, and I spent Christmas day with them. A few other friends became part of my life and made it more pleasant than it would have been otherwise; we have remained friends.

I knew some lower-class Europeans but not as many as I would have liked. Class distinctions in this small British community were tightly drawn, and it was not easy to move freely from one class to another. However, I became rather well acquainted with one lower-class couple, who were rewarding for data. Contact with them began accidentally. I had met them on the cinema van tour in the rural area and we had given them some assistance when their lorry broke down. Then in Luanshya, I happened to meet him on the street and he immediately asked me to come to tea with him and his wife. I did so, and then dropped in for tea several times a month, because they were ideal informants, even though their point of view did not represent the norm. Its very exaggeration highlighted the more run-of-the-mill members of their class.

The man was English of working-class background and his wife South African of the same class. During World War II he had been sent to Africa and had stayed there when it ended. He served in the police force of Southern Rhodesia for a while, and then began adventuring: prospecting for minerals, hunting crocodiles, trying to farm—all unsuccessfully. He had a deep sense of frustration and his bitterness and feelings of violence were extreme. His hatred of the "Kaffirs," as he called Africans, pervaded his whole being. He also hated the Europeans and said the D.C.'s and the D.O.'s were pro-African, and that mine management wanted to oust the Europeans from their jobs and give them to Africans. The wife was full of the same hate and boasted about how she cursed the house-boy. Both the man and his wife were violent people and, I think, would have been so in any environment. They felt particularly thwarted in Africa because of their lack of success and because they seemed to have an image of Africa as a place for violence. I do not think they knew much about what I was doing. They never asked me and seemed uninterested. They said they enjoyed my visits because they could talk freely to me; he was afraid of being fired if he expressed himself on the job and had already been reprimanded for using abusive language to Africans. I asked only a few questions directed to learning about their background, hoping to find some connection between it and the violence which poured from them compulsively.

Other European miners in the same class, whom I knew more or less casually, feared African advancement and looked down on the African people as innately inferior, but their anxieties and hostilities were not as extreme. I had a friendly social relationship with one couple, in which the husband was active in the European miners' union and the wife interested in community affairs. Through them I met a few others. I attended a few of the classes on race relations given to the European miners; the expression on their faces and their questions after the lecture indicated an unsympathetic reaction to the benevolent attitude of management to Africans.

I wanted to learn more about this group, many of them "gangers," the lowest level of European supervisor. About half-way through the study I realized that the main focus of communication between both races was in the relationship between the "ganger" and the African "boss boys," who headed a group of fourteen to fifteen African workers. It occurred to me that a study of the "ganger-boss boy" relationship might be a fruitful way of studying the communication of Western culture. (Considerably earlier, I had realized that the problem could not be limited to the mass media.) I thought of a way that Phiri and I could work on this new angle. Since I had known nothing of "gangers" or "boss boys" before coming to the mine township, the subject was not part of the plan discussed with Sir Ronald Prain in Lusaka or with the general manager of the mine in Luanshya. The contemplated expansion of the project was such a radical departure from the original plan that I felt ethically bound to tell the latter about the proposed new direction. The general manager's reaction was immediate: strong disapproval. He stood up, as if to emphasize his words: "As the general manager, and as your friend,

I must tell you that such a study can not be done." He feared
its execution would cause trouble. The European miners were
restless over the company's plan to advance the African workers, and talk of a possible strike of Europeans was in the air.
I was sure that my new plan would not change the situation
in any way, but I could not convince the general manager.
Reluctantly, I decided to drop the new plan.[1] Perhaps I
could have carried it through without the general manager's
knowledge, although that is doubtful, but I felt a need—both
personal and as a field worker—to play fairly. In the end I
think it paid off on both levels: I was more comfortable and
it was possible to continue working within the complex power
structure of this company town. And, of course, I had plenty
of other things to do.

Continuous observation of Europeans was part of the field
work. I noted and recorded whatever I saw and heard, as I
walked through the streets of the European shopping center,
went into the shops, attended informal and formal gatherings.
The note-taking was as full and detailed as when I had walked
through the village of Lesu. The kick of a European man to an
African sitting on the pavement, selling wooden animals in front
of a large shop, to get him to move, the butcher kicking his
assistant to get his attention, and similar incidents made me
realize that the kick was one of the forms of communicaticn
used by Europeans. Obviously, I could not have learned this
through interviews or by a survey.

Listening to Europeans address Africans and talk spontaneously about them always provided data. Attending the laying
of a corner stone for a European church, I heard a European
woman address two middle-aged ordained African ministers
as "boys," and it was clear from the tone of her voice and the
expression on her face that she had no idea that she was insult-
ing them. I knew the African ministers had been invited at the
insistence of the European minister, against the wishes of some

---

[1] Considerably after I left Luanshya, the mines on the Copperbelt employed a commercial polling organization to make a study of the attitudes
of "gangers" and other Europeans to African advancement. The report
was confidential.

members of his board. I went to the ceremony, partly out of curiosity and partly out of politeness to the minister, with whom I had a cordial relationship.

Europeans (as well as the Africans) took me more or less for granted after I had been there a few months, and they accepted the unique situation of a white woman driving alone around the compound, visiting in African homes, having a cup of tea or smoking a cigarette with them, inviting Africans to her home, attending African movies, and other social affairs. But I knew that in this kind of community, the acceptance of each group could be lost if any act of mine caused suspicion. This could happen inadvertently, and I knew it had happened to others. I took the simple precaution of frequently telling Europeans and Africans in leadership positions what I was doing, thinking this would reduce the need to speculate and gossip about my activities.

But all my precautions did not preclude trouble. I was startled one day to hear a rumor among Europeans that I had done a hula hula at a Saturday night African dance, shortly after I had attended my first one at the African welfare center. I had thought it might be an interesting contrast to the tribal dances which took place on Sunday afternoons. Accompanied by several Africans (Phiri, the cook, a couple of their friends), we arrived at the dance hall about nine o'clock. A European policeman on the veranda looked startled at my appearance. Most of the policemen knew me, but he was new. I immediately explained who I was and what I was doing. Mr. Howie, the European director of welfare activities, had not yet arrived. We entered the hall and sat sedately in chairs along the wall. The Africans with me did not care to participate and we all thought the dance a "wash-out," because of its small attendance. Mr. Howie arrived about fifteen minutes later. We stayed only long enough to be polite, until about 10:30. The next day, we heard that a crowd began to come at midnight, and that the dance became gay and more interesting.

In the feeling-tone of the European community, the hula hula story was disturbing. I immediately went to see a good European friend in the African personnel department. His reaction was, "So you've heard about it!" More mystified than

ever, I asked, "But what is behind this tale?" I learned that at
a regular meeting of the European staff in the African personnel department, one of its members presented the charge that
I had done a hula hula at the Saturday night African dance
and that I had, accordingly, endangered and lowered the Europeans' status. Something should be done to stop my working
among Africans. The head of the African personnel department
was the kind of man who would go along with whatever was
the prevailing sentiment. Fortunately, I had two good friends
on the staff. They said the story was ridiculous and demanded
proof from the accuser. The policeman and Mr. Howie were
called to testify. Both denied the hula hula story and said that
I had been a wall flower at the dance. The charge against me
was withdrawn, and I was not supposed to know anything
about it.

As near as my friend could reconstruct what had happened,
after the African dance was over the policeman had gone to
the bar at the European club, filled with the usual Saturday
night group of men enjoying their drinks. The policeman had
told them of his great shock at seeing a "European" woman
accompanied by Africans entering an African dance hall. The
story was enlarged as it passed gaily around the bar and
emerged with "the American doing a hula hula at an African
dance." This was what the man who presented the charges
heard. I later became acquainted with him and discovered
that he was far more suspicious than the average European
mine official. But his charge had been taken seriously; the
general manager had been told of it. I might have been in a
bad way if I had not had friends "at court." The general manager was sufficiently concerned, even though the charge was
proved false, to advise me to have a European escort when I
went to the African township at night. It was necessary to
disregard this advice.

In spite of the suspicious tone of the community, I was
persona grata and able to work steadily. I ranged back and
forth between the two races, and between different classes in
each. Sometimes, as in other field trips, I grew tired of the
incessant note-taking. I remember one escape on a Sunday
afternoon, when my Canadian friend and I drove over to
Ndola to see a football game between opposing African teams.

I've never followed a football game so intently. I kept my eyes on the ball, following its every move, made almost no observations on the spectators, and came home refreshed.

My sabbatical was almost over. The problems with which I started had become more definite, and new ones had opened up. More data were needed on all of them. I wished that I had planned to stay for two years. The ideal would have been to take a vacation for a couple of months, and then return to Luanshya for another year's work. But the Guggenheim grant was for a year only, and it was too late to apply to them or elsewhere for another grant when I thought of extending the time. So the exploratory study ended.

XXVI

WRITING *COPPER TOWN*

Difficulties began after I arrived home and started to read the field notes and to organize them for writing. It was relatively easy to code the essays and interviews and establish the patterns in them. The work on the essays resulted in a compact paper on the imagery and values of teen-age Africans in the mining community.[1] But writing the book presented three major dilemmas: (1) how to integrate meaningfully the many different kinds of data—quantitative, qualitative, impressionistic, historical, contemporary conversations, and so on; (2) what did it all mean, i.e. how to interpret; (3) how to keep the human quality of life on the Copperbelt and at the same time be scientific—to present the inside and the outside views.

The problems of presentation seemed hopeless because of the greater than usual diversity of data. I thought of two books. One would be a scientific monograph centered around communication of Western values through the mass media and other means. The other, I thought of as more literary, to be called "Africans Talk," and based on the intra-African conversations. I began both. After editing some of the conversations to delete repetition, I asked two colleagues whose areas were not Africa and one non-anthropologist friend to read them. To my surprise, the conversations did not make much sense to any of them; the setting and necessary background were missing. I therefore began writing an introduction and after a hundred or

---

[1] "Social Change through Imagery and Values of Teen-Age Africans in Northern Rhodesia," *American Anthropologist*, LVIII (1956), 5. A rather general paper which I gave to the Anthropology Section of the New York Academy of Sciences shortly after my return was published as "Communication and Social Change Based on a Field Study in Northern Rhodesia," *Transactions N.Y. Academy of Sciences*, Ser. II, Vol. 17, No. 5 (March 1955).

so pages, realized that I was writing another book. I had also started the monograph and it seemed hopelessly dull to me. Finally, I settled the technical problem of combining many different kinds of material in one book by the decision not to bother about consistency of form, allowing it to be dictated by the diverse data.

I also began to read widely in the history and ethnology of this part of Africa, reading almost everything that had been written on it. Much of this reading should have preceded the field trip, but the necessary change of locale had made that impossible, and time for reading was limited in the field. As I read, the contemporary scene which I had studied became more firmly anchored in its background, and I saw modern problems more clearly.

The most difficult questions were those concerned with the "Why" and the "How" of social change. The theoretical problem was the same for both Africans and Europeans living on the Copperbelt, and not limited to them since all of us live in a period of revolutionary change. I moved away from the structural functional approach concerned primarily with the interrelations of roles and of institutions because it was inadequate for understanding problems of change. These had to be related directly to people rather than to roles. Why should some individuals want to change and others resist it? The answers could lie only in an integration of psychological and social processes in theory, as they are integrated in reality. I re-read some of the psychoanalytical work concerned with identity and individual change: mainly Freudian theory, and Erikson's papers on the subject. Among the latter were "Growth and Crises of the Healthy Personality" (which I had used in my course on Culture and Personality), "The Problem of Ego Identity," and, then, for the first time, "Ego Development and Historical Change."[2]

I began to think about what a model life history in tribal society might have been and to try and understand the loose "fit" of infantile and childhood conditioning with adult social

[2] These and other papers are reprinted in *Identity and the Life Cycle. Selected Papers by Erik H. Erikson, with a Historical Introduction by David Rapaport.* Psychological Issues, I. 1. Monograph I (New York: International Universities Press, Inc., 1959).

patterns. From there I moved to the contemporary society I had studied on the Copperbelt and its major changes from tribal life, seeing in them an extension of the areas of self-awareness, of perception, of action, and of the range of identifications. The last point, which had come out clearly in the intra-African conversations about the strike, was explicit and implicit in much of the other data. Teilhard's *Phenomenon of Man* [3] was published while I was making the attempt. His stress on the themes of selective differentiation, followed by convergence and incorporation of differentiation into an organized pattern underlying biological, psychological, and social change, tied together a number of ideas from other sources, and illuminated my data.

On the Copperbelt and in much of rapidly changing Africa, adult socialization, which included ever-widening areas of choice, could certainly not be omitted from any theory of change. Here, the work of Kenneth Boulding and Neil Smelser were of great help and I borrowed from them.[4] I re-read Josef Pieper's classic, *Leisure, the Basis of Culture.*[5] Other books, some new and some old, which contributed to my thinking are too numerous to mention in this context.

The evolution of my theoretical approach was not as logical as the above account might indicate. I went backwards and forwards, constantly revising and changing. I gave papers on selected aspects at various meetings and profited by comments, as I did even more from discussions with colleagues and friends who were kind enough to read early drafts. The complexities of the problem, the limitations in my data, and the state of our knowledge made definitive answers impossible. But I struggled. Knowing my limitations, I had no idea of evolving a new theory of change. But I had to explain the data to myself, and to do this I attempted to integrate concepts from many sources. The problem of integrating psychological and social theories to answer questions of "Why" and "How" in social change still continues for myself and for others.

---

[3] Pierre Teilhard de Chardin, *The Phenomenon of Man.* Trans. Bernard Wall. Introduction by Julian Huxley, (New York: Harper and Bros., 1959).
[4] Kenneth Boulding, *The Image* (Ann Arbor: University of Michigan Press, 1956) and Neil J. Smelser, *Social Change in the Industrial Revolution* (Chicago: University of Chicago Press, 1959).
[5] London: Faber and Faber, 1952.

The uniqueness of the book is perhaps the inside view of life on the Copperbelt at the time of my study. The intra-African conversations which form a large part of the book present a many-dimensioned picture of human realities. In them are the half-uttered as well as the fully uttered expressions of values, the small actions, the words used with special frequency, and other subtleties which Lionel Trilling called (in a quite different context) "a culture's hum and buzz of implication." Individuals stand out as unique personalities in the conversations. New abstractions can still be made from the published (and unpublished) conversations. In the meantime, and for all time, a group of Africans, in the midst of dramatic social change, are alive through what they say and do in small, intimate groups.

This book took longer to write than any previous one. Partly it was due to the complexity and breadth of the problems, to limitations of data, and to the enormous amount of reading I did after I returned from the field. Teaching and other normal duties at the college cut my time drastically, although having to prepare (for the first time) a course on African peoples and cultures contributed to the book. I tried out some of my ideas in the "Culture and Personality" course. But there were other courses during this period which had no relation to the book. Summers were the best time for writing, and I took one semester off without pay.

The situation I was writing about and trying to make meaningful was rapidly changing. The field work was done in 1953–54 and the book was published in 1962. I endeavored to keep up with the changes through newspapers from the area and elsewhere, journals, books and letters with African and European friends. I updated data, particularly statistics on population, wages, housing conditions, welfare activities, education, from annual reports of the mine company, government census, and other bulletins. I was in constant correspondence with my alter ego, Phiri, and he checked some points and answered questions on others. Yet, I knew that some unsympathetic reviewer would say that the study was dated. In the past an anthropologist might, and often did, publish a tribal study ten or twenty years after it was done, and it made little difference. But I was writing about contemporary Africa and a changing culture, in which many people besides anthropologists were interested. However, I thought it better not to publish as a journalist would. The problem of social change is *the* problem of our era, not fundamentally different from one decade to another. My fascination with the problem, with its many ramifications, kept me working through periods of discouragement until I completed the book.

Although I knew the gaps, the tentativeness of hypotheses, and other weaknesses, yet I was not displeased with the book. In the field, I had managed, to some extent, to overcome the handicap of not knowing the vernacular language, and I was able to get an inside view. The problem on which I worked was more sophisticated and complex than that of my previous studies. I had learned more in the writing than in any of the other books.

EPILOGUE

The participant observation method was forged in the study of small homogeneous societies, in which the anthropologist lived for an extended period of time, participated in them, learned the language, interviewed, and constantly observed. He followed long and devious sequences, such as those involved in initiation rites, which might be six or more months in preparation, and observed the minutiae of daily life in which they occurred. His record and observations of life were not unlike those of the natural historian. But he went beyond that and worked on anthropological problems such as kinship systems, forms of marriage and of residence, economic and political organization, religious and magical beliefs and rituals, myths and folk tales, and many others. He asked questions in structured and unstructured interviews, and noted whether or not the answers agreed completely with the actual behavior. He made mistakes and learned from them. Often he stumbled upon facts and problems about which he would not have known enough to ask in advance. Usually he had a close friendship with a few of the indigenous people, and he knew more or less well a considerable number of others. In a small community such as Lesu, it was possible to know almost everyone; all of its population appeared in my genealogical charts.

It is easier to use the participant observation method in small communities, tribal or modern, than in large ones. Problems of sampling and the need for quantified data become apparent as anthropologists move from small tribal villages to the study of larger and more stratified social units. However, the survey cannot substitute for the participant observation method; when necessary, they should be combined. A survey could give statistics on the percentage of literate people, of radio listeners, and of movie goers among the Africans. But it was interviewing and participant observation that provided

an understanding of what it meant to become literate in a
pre-literate society, and of the functions of radio listening
and of going to movies for the pre-literate and the literate.

Whether the contemporary community is small or large,
problems have become more complex. All people (tribal, peasant, and modern) have been more or less affected by the recent
revolutionary changes in technology, ideology, and communication. It is difficult to omit the phenomenon of social change
from any contemporary field research, or to find a situation
which escapes biracial strains or hostilities between opposing
power structures or ideological systems. In the 1930 study of
Lesu, all these problems were too minimal to affect field work
there. Later, in order to work effectively—or even to continue
working—in Mississippi and in Northern Rhodesia, I had
the problem of not disturbing the security of the dominant
white group any more than was absolutely necessary. In Hollywood, the power struggle was so intense that it became the
dominant theme in the research. The study of social change
was part of the research in two communities and was *the* problem on the African Copperbelt. Although participant observation was more difficult in the research which followed Lesu, it
was no less necessary.

Like everything else, anthropology grows, changes, and de-
velops. New problems appear and new techniques are developed. My assumption is that the participant observation
method of which intensive interviewing is a part continues to
be basic to meaningful field work, often in combination with
other methods.

Essential to participant observation is the need for communication between the investigator and the people being studied,
an important distinguishing point between the social and natural sciences. There is no reciprocal personal communication
between the physicist and atoms, molecules, or electrons, nor
does he become part of the situation studied. As Northrop has
remarked, "A subject becomes scientific . . . by beginning with
the peculiar character of its particular problem." [1] A peculiar
character of field work in anthropology and in other social
sciences is that the scientist has to communicate with the ob-

---

[1] F. S. C. Northrop, *The Logic of the Sciences and the Humanities* (New
York: The MacMillan Co., 1947), p. 274.

jects studied and they with him, and that he is part of the
situation studied. The communication varies from spontaneous
to planned, from superficial to deep, from subjective to objective areas of interest, from purely verbal to more subtle and
emotional expression. The range for an effective field worker
usually will include the whole continuum in any one field
situation.

The conditions for successful mutual communication include
1) physical proximity of the field worker to the people he
studies, 2) knowledge of their language, and 3) psychological
involvement. (The above order is not one of priority or of
significance.) In my four field experiences each of the three
conditions was met in different degrees. The overall communication seemed to have been most effective in Lesu, followed
by Mississippi (a close second), Northern Rhodesia, and Hollywood.

Lesu was the ideal in terms of physical proximity. Living in
the center of a small tropical village in which all social life was
outdoors, I could see and hear most everything that went on
publicly. I was with the Melanesians during big and little
rituals, in their gardening and fishing, as they prepared food
for the evening meal or for a feast, as they took their ease,
loafed and gossiped. When I was at home, they were constantly
in and out of my house except when I was typing notes or
asleep. Although the social life of men and women was sharply
differentiated, I was fortunate in having access to both groups,
though more formally with the men than with the women. It
would have been difficult to have escaped the company of the
Melanesians if I had wanted to, and, generally, I did not
want to.

In Mississippi, the proximity was almost, but not quite, as
good as in Lesu. I was continually with either the white or
Negroes, both of whom I was studying, and I could also observe their reactions to each other. Living in a white boarding
house gave the advantage of observation of fellow boarders,
and casual participation in social life among other whites provided much data. Sometimes the more casual the participation, the easier it is to get data on attitudes and values. Over
a Coke in a drug store a white man would be more expansive
on his opinions about Negroes than he would have been in a

formal interview. To be with Negroes I had to go across the tracks or drive out to see the rural sharecroppers. Most of my time was spent with the Negroes, but I did not have my own house, with the freedom to have Negroes come and go in it. However, I was totally immersed in the society—Negro and white—of Indianola and its surrounding rural area.

In Hollywood, no physical community existed—a serious handicap. Studios and homes of the movie-makers were scattered over the eighty-odd mile-long area of Los Angeles. Nor were people indigenous; there was a coming and a going. Casual mingling in the daily lives of the movie-makers and any significant degree of participation was not possible. All interviews had to be carefully planned and set up far in advance.

In Northern Rhodesia, I had my own house, and Africans could come and go in it. I observed African-European relations by walking down the street and, as already described, through participation in community life. I studied the white people as I had in Mississippi, by being part of their social life. But the African township was five miles away from my house. Moreover, I could not roam about it as freely as I did among the Negroes in Mississippi for a number of reasons: the much larger size of the African community; the tight specific controls of a company town; the greater formality of the Africans; and, in the beginning, their suspicions of me, as a white person, and of the purpose of my research. The work of African assistants and the recorded conversations of daily life helped reduce the disadvantages of not being more constantly in the African community.

Knowing the language of the people studied is so manifestly an important part of communication that the point needs no elaboration. In Mississippi and Hollywood no linguistic problem existed since everyone spoke English. In Lesu I had to learn a language which had not been recorded, and I lacked linguistic training. It was a difficult task, but I managed to learn to speak sufficiently well to make myself intelligible and to understand most of what went on. But my linguistic ability was within definite limits, of which I was well aware. My speech was a combination of the native language and pidgin English, with the proportion of the former increasing with time.

For reasons, discussed earlier, I did not speak Bcmba in Northern Rhodesia. Direct verbal communication was limited to those Africans who spoke English, the educated, a sizeable minority. The handicap of not being able to speak to other Africans was partly offset by using trained Africa assistants, one of whom was an alter ego, serving as eyes and ears for me.

Language is only one form of communication, the most obvious. The more subtle and often deeper levels are conveyed consciously and unconsciously by nuances of behavior, such as the facial expression, tone of voice, and gestures. The desire to communicate and an alertness or sensitivity (on both verbal and nonverbal levels) to communication from others are likewise an essential part of the process. We all know people who speak our language perfectly but with whom any significant communication is impossible. Some degree of personal involvement is essential for successful nonverbal, and even for much of verbal, communication. (The two can rarely be completely separated.) In spite of the fact that no language problem existed in Hollywood, communication with informants was less than in any of the other field experiences.

More complex than physical proximity and linguistic ability, and more difficult to explain, is the psychological involvement which underlies communication. The problem includes the field worker's self image of himself and of the situation, which as Goffman has pointed out, any individual "knowingly and unwittingly projects" when he appears before others.[2] The self is basically no different in the field than elsewhere. It is an integration of many roles and of the identities that go with them.[3] The individual plays many roles, the choice depending on the expected behavior in the situation and on his needs. The reasons for playing any role may be personal, sometimes neurotic, and at the same time, the performance may be rational, in keeping with the demands of the situation. The self concept of many anthropologists seems to have one character-

---

[2] Erving Goffman, *The Presentation of Self in Everyday Life* (New York: Doubleday & Co. [Anchor Books], 1959), p. 242.

[3] This concept differs from that of Goffman's view in *The Presentation of Self in Everyday Life,* in which the self appears to be a bundle of many masks and characters, behind which hides a fearful performer for whom interpersonal relations are treacherous.

istic in common: the image of stepping in and out of society, of being involved and detached. This image is apt to be part of the field worker's personality before he becomes an anthropologist and to be one of the motives (often unconscious) for entering that discipline. (See Chapter I.) The role is then strengthened by academic training and by field experiences.

Other parts of the self-image are personality characteristics which vary from one field worker to another. People differ, for instance, in their degree of reticence, of being outgoing or withdrawn. At the beginning of all my field work, I hesitate to interview people. With some effort I overcome it and proceed from impersonal questions to personal questions without feeling impertinent. I know that most people love to talk about themselves and never have enough opportunity. The field worker is an ideal listener. But several anthropologists, whose personality is fundamentally more reticent than mine, have told me that they find it impossible ever to ask really personal questions. If they forced themselves to do it, the resulting tension in them might adversely affect communication with their informants.

The choice of close friends in the field depends on subtle and often intangible personality qualities which underlie friendships anywhere. The intimate inside view which a field worker receives from his close friends must therefore differ somewhat from what another anthropologist would get from different types of intimates in the same field situation.

In general it is easier for the field worker to make effective communication if he likes himself, if he expects others to like him, if he can communicate easily and directly. Africans in a rural Ghana community told a field worker that they liked him because he was a "simple" person, by which they meant they could talk to him simply and he talk to them in the same way. This was their concept of a good chief. Actually, my impression of this field worker is of a complex person, who has attained a kind of simplicity in relating to others. Those with more unresolved complexities may be arrogant or fearful of contacts with others. Another field worker was told by "his" people in southeast Asia that they liked him because he had a "good heart." Kindness is an inherent part of his personality. Patience, tact, good manners, and a fresh but not innocent eye, are all desirable characteristics for a field worker. Combined with these rather general qualities, may be idiosyncratic characteristics, useful in one field situation and not in another. The ability to be psychologically mobile is important in hierarchical situations where it is necessary to move easily between different levels in the power structure. Some field workers identify so completely with the underdog that they are unable to make effective contacts with those on the top level of the social (or political) hierarchy. Field workers without high social status in their own society may have satisfaction (often unconscious) in the prestige of being a white man, a *bwana* (using the term formerly common in Africa) among black men. As social distinctions between races disappear (or become inverted!), this satisfaction will be lost. For others, who prefer working among their peers, or, rather, who regard all people as their peers, satisfactions will be increased. The only field work where psychological mobility presented a real problem for me was Hollywood, primarily because of my hidden involvements and inability to overcome ideological centricity, far more difficult to surmount than ethnocentricity. The ideal is a sense of compassion and of a common humanity with all men, one of the axioms of anthropology.

Tensions are inevitable for a field worker who spends most of his waking hours with the people he studies and who is continuously stepping in and out of their society, endeavoring to understand it from their point of view and to then bring the data into an ordered anthropological frame of reference. The degree of tension, awareness of it, and the handling of it varies from one field worker to another and from one field situation to another for the same person. A high degree of tension can make communication difficult in the field, or out of it.

Goffman puts the problem neatly when he notes that tension occurs when spontaneous and unspontaneous (playing the rules of the game, in his terms) involvement are incongruent, and that there is ease when the two involvements coincide.[4] I experienced less tension in Lesu than in any of the other field experiences. Only two high points of tension occurred in the

[4] Erving Goffman, *Encounters—Two Studies in the Sociology of Interaction* (New York: Bobbs, Merrill & Co., 1961), pp. 41–2.

Melanesian village, and these were opposite sides of the same coin. The first night alone I feared being isolated, not relating to the Melanesians. The tension which preceded dancing with my clan "sisters" at the boys' initiation rites was caused by fear of losing the role of observer, of a too-intense intimacy. The incongruence of being a modern American, of conventional family (I "saw" my family watching my performance), a "self" who stepped in and out of society, performing in the largest and one of the most significant rites in the Melanesian society, overwhelmed me with ambivalence and self-consciousness. The first crisis was over when Ongus and Pulong and their daughter came to see me, and I found I could relate to them easily. At the time of the second crisis, in spite of my tension, I went through with the dancing role because my Melanesian friends expected it of me, and, then, to my pleased surprise, the anxiety disappeared, and I enjoyed the experience. The tension vanished. I liked the Melanesians and most of the time in Lesu, I was completely at home in my role of participant observer and involved in learning as much as possible about the people and their society. I became fed up with the continuous note-taking, but that was different from tension.

In Mississippi there was a small feeling of tension in "carrying" two groups mutually hostile and fearful of each other. It was as if the Negroes were on one shoulder and the whites on the other. My identifications with each were quite conscious, and, as I have already reported, I sometimes wondered whether I was Negro or white. But that question caused no anxiety. I could be either psychologically. Tension was usually absent with the Negroes. Their acceptance of me had been immediate and whole hearted. I gave them the status which was rightfully theirs, but denied to them by other white people. This was a spontaneous personal involvement on my part and coincided completely with the role of field worker. But with the whites, I sometimes knew tension. There was occasional fear of what would happen if they knew I was breaking their taboos, and this fear was not totally unrealistic. But often the situation only amused me, such as when I was a guest for dinner in a white woman's home and the servant waiting on the table had entertained me the preceding day in her home. I was, of course, constantly aware of the taboo between Negro men and white

women, and of the need to be circumspect because of the potential dangers for them. But this did not cause anxiety. The
high point of tension in Mississippi was in the meeting of a
would-be lynching gang on the road, which occasioned the
emergence of totally conflicting roles: to step into the situation
and try to save the Negro or to remain outside and study it.
The open tensions were resolved by my recognition that I did
not have the power to save the Negro and that the only rational
role open to me was that of the observer of the whites in the
situation. In Mississippi, the tensions of the white people, of
the Negro men, and of myself were all sources of data.

In Hollywood I do not remember experiencing any conscious
tensions. There, all feelings were muted. The hidden nature of
some of my involvements that prevented the tensions from
coming to the surface, to the detriment of the research, have
already been described.

In the African field work tensions inherent in a biracial
situation were far less than in Mississippi. Less hostility existed between the two races in Northern Rhodesia than in our
deep South, and the situation was more open in Africa. The
white people there knew that I entertained Africans in my
home, went around the African township by myself and at
night—all contrary to the local mores—but accepted the situation. The upper levels of the white hierarchy were more sophisticated as well as less fearful than the Mississippi whites, and,
even more important, an anthropologist was not a new phenomenon to them. The head of a department on the mine
rebuked an unusually liberal employee sitting on a bench and
smoking a cigarette with an African during the lunch hour,
by saying, "You looked like an anthropologist!" In Indianola,
on the other hand, no precedent existed for me. I was the first
social scientist to be in their community. Having been accepted
so easily by the Negroid Melanesians and by the Mississippi
Negroes, I was unprepared for the Africans' suspicions of me
as a white person and of the purpose of my research. But their
suspicions eventually faded or disappeared, primarily, I think,
because my involvement with the Africans was spontaneous
and congruent with the role of field worker.

The role of anxieties and tensions in field work can be explored further. In an unusually frank statement, Peter Blau,

the sociologist, discussing his study of a bureaucratic group in a federal agency, describes his insecurity as an outsider in the midst of an integrated group of officials and his uncertainty about attaining his research goals in the limited time available. Reconstructing his mental processes of this period as far as he can remember them, Blau writes that he seems to have coped with his anxieties by turning too soon from exploratory observations and imposing a rigid structure on his research activities. To the irritation of his informants, with whom he had not yet established sufficient rapport, he began systematically to observe and record all social contacts among officials. This precisely circumscribed and routine task of recording interaction frequencies Blau now regards as premature and a blunder.[5]

Blau's insecurities were similar to those of many anthropologists in the beginning of their field work. We, too, are strangers in the midst of a close-knit group, and we are always worried about how little time we have to do so much. We, too, often assuage our anxieties by getting some relatively easy quantifiable data, which is, however, not necessarily a blunder in technique. In Lesu, I began by taking a census, too impersonal to irritate the Melanesians; in Mississippi, overwhelmed by the biracial difficulties, I spent the first few weeks securing statistical data about the distribution of landowners, renters, and sharecroppers among Negroes and pored over the census and statistical reports on education. The statistical data were, of course, useful. But their psychological function for Blau and myself may provide some understanding of those field workers who, although not primarily statisticians, never depart from a structured survey or statistical approach.

A possible psychological hypothesis for these social scientists is that direct contact with the people studied makes them uncomfortable. Another type of personality is equally uncomfortable unless he makes direct contact and is involved. The premise is that both types are conditioned by different needs, conscious and unconscious. The exclusive reliance on questionnaires can be a way of erecting a barrier between the in-

---

[5] Peter M. Blau, "The Research Process in the Study of The Dynamics of Bureaucracy," in Sociologists At Work: Essays on The Craft of Social Research, Phillip E. Hammond, ed. (New York: Basic Books, Inc., 1964), pp. 27–28.

vestigator and his subjects and to keep him from being involved with them. He is even more removed if the questions are asked through an interpreter or if the survey is made by a native staff. Such a survey is often necessary, and I made one in Northern Rhodesia. A scientific problem occurs when field work is limited to surveys. One social scientist who took pride in using only what he considered rigorous scientific methods returned from Africa after spending considerable time making surveys and reported that Africans were not verbal. Almost anyone, with even limited research experience with Africans, knows that they are exceptionally verbal. But no Africans had apparently talked to the scientist or to each other while they answered questions in the survey administered through an interpreter, and the field worker's method apparently did not go beyond the surveys. The detached social scientist, using only techniques he considered scientific, made a highly subjective and incorrect observation because he was so uninvolved with Africans.

Whatever the level of involvement—superficial or deep— the participant observer is also detached. The anthropologist's involvement and detachment is similar in some respects to the immersion of the historian in the written records of a particular period. He, too, is studying culture. A distinguished historian, Sir Keith Hancock, perceptively discusses this topic in writing about his study of the *Risorgimento*, the nineteenth-century movement for the independence and unity of Italy.[6] Sir Keith writes that he made (for the time being) the point of view of each faction his own: the House of Austria, the House of Savoy, the Papacy, the Mazzinian people, and half a dozen brands of liberalism and democracy. He was thus able to understand each and report it fairly. Then he detached himself from all of them, related each to the *Risorgimento,* and was able to see it in what he calls "span," i.e. in the wider map of human experience. For Sir Keith, "getting inside the situation is the opening movement; getting outside of it is the concluding one."[7]

---

[6] W. K. Hancock, *Country and Calling* (London: Faber and Faber, 1954), pp. 214–222.
[7] *Ibid.*, p. 221.

The involvement and detachment of the anthropologist and historian have likewise something in common with the relationship between the psychoanalyst and his patient, although the goals are very different. The analyst must be sufficiently involved with the patient to understand his problems and, at the same time, be detached in order to help the patient increase his self-understanding. The anthropologist is primarily not interested in helping his informants, although he may do so inadvertently. His motivation is to secure data. Likewise, the position of the patient with the analyst is far different from that of the informant with the anthropologist. The informant may receive some catharsis from talking about himself to a sympathetic stranger, but this is not usually the primary motivation; basically he is the teacher, informing the anthropologist, his student. The best data is usually obtained from those who enjoy this role and become involved in the research, which may, or may not, be combined with pecuniary rewards. These and other characteristics set off the therapeutic relationship between psychoanalyst and patient from the research process in which anthropologist and informant are involved.

The novelist and playwright, as well as the anthropologist, write out of their immersion and participation in a particular situation from which they have been able to detach themselves. But they write of the particular; if they are gifted, the particular illuminates the human condition. The anthropologist starts with particulars, and then analyzes, generalizes, and compares; the gifted ones may also illuminate the human condition.

Enough has been written to indicate that an anthropologist in the field is all too human an instrument. Traditionally, the self image of the anthropologist has been that of humanist and scientist, and he did not see any necessary contradiction between the two approaches. As Eric Wolf writes, anthropology has been "a bond between subject matters . . . in part history, part literature; in part natural science, part social science; it strives to study men from within and without . . . the most scientific of the humanities, the most humanist of the sciences." [8]

However, a current trend moves away from this position.

---

[8] Eric R. Wolf, *Anthropology, Humanistic Scholarship in America*, The Princeton Studies (Englewood Cliffs, N.J.: Prentice-Hall, 1964), p. 88.

Many anthropologists now see an unresolvable contradiction between the humanistic and scientific approach. They would agree with a sociologist's criticism of their humanism: "The humanistic element in cultural anthropology is more disturbing than the biologic because it has offered an easy method for neglecting scientific methodology while claiming scientific status." [9]

The emulation of the natural sciences by social scientists is not surprising. The form of our age has been largely shaped by the advances of the former, and by an awareness of their even greater potentialities. A sincere belief in the power of those methods which have produced such remarkable results motivates many people. Then, too, the methodology of the natural sciences, particularly of mathematics and physics, is the new Establishment, and, naturally, many want to enter. Its high prestige and relative assurance for foundation support may not also be without influence. These motivations have more or less validity. Criticism is of the naïve worship of methodology. Unimportant problems are frequently selected because they fit a method, not realizing that advances of science usually occur through the imaginative development of new problems. But methodology is the tail that now wags the dog.

The issue is further complicated by the emulation of the methods and spirit of the natural sciences of the nineteenth century rather than of the mid-twentieth. In the preceding century scientific method was dominated by mechanistic ideas and notions of permanence and of strict causality. But these have been replaced by principles of indeterminacy, and there has been a shift from exactness to probability curves. Natural scientists no longer speak of their discipline as "exact." But, as the sociologist Melville Dalton writes, "Influenced by the dogmatism of nineteenth century science, research methodology in the social and psychological sciences is now more cocksure than in the increasingly humbler physical sciences." [10] Jacob Viner the economist makes a similar point when he

---

[9] Bryce Ryan, "The Application of Anthropological Knowledge to Modern Mass Society, a Sociologist's View," *Human Organization*, XV (1957), no. 4, p. 33.
[10] Melville Dalton, *Men Who Manage; Fusions of Feeling and Theory in Administration*. (New York: John Wiley & Sons, 3rd ed., 1964), p. 273.

questions that "the progress of scientific analysis is marked by the substitution of simple for complex solutions to problems, and of precise and definite for qualified and contingent answers to questions."[11]

The schoolbook image of a neutral, antiseptic scientist who, by some mechanical process, discovers and collects facts has been dispelled by Einstein who talked about the "underlying uncertainties of all knowledge and the function of intuition resting on a sympathetic understanding of experience." A mathematical biologist declares that "no scientist follows cut-and-dried procedure. Intuition and idiosyncrasies probably play as important a part in the work of the scientist as they do in the work of the artist."[12] The similarities in the process of creation by scientists and by artists are being constantly documented.[13] Only a very few men in the sciences and the arts are geniuses, but many can be creative.

The Scientific Revolution can be said to have begun in 1543 with the thesis of Copernicus that the earth moves around the sun. According to Bronowski, Copernicus did not make this discovery through routine calculations. "His first step was a leap of imagination—to lift himself wildly, speculatively into the sun. 'The earth conceives from the sun,' he wrote; and 'the sun rules the family of stars.'"[14]

The stress on the humanistic elements in anthropology does not deny the need for development and refinement of methodology. There are a number of new approaches, only a few of which can be discussed in an Epilogue, and these are further restricted to those currently in favor with American anthropologists.

One of the promising new techniques is concerned with the analysis of data by computers. Their use permits the analysis of

[11] Jacob Viner, *International Trade and Economic Development.* (Oxford: Clarendon Press, 1953), p. 2.
[12] Quoted from Anatol Rapaport, *Operational Philosophy,* 1954, p. 48, in Dalton, *op. cit.,* p. 273.
[13] See Arthur Koestler, *The Act of Creation: A study of the conscious and unconscious processes in humor, scientific discovery and art,* (New York: Macmillan & Co., 1964).
[14] J. Bronowski, *Science and Human Values* (New York: Harper and Row, 1965) pp. 11–12. The author writes that this point has been well documented by Thomas S. Kuhn in *The Copernican Revolution* (Cambridge: Harvard University Press, 1957).

large masses of data (whether collected by one person or by a
team) quickly and efficiently. The industrial revolution has
hit anthropology! Computers not only save time in analyzing
certain types of data but permit an extension of problems and
a breadth of results not possible by hand work. Coult and Ran-
dolph have briefly described the use of computer methods for
analyzing genealogical space.[15] The data were taken directly
from field notes not written in anticipation of computer proc-
essing. This method permitted a far more intensive empirical
analysis of genealogical data and of endogamic marriage than
could have been done through a study of actual marriages and
such indirect indicators as rules, preferences, and kinship terminology. The preparation of data required by the program
took approximately twelve-hours, and the running time for
tracing relationships through ten links for a population of five
hundred took about forty-five minutes.

Computers can also be used to analyze data on broader cultural and social psychological problems. The work of Benjamin
Colby and of his associates is of particular interest.[16] In work
still in progress, they are attempting "to discover those themes
that distinguish the folk tales of one culture (or sub-culture)
from those of another. Clusters of such themes provide insight
into the ways cultures conceptually organize the world around
them." [17] The work is focused on implicit, affective elements, as
well as explicit, cognitive ones. A computer is used to point out
thematic patterns within the folk tales by counting groups of
words and running statistical tests of significance. Dr. Colby
has the advantage of large collections of folk tales collected by
other field workers and of their intensive field studies of the
cultures. He informs me (in personal communication) that while
the computer does work that could not otherwise be done, the

---

[15] "Genealogical Space," *American Anthropologist*, Vol. 67, No. 1 (Feb.
1965), pp. 21–9.
[16] See B. N. Colby, George A. Collier, and Susan K. Postal, "Comparison
of Themes in Folktales by the General Inquirer System," *Journal of
American Folklore*, Vol. 76, no. 302, (Oct.–Dec. 1963), pp. 318–23.
B. N. Colby and Mark D. Menchik, "A Study of Thematic Apperception
Tests with the General Inquirer System," *El Palacio* (Santa Fe: Museum
of New Mexico Press, 1964).
B. N. Colby, "The Analysis of Culture Content and Native Concern in
Texts," to be published in the *American Anthropologist*.
[17] Colby, *et al.* (1963), p. 318.

time it takes (for both preparing and running the data), is only, at most, about 5 per cent of the total research effort. Once the thematic patterns have been indicated by the computer, he immerses himself in the folk tales and the cultures, both for a more holistic understanding of the themes and a more complete definition of them. This immersion is similar to that of the participant observer in the field, or to any other researcher in his data.

The above examples are cited to counter the naïve notion that computers can do the work of anthropologists or of any other social scientists. Their use is limited to a quick, efficient, and broad analysis of data which have already been collected without, necessarily, any reference to computers. They permit an anthropologist to then spend more of his time immersed in the data, and in imaginatively viewing and expanding the problems. Computers do not replace men who sniff and hunt for clues and who ponder the imponderables. The danger is, and it has already happened, that problems will be picked, not because of their significance, but because data on them can be programmed for computers. In such a situation, anthropology would be reduced to the work of technicians. However, bastardization is a danger for any method or technique and is not an inherent criticism of either.

Ethnographic semantics, called also the "New Ethnography" —a wave of the present—is concerned both with field methods and with the analysis of data. The linguist Dell Hymes describes the goal as an effort to improve techniques "for tapping, through linguistically expressed categories, the cognitive worlds of participants in the culture; and the thoroughgoing avoidance, through command of verbal detail, of the imposition of alien descriptive categories on those worlds." [18]

No anthropologists would quarrel with this aim. But the goal of understanding "how a native thinks" through a study of his language is hardly new. It is more or less common knowledge that the social and psychological components of speech are necessary for understanding, but it is also usually accepted that

---

[18] Dell H. Hymes, "A Perspective for Linguistic Anthropology," in *Horizons of Anthropology,* Sol Tax, ed. (Chicago: Adline Publishing Co., 1964), p. 95.
[19] Boas, Malinowski, and Sapir all made these points. See B. N. Colby, "Ethnographic Semantics: A Preliminary Survey," to be published in *Current Anthropology.*

we can never know nor enter completely into the speaker's world.[19] Critics, such as Robbins Burling, question whether the practitioners of ethnographic semantics are really "discovering the cognitive system of the people," as they claim, or "fiddling with a set of rules which allow them to use terms the way others do." The latter, he contends, is a realistic and valid goal, while the former is illusory.[20]

The model building in the "New Ethnography" through componential and other forms of analysis represents a refinement of method, and its major contribution has been an economical and rigorous form of presentation, particularly applicable to kinship systems. For instance, Lounsbury's formal account of the Crow- and Omaha-type kinship terminologies [21] is different from a functional, historical, or any other kind of causal account, and it succeeds in its aims, "to tell one the exact minimum he will need to know in order to predict accurately who gets called what in such and such a system of kinship terminology." [22] The advantage of Lounsbury's diagrams are their neatness and economy.

But outside of these advantages, the "New Ethnography" has not proved its usefulness. It has not been productive in studying affective aspects of cultures, such as values, motivations, and other important social psychological themes. Colby makes a similar point when he writes, "It seems to me that the greatest significance of componential analysis is linguistic rather than anthropological—in its delineation and clarification of semantic problems rather than in its revelation of psychological reality." [23]

It is indeed paradoxical that the ethnographic semanticists apparently do their field work in the participant observer tradition and relate to the people they study. For instance, Ward Goodenough, a leading member of this group and a very able anthropologist, who worked on Truk (an island in Micronesia), became a "brother" to a Trukese of about his age which in-

---

[20] Robbins Burling, "Cognition and Componential Analysis; God's Truth or Hocus-Pocus," *American Anthropologist*, Vol. 66, No. 1 (Feb. 1964), p. 27.
[21] Floyd L. Lounsbury, "A Formal Account of the Crow- and Omaha-type Kinship Terminologies," in *Explorations in Cultural Anthropology, Essays in Honor of George Peter Murdock*, Ward E. Goodenough, ed. (New York: McGraw-Hill, 1964), pp. 351–93.
[22] *Ibid.*, p. 386.
[23] "Ethnographic Semantics." See note 19.

creased his participation in the social system of relationships and through it he discovered another type of kin group.[24] But he scorned to convey the vibrancy of Trukese life. His goal was to present Trukese culture only as his analysis revealed it —the rules of behavior comparable to a linguistic grammar— and not as Trukese saw it; he stated that his aim was not to make the Trukese people "come to life." [25] There is no reason why Goodenough, or any other anthropologist, could not give an analysis of rules and make a people "come to life," if anthropology is accepted as a humanistic discipline.

In evaluating the work of the ethnographic semanticists and other model making, a crucial question is whether the models necessarily contribute to understanding the culture patterns. For example, Goodenough, whose work has already been mentioned, analyzes an emotional situation which occurred during his field work on Truk in terms of status and role models.[26] But I was able to understand the incident and its implications from his description without any reference to his models, and the latter would have meant little without the description.

Anthropologists have been studying rules since the beginning of the discipline. Should we not also begin to ask new questions as, for example, why this rule and not that one? Should we not likewise go beyond a study of the rules themselves? The study of man is far broader than the rules of behavior. In no society are all rules obeyed all the time by all people. Why do people sometimes follow the rules and other times depart from them? An intriguing question is how do some people "get by" in consistently breaking a rule which others follow. The answers to such questions lie partly in the study of motivations, for which psychological theories should be among those tools used. But the use of psychological theory, which leads to the study of men as individuals, is currently not fashionable in anthropology. Why cannot both men and rules be studied and described?

---

[24] Ward E. Goodenough, *Property, Kin and Community on Truk* (New Haven: Yale University Publications in Anthropology, 1951), No. 46, p. 9.
[25] *Ibid.*, p. 11.
[26] Ward H. Goodenough, "Rethinking 'Status' and 'Role' Toward a General Model of the Cultural Organization of Social Relationships," in *The Relevance of Models for Social Anthropology*. A. S. A. Monograph I (New York: Frederick A. Praeger Publishers, 1965), pp. 1–24.

It happens that most of the ethnographic semanticists are in the generation born approximately between 1915 and 1930. I have a quite tentative hypothesis that some of the diverse trends in anthropology can be understood in terms of generation differences and in the accompanying changes in the culture. Anthropologists and sociologists have long used age groups as a way of studying social change. Why can we not have a similar sociology of anthropology? The following ideas are decidedly not that but only a few notions to suggest possible lines of inquiry.

Anthropologists born before 1915 could not have been much concerned about economic security, because they entered a profession in which the latter was rare. Before World War II earning a living in anthropology was decidedly uncertain. The subject was seldom taught in undergraduate colleges, or at best, there might be one course in introductory anthropology, often taught by a sociologist. No one thought then of anthropologists working in industry or government (except in the Indian Bureau). This generation of anthropologists apparently accepted these risks quite easily, perhaps because the subject filled certain deep needs, conscious and unconscious. Before becoming anthropologists many of the men and women of this group seem to have had problems with authority, and stood to a considerable degree outside of their culture. (See the discussion in Chapter I). Anthropology is a profession in which it is an asset for the practitioners to be somewhat outside of their own society and of the ones they study, and yet be able to step into them and relate to people. Certain personality types carry this dual role of involvement and detachment more easily than do others and even enjoy it.

The generation of anthropologists born between 1915 and 1930 entered the discipline when its economic aspects were quite different. World War II had drastically changed them. Anthropologists knew more about many parts of the world where the war was being fought than anyone else; they had experience in learning languages without recorded grammars; they had worked with tribal peoples, some of whom were involved in the war. After the war, new fields continued to open for anthropologists; the discipline became an accepted part of undergraduate curriculums; and graduate departments expanded. Funds for field work (pre-doctoral and post-doctoral) became readily available. Today, there are far more jobs in anthropology than trained people to fill them. The profession offers safety and security in a way that it did not do in the past.

It is perhaps no accident that many of the anthropologists in the generation born between 1915 and 1930 attempt to secure definitive "answers," which can be cast into elegant models, formal rules, and neat diagrams. These could possibly answer a need for certainty and a fear of ambiguity. One can understand both the needs and the fears. This generation likewise seems to be more truly a part of their own society, desiring to enter the Establishment rather than rebelling from it as did many members of the preceding generation. Moreover, the dehumanizing character of much of the work of the generation born between 1915 and 1930 resembles a similar tendency in the arts and in social life today.

Obviously these ideas about differences in personality types between two generations are only speculations about trends, to which there can be many exceptions. But some of us in the generation born before 1915 think differences do exist. This point could be documented or disproved by a study similar to that done in the early fifties by the psychologist Anne Roe of eminent anthropologists and other scientists.[27] A better study could be done today because of improved methods.

The generation born after 1930 seems different from the preceding one. There appears to be a trend among its members to explore broader and deeper problems. They attempt to refine their methods and make them more rigorous but not necessarily to imitate the methods of linguistics or those of natural sciences. They recognize the unique characteristic of the subject matter of anthropology: man—a thinking and feeling being. They select problems of theoretical interest and do not appear too concerned that their results are in terms of probabilities. Sol Tax, an eminent senior anthropologist, wanted some of his younger colleagues as contributors to *Horizons of Anthropol-*

---

[27] Anne Roe, "A Psychological Study of Eminent Psychologists and Anthropologists, and a Comparison with Biological and Physical Scientists," *Psychological Monographs* (American Psychological Association), No. 352, 1953, pp. 1–55.

ogy.[28] He selected five and asked them to choose the others to make nineteen—men still in their thirties whose work was interesting and significant. They were asked to put their contributions in a "whole-human" frame,[29] which they were able to do.

Since students—still another age group—have not yet published anything, impressions are very limited. However, it may be significant that a *Fellow Newsletter* of the American Anthropological Association stated in 1963 that contemporary students prefer the monographs of the past which give detailed descriptions of people and their society to the narrower problem-oriented studies of the present.[30] It is my general impression that students often chose anthropology over sociology because of its breadth of scope and depth in time, its holistic approach and its fewer pretensions to being a science in the sense that mathematics and physics are.

But as some anthropologists take on these pretensions a new trend begins in sociology. In the not too distant past sociologists were far more intent than anthropologists in stressing the non-humanistic aspects of their discipline. The emphasis was on a quantified methodology for small specific problems. But in 1963 Everett Hughes, outgoing president of the American Sociological Society, suggested in his presidential address that the sociological imagination has been so restricted by empirical concepts, "limited to little bundles of facts applied to little hypotheses, that we (sociologists) are incapable of entertaining a broad range of possibilities, following out the madly unlikely combinations of social circumstances." [31] Hughes would probably not deny that the little bundles of facts and the little hypotheses have their usefulness, but the ideal of narrow exactitude may exclude the use of the imagination to formulate new and significant problems.

The presidential address of George Homans to the same society the following year was titled "Bringing Men Back In,"

---

[28] Sol Tax, ed. *Horizons of Anthropology*. (Chicago: Adine Publishing Co., 1964).
[29] *Ibid.*, pp. 5–6.
[30] Vol. 4, No. 3 (March 1963), p. 2.
[31] Everett C. Hughes, "Race Relations and the Sociological Imagination", *American Sociological Review*, Vol. 28, No. 6 (Dec. 1963), p. 889.

and its thesis was the need to study the behavior of men—individual men—using psychological propositions to do so. He advocated going beyond the functional studies of interrelations and asking questions concerned with the why of human relations. He points out that it is the needs of men rather than the needs of society which explain the relationships.[32] The problem is the same in anthropology.[33]

The Epilogue began with the observation that underlying all field work is the necessity of reciprocal communication between a field worker and the people he studies. To openly recognize and use as part of the research the humanness of the investigator, as well as of the people he studies, is sometimes considered old fashioned by those who would depersonalize both. But the constants underlying effective field work know no fashion.

There are many levels of communication, understanding, and of generalization. Semantic codes, models, statistical tables are but a few. To capture, as far as possible, through empathy and compassion (as well as with techniques and methods appropriate to the situation) the life of a people as seen through their eyes and to present it vividly, is another level and a significant one. This kind of understanding and description does not prohibit the making of hypotheses or generalizations and the best monographs combine both. But there are some anthropologists who rather arbitrarily reserve the label "scientific" for nonhumanistic studies. A scientific attitude ignores no level of understanding.

Anthropologists (particularly in the United States) have enjoyed a broad catholicism in problems, methods, and interests. If the dual nature of anthropology—an art and a science, a humanistic science—is accepted, there is no reason why each cannot be expanded. The inherent ambiguities of this approach are only a reflection of those which exist in life itself.

---

[32] George C. Homans, "Bringing Men Back In", *American Sociological Review*, Vol. 29, No. 6 (Dec. 1964), pp. 809–18.

[33] In a recent publication two anthropologists, Conrad Arensberg and Solon Kimball, make a somewhat similar point in their discussion of community-study method. They suggest that behavior and attitudes should be studied *in vivo* through observation rather than *in vitro* through isolation and abstraction or in a model through experiment. Conrad M. Arensberg and Solon T. Kimball, *Culture and Community,* (New York: Harcourt, Brace, & World, Inc., 1965), p. 29.

SELECTED BIBLIOGRAPHY
FOR METHODS
OF FIELD WORK

Adams, Richard N., and Jack J. Preiss (eds.). *Human Organization Research*. Homewood, Ill.: The Dorsey Press, 1960.

Arensberg, Conrad M., and Solon T. Kimball. *Culture and Community*. New York: Harcourt, Brace & World, Inc., 1965, pp. 28–47.

Bain, Robert K. "The Researcher's Role: A Case Study," *Human Organization*, Vol. 9, No. 1, 1950, pp. 23–28.

Bartlett, F. C., *et al*. *The Study of Society: Methods and Problems*. London: Kegan Paul, Trench, Taubner and Co., 1939.

Bateson, Gregory. "Experiments in Thinking about Observed Ethnological Material," *Philosophy of Science*, Vol. 8, No. 1, 1941, pp. 53–68.

Beals, Robert L. "Native Terms and Anthropological Methods," *American Anthropologist*, Vol. 59, No. 4, August 1957, pp. 716–717.

Becker, Howard S. "Participant Observation: the Analysis of Qualitative Field Data," *Human Organization Research*, R. N. Adams and J. J. Preiss (eds.) Homewood, Ill.: Dorsey Press, 1960, pp. 267–289.

————. "Problems of Inference and Proof in Participant Observation," *American Sociological Review*, Vol. 23, No. 6, December 1958, pp. 652–660.

Becker, Howard S., and Blanche Geer. "Participant Observation and Interviewing: A Comparison," *Human Organization*, Vol. 16, No. 3, 1957, pp. 28–32.

Bennet, John. "The Study of Cultures: A Survey of Techniques and Methodology in Field Work," *American Sociological Review*, Vol. 13, No. 6, December 1948, pp. 672–689.

Bennet, John, and Kurt H. Wolff. "Toward Communication Between Sociology and Anthropology," *Current Anthropology*, Supplement to *Anthropology To-day*, W. L. Thomas (ed.). Chicago: University of Chicago Press, 1956, p. 340.

Berreman, G. D. *Behind Many Masks: Ethnography and Impression Management in a Himalayan Village*. Ithaca, N.Y.: Society for Applied Anthropology, 1962.

Boaz, Franz. "The Method of Ethnology," *American Anthropologist*, Vol. 22, No. 4, October–December 1920, pp. 311–321.

Bowen, Elenore Smith (pseudonym). *Return to Laughter*. New York: Harper and Bros., 1954.

Casagrande, Joseph B. (ed.). *In the Company of Man*. New York: Harper and Row, 1960.

Chapple, Eliot D., and Conrad Arensberg. *Measuring Human Relations*. Provincetown, Mass.: The Journal Press, 1940.

Dalton, Melville. *Men Who Manage; Fusions of Feeling and Theory in Administration*. New York: John Wiley and Sons, 1959.

Davis, Allison, Burleigh B. Gardner, and Mary R. Gardner. *Deep South: A Social Anthropological Study of Caste and Class*. Chicago: University of Chicago Press, 1941.

Dean, John P., and William F. Whyte. "How Do You Know if Your Informant is Telling the Truth?" *Human Organization*, Vol. 17, No. 2, 1958, pp. 34–38.

DuBois, Cora. "Some Psychological Techniques and Objectives in Anthropology," *Journal of Social Psychology*, Vol. 8, No. 3, 1937, pp. 285–300.

———. *The People of Alor: A Social Psychological Study of an East Indian Culture*. Minneapolis: University of Minnesota Press, 1944.

Eggan, F. "Social Anthropology and the Method of Controlled Comparison," *American Anthropologist*, Vol. 56, No. 5, 1954, pp. 743–763.

Ehrlich, June Sachar, and David Riesman. "Age and Authority in the Interview," *Public Opinion Quarterly*, Vol. 25, No. 1, Spring 1961, pp. 39–56.

Embree, John F. *Suye Mura: A Japanese Village*. Chicago: University of Chicago Press, 1939.

Evans-Pritchard, E. E. *The Nuer*. Oxford: Oxford University Press, 1940.

Firth, Raymond. *We, The Tikopia*. London: George Allen and Unwin, 1936.

Gillin, John. "Methodological Problems in the Anthropological Study of Modern Cultures," *American Anthropologist*, Vol. 51, No. 3, July–September 1949, pp. 392–399.

Goffman, Erving. *The Presentation of Self in Everyday Life*. Edinburgh: University of Edinburgh, Social Sciences Research Centre, 1956.

Gold, Raymond L. "Roles in Sociological Field Observations," *Social Forces*, Vol. 36, No. 3, March 1958, pp. 217–223.

Gouldner, Alvin. "Appendix," *Patterns of Industrial Bureaucracy*. Glencoe, Ill.: Free Press, 1954.

Hammond Phillip E. (ed.). *Sociologists at Work: Essays on The Craft of Social Research*. New York: Basic Books, 1964.

Haring, Douglas G. "Comment on Field Techniques in Ethnology: Illustrated by a Survey in the Ryuku Islands," *Personal Character and Cultural Milieu*, D. G. Haring (ed.). Syracuse: Syracuse University Press, 1956.

Herskovits, M. J. "The Ethnographer's Laboratory," *Man and His Works*. New York: A. A. Knopf, 1948, pp. 79–93.

Holmberg, Allan. *Nomads of the Long Bow*. Washington, D.C.: U.S. Government Printing Office, 1950.

————. "The Research-and-Development Approach to Change: Participant Intervention in the Field," *Human Organization Research*, R. N. Adams and J. J. Preiss (eds.). Homewood, Ill.: Dorsey Press, 1960, pp. 76–89.

Homans, George C. "Bringing Men Back In," *American Sociological Review*, Vol. 29, No. 6, December, 1964, pp. 809–818.

Hyman, Herbert H. *Interviewing in Social Research*. Chicago: University of Chicago Press, 1954.

Janowitz, Morris, "Anthropology and the Social Sciences," *Current Anthropology*, Vol. 4, No. 2, April 1963, pp. 149–154.

Junker, Buford H. *Field Work—An Introduction to the Social Sciences*. Introduction by Everett C. Hughes. Chicago: University of Chicago Press, 1960.

Kaufmann, Felix. *The Methodology of the Social Sciences*. New York: The Humanities Press, 1958.

Kluckhohn, Clyde. "Participation in Ceremonials in a Navajo Community," *Personal Character and Cultural Milieu*, D. C. Haring (ed.). Syracuse: Syracuse University Press, 1956, pp. 67–77.

————. "The Personal Document in Anthropological Science," *The Use of Personal Documents in History, Anthropology and Sociology*, L. Gottschalk, C. Kluckhohn, and R. Angell. New York: Social Science Research Council, 1945, pp. 79–173.

Kluckhohn, Florence R. "The Participant-Observer Technique in Small Communities," *American Journal of Sociology*, Vol. 46, No. 3, November 1940, pp. 331–343.

Kolaja, J. "A Contribution to the Theory of Participant Observation," *Social Forces*, Vol. 35, No. 2, December 1956, pp. 159–163.

Lazarsfeld, Paul F. "Problems in Methodology," *Sociology Today*, R. K. Merton, L. Broom, and L. S. Cottrell, Jr. (eds.). New York: Basic Books, 1959.

————. "The Art of Asking Why," *National Marketing*, Vol. 1, 1935, p. 1.

Lewis, Oscar. "Controls and Experiments in Field Work," *Anthropology Today*, A. L. Kroeber (ed.). Chicago: University of Chicago Press, 1953, pp. 452–475.

Lohman, Joseph D. "The Participant Observer in Community Studies," *American Sociological Review*, Vol. 2, No. 6, December 1937, pp. 890–897.

Maccoby, Eleanor, and Nathan Maccoby. "The Interview: A Tool of Social Science," *Handbook of Social Psychology*, Gardner Lindzey (ed.). Vol. 1, Cambridge, Mass.: Addison-Wesley Publishing Co., 1954, pp. 449–487.

Malinowski, B. *Argonauts of the Western Pacific*. New York: E. P. Dutton and Co., 1922, pp. 5–25 and *passim*.

Mead, Margaret. *An Anthropologist at Work: Writings of Ruth Benedict*. Boston: Houghton Mifflin Company, 1959.

————. "More Comprehensive Field Methods," *American Anthropologist*, Vol. 35, No. 1, January-March 1933, pp. 1–15.

Merton, Robert K. "Foreward," *Science and the Social Order*, Bernard

Barber. Rev. ed. New York: Collier Books, 1962.

Merton, Robert K., and Patricia L. Kendall. "The Focused Interview," *American Journal of Sociology*, Vol. 51, No. 6, May 1946, pp. 541–557.

Miller, S. M. "The Participant-Observer and 'Over-rapport'," *American Sociological Review*, Vol. 17, No. 1, February 1952, pp. 97–99.

Nadel, S. F. "The Interview Technique in Social Anthropology," *The Study of Society*, F. C. Bartlett *et al.*, (eds.). London: K. Paul, Trench, Taubner and Co., Ltd., 1939.

Nash, Dennison. "The Ethnologist as a Stranger: An Essay in the Sociology of Knowledge," *Southwest Journal of Anthropology*, Vol. 19, No. 2, Summer 1963, pp. 149–167.

Osgood, Cornelius. *Ingalik Material Culture*. New Haven: Yale University Press, 1940, pp. 50–55.

————. *The Koreans and Their Culture*. New York: Ronald Press, 1951.

Paul, Benjamin D. "Interviewing Techniques and Field Relationships," *Anthropology Today*, A. L. Kroeber (ed.). Chicago: University of Chicago Press, 1953, pp. 430–451.

Piddington, Ralph. "Methods of Field Work," *An Introduction to Social Anthropology*. Vol. 2. New York: Macmillan, 1957, pp. 525–596.

Polanyi, Michael. *Personal Knowledge*. Chicago: University of Chicago Press, 1958.

Radcliffe-Brown, A. R. *The Andaman Islanders: A Study in Social Anthropology*. Glencoe, Ill.: Free Press, 1948.

Radin, Paul. *The Method and Theory of Ethnology*. New York: McGraw-Hill Book Co., Inc., 1933.

Redfield, Robert. "The Art of Social Science," *American Journal of Sociology*, Vol. 54, No. 3, November 1948, pp. 181–190.

Richards, A. I. "The Development of Field Work Methods in Social Anthropology," *The Study of Society*, F. C. Bartlett *et al.* (eds.). London: K. Paul, Trench, Taubner and Co., Ltd., 1939, pp. 272–316.

————. "The Village Census in the Study of Culture Contact," *Africa*, Vol. 8, 1935, pp. 20–33.

Riesman, David, and Mark Benney. "The Sociology of the Interview," *Midwest Sociologist*, Vol. 18, 1956, pp. 3–15.

———— (eds.). "The Interview in Social Research," *American Journal of Sociology*, Vol. 62, No. 2, September 1956, pp. 137–252.

Riesman, David, Robert J. Potter, and Jeanne Watson, "Sociability, Permissiveness and Equality: A Preliminary Formulation," *Psychiatry*, Vol. 23, No. 4, November 1960, pp. 323–340.

————. "The Vanishing Host," *Human Organization*, Vol. 19, 1960, pp. 17–27.

Roberts, John. *Zuni Daily Life Notebook No. 3*. Laboratory of Anthropology, University of Nebraska, 1956.

Schwartz, Morris, and Charlotte Schwartz. "Problems in Participant Observation," *American Journal of Sociology*, Vol. 60, No. 4, January 1955, pp. 343–353.

Selltiz, Claire, Marie Jahoda, Morton Deutsch, and Stuart W. Cook.

Research Methods in Social Relations. New York: Henry Holt and Company, Inc., 1959.

Shils, Edward. "Primordial, Personal, Sacred and Civil Ties," *British Journal of Sociology,* Vol. 8, No. 2, June 1957, pp. 130–145.

Spencer, Robert F. (ed.). *Method and Perspective in Anthropology.* Minneapolis: University of Minnesota Press, 1954.

Stycos, J. Mayone. "Interviewer Training in Another Culture," *Public Opinion Quarterly,* Vol. 16, No. 2, Summer 1952, pp. 236–246.

Thomas, W. I., and F. Znaniecki, "Methodological Note," in *The Polish Peasant in Europe and America,* Vol. 1. Chicago: University of Chicago Press, 1918, pp. 1–86.

Vidich, Arthur J. "Participant Observation and the Collection and Interpretation of Data," *American Journal of Sociology,* Vol. 60, No. 4, January 1955, pp. 354–360.

Wagley, Charles, and Edwards Galvai. "Preface," *The Tenetehara Indians of Brazil: A Culture in Transition.* New York: Columbia University Press, 1949.

Wax, Rosalie Hankey. "Reciprocity as a Field Technique," *Human Organization,* Vol. 11, No. 3, 1952, pp. 34–37.

West, James. *Plainville, U.S.A.* New York: Columbia University Press, 1945.

Whyte, William F. "Interviewing for Organizational Research," *Human Organization,* Vol. 12, No. 2, 1953, pp. 15–22.

————. "Methodological Appendix," *Street Corner Society.* 2nd ed. Chicago: University of Chicago Press, 1955.

————. "Observational Field Work Methods," in M. Jahoda, M. Deutsch, and S. W. Cook. *Research Methods in Social Relations.* Vol. 2. New York: The Dryden Press, 1951, pp. 493–514.

————. "On Asking Indirect Questions," *Human Organization,* Vol. 15, No. 4, 1957, pp. 21–23.

INDEX

313